The Sephardic Jews of Bordeaux:

Assimilation and Emancipation in
Revolutionary and Napoleonic France

The Sephardic Jews of Bordeaux:

Assimilation and Emancipation in Revolutionary and Napoleonic France

Frances Malino

The University of Alabama Press
University, Alabama

Library of Congress Cataloging in Publication Data

Malino, Frances
   The Sephardic Jews of Bordeaux.

   (Judaic studies; 7)
   Bibliography: p.
   Includes index.
   1. Jews in Bordeaux—History. 2. Sephardim—France
—Bordeaux—History. 3. Assemblée des Israélites de
France et du royaume d'Italie, Paris, 1806-1807.
4. Paris, Sanhédrin, 1807. 5. Bordeaux—History.
I. Title. II. Series.
DS135.F85B65   323.1'19'2404471   77-22659
ISBN 0-8173-6903-1

Contents

To My Parents
With Love and Admiration

Preface

This book focuses on a small community of French Jews, the first in Europe to encounter the requirements of an emerging nation-state and to be recognized by that state as full and equal citizens. The Sephardim of Bordeaux were typical of neither the majority of the Jews of France nor those of Western Europe. They had entered France as Catholics; only after more than a century of public adherence to Catholicism was their community officially recognized as Jewish. Nevertheless, their assimilation and conformity to the standards of French society as well as their commitment to a Judaism fashioned as much by contemporary political and economic concerns as by tradition reveal a legacy bequeathed to French Jewry and an important model for the development of the modern Jew.

My interest in the Jews of Bordeaux began during my years of graduate study at Brandeis University. There I enjoyed the encouragement of Professors Alexander Altmann, Nahum Glatzer, Benjamin Halpern, and Nahum Sarna. To these learned scholars I am deeply indebted.

A grant from the National Foundation for Jewish Culture and the help of Mr. Zosa Szajkowski and the Jewish Theological Seminary of New York enabled me to begin my work. The main research was done in Paris and Bordeaux during the academic year 1968–69 and the summer of 1972. I am grateful to the Fulbright Commission and the University of Massachusetts whose fellowships made my travel and research possible.

It would have been difficult to benefit from the material available in this field without the help of MM. Bernhard Blumenkranz, Gérard Nahon, and Georges Weill as well as from M. Jean Cavignac, who arranged for me to have complete access to the Departmental Archives of Bordeaux and the city archives.

My research also took me to Israel where with the help of M. Simon Swartzfuchs I was introduced to M. Pascal Thémanlys, whose kindness and generosity in permitting me to examine his family archives will never be forgotten.

I owe the deepest gratitude to my friends. It was their support which sustained me as I prepared this manuscript and their criticism which helped me to clarify my ideas. A final thank you must go to Daniel and Elizabeth who, although too young to understand, nevertheless gave to their mother an abundance of joy.

The Sephardic Jews of Bordeaux:

Assimilation and Emancipation in
Revolutionary and Napoleonic France

1

The Establishment of the Portuguese NATION in Southwestern France

From the splendor of the courts of medieval Muslim Spain to the war-weary port of the city of Bordeaux represents a long and eventful journey filled with conversion, expulsion, and the unrelenting threat of the Inquisition. What led the Marranos of Spain and Portugal to Bordeaux? How, despite the fact that France had expelled her Jews in 1394 and showed no intention of reversing that decision, were they able to establish a Jewish community which by the eve of the Revolution was intellectually enlightened, economically prosperous, and socially and politically prepared to enter the emerging nation-state? It is these questions which will occupy us as we trace the early development of the Bordeaux community.

For a few centuries there had existed in medieval Muslim Spain a dynamic rapport between the Jews and their Arab and Christian neighbors. This rapport minimized the restricting impulses of separate theologies and elicited an intellectual, poetic and commercial efflorescence. As the Spanish Umayyad caliphate gave way to the fanatical Berber dynasties, however, Jews were increasingly persecuted. Many left southern Spain for areas in the north recently reconquered by the Spanish Christians. There they reestablished their prestige and influence.

Political instability, Catholic zeal, and the examples set by the Christians of Europe soon undermined the security of the Jewish communities. In 1391 persecutions and massacres spread throughout Christian Spain, creating in their wake converts to Christianity known as New Christians or *Conversos*. These former Jews, many although not all of whom retained their commitment to Judaism, saw their numbers increased with the persecutions of 1411. No longer protected as infidels, these New Christians were soon subjected to the punishments reserved for heretics.

In 1492, Ferdinand and Isabella completed the *reconquista* with the defeat of the only surviving Muslim stronghold of Granada and the expulsion of all Muslims and Jews. Unable to rescind the decree of March 30, the Jews of Spain were required to convert or emigrate. While some converted, others made their way to Portugal, where Emmanuel, unwilling to deprive his realm of a needed middle class, forcibly baptized the entire community. By the middle of the 16th century, both Spain and Portugal (united in 1580) had "cleansed" their realm of the Jews; they were confronted, however, with a large and increasingly influential community of New Christians, derisively labelled Marranos. Throughout the following centuries the Inquisition would seek to ferret out those among these converts who were suspected of Judaizing.

The social climate of Bordeaux and its unique potential for commercial growth were such as to provide a receptive environment for those fleeing the arms of the Inquisition. Bordeaux had prospered during the years of English rule (1152–1293, 1303–1453), but the definitive victory by France and the subsequent emigration of many who had remained loyal to England had left her depopulated and impoverished. In June 1472 and February 1474, Louis XI, aware of the potential significance of Bordeaux to France, promulgated two significant ordinances. Foreigners, excluding the English, could now dwell in Bordeaux with the privilege of being exempt from the *droit d'aubaine* (according to French law, the estate of a deceased foreigner belonged to France), and with the right of disposing of goods without letters of naturalization.

The motivations underlying these two decrees, namely the desire to populate Bordeaux with enterprising foreigners and to stimulate a revitalization of her commerce, were to remain powerful during the next two hundred fifty years. We shall see that they explain both the initial settlement of the *nouveaux Chrétiens* (New Christians) in Bordeaux, despite a suspected Judaism, and the retention of their privileged status, despite pressures to revoke it.

Shortly after their arrival in Bordeaux, the *nouveaux Chrétiens* grew dissatisfied with their unofficial status. Choosing as their spokesman André Govea, a renowned professor at the College of Guyenne and the commercial liaison between the king of Portugal and Bordeaux, they sought to prove to Paris that their existence in Bordeaux was useful to the economy of that city. Henri II, convinced by the arguments of Govea and willing to ignore rumors of a crypto-Judaism, agreed to issue the *Lettres Patentes* of 1550. The *nouveaux Chrétiens*, now officially recognized and protected, were to enjoy all the rights of privileged Frenchmen—they were free to come and go as they pleased, engage in commerce, and acquire property—and in addition were not to be required to pay for these rights.[1]

Henri's generous welcome notwithstanding, the "Marchands et autres Portugais" could not assume that their future was secure. Acceptance had been predicated upon their usefulness to the king; their future status would depend on this continued usefulness.[2] Henri's right to grant the privileges, moreover, became his or his successor's right to revoke them.

During the next one-hundred and thirty years, the actions taken by the king, the Bordeaux *Parlement* and *jurats,* and the Bordelais merchant guilds (on one side of the political board) and the *nouveaux Chrétiens* (on the other) consistently reflect their respective roles within French society. The kings were restricted to assuring themselves that the *marchands Portugais* were protected adequately enough to enrich France, and that in fact at all times France benefited as much as was possible. The *Parlement,* with its "long arms, large conscience, and narrow devotion" concerned itself with the benefits to Bordeaux commerce.[3] This often meant blocking the effects of those decrees which would be injurious to the well-being of the *nouveaux Chrétiens* and always meant preventing the merchants from destroying the *Portugais* as a privileged group. The bourgeois, sitting as both members of *Parlement* and as *jurats,* felt free to move in any direction which their economic interests took them. In contrast to this rampant flexibility stood the strict regulation of the merchant guilds. Theirs was a commitment to preserving the existing inequalities. Honest, hardworking, and parochial in all spheres of their life, the merchants could never find reason for tolerating the intrusion and subsequent competition of a non-French, suspiciously non-Catholic, privileged group.

The *nouveaux Chrétiens,* facing these varied arbiters of their destiny, carefully designed their moves. To the king they strove to appear useful but never wealthier than he suspected. To the *Parlement* they strove to justify the continued protection they received with a special devotion to the commercial development of Bordeaux. To the merchants they strove to make their presence as unobtrusive as possible and to accept simultaneously many of the limits which the guilds placed upon their supposedly all-inclusive privileges.

By 1574, the *Lettres Patentes* of 1550 had been registered only in Paris and thus had no validity in Bordeaux.[4] (The law of the *ancien régime* required that for royal decrees to be valid in any specific province, they must be registered by the *Parlement* of that province.) The prolonged period between the enactment of these privileges and their subsequent registration in Bordeaux reflects the unwillingness of the

Bordelais community to accede to the demands of its king. On March 17, however, the Bordeaux *Parlement*, at the behest of the *marchands Portugais*, promulgated the first protective ordinance in which it was prohibited "to all residents regardless of status either to molest the *nouveaux Chrétiens* or to force them to leave the city."[5] The following November 11, King Henri III issued two ordinances, one directed to the Bordeaux *Parlement* and one to the *Parlement* and *Grand Sénéchal* of Guyenne.[6] Both ordinances reaffirmed the privileges of 1550 and made clear that the *nouveaux Chrétiens*, who had begun justifiably to fear for their safety, must be protected.[7] The two ordinances of the king and the *Lettres Patentes* of 1550 were finally registered in Bordeaux on April 19, 1580.[8]

Scarcely fifty years after the first *Lettres Patentes*, those *nouveaux Chrétiens* who had been in Bordeaux for less than ten years were asked to leave. Most of them settled in Peyrehorade, Bidache, and Bayonne.[9] France was at war with Spain and, according to one source, the citizens of Bordeaux feared the possibility of traitors among the more recent Spanish arrivals.[10] Other sources, however, state that the *nouveaux Chrétiens* themselves asked for the decree because of commercial jealousy between them and the new arrivals.[11] A third explanation, advanced in the Sephardic *mémoire* to the Malesherbes Commission in 1788, stated that the government had been seeking to avoid concentration of industry in one place.[12] It appears most likely that the fear of traitors, if seriously advanced at all, was merely an opportune excuse used by the Bordelais and subsequently Bayonnais inhabitants.[13] The explanation offered by the Sephardim themselves seems no more tenable.

On April 23, 1615, Louis XIII published an edict demanding that all Jews, disguised or not, leave France in one month.[14] By this time, however, the *Parlement* of Bordeaux was firmly committed to supporting the commercial activities of the *nouveaux Chrétiens* and successfully prevented the edict from being executed, much to the dismay of the Bordeaux merchants who, in 1630, complained that the city had not yet been emptied of the Portuguese competitors.[15] The *Parlement* continued in its role as protector when, on May 14, 1625, it ignored an ordinance of the king which demanded an inventory of all the possessions of the *nouveaux Chrétiens*.[16] In addition to finding themselves thus protected, the Portuguese merchants were admitted in August 1615 as bourgeois of Bordeaux. This political and economic privilege, costing each of them three-hundred francs, soon became a requirement for those who wished to open retail stores.[17] By this time, the "*étrangers naturalisés*" numbered two-hundred and sixty individuals.[18]

Despite these episodic indications by the government that the privileges granted to the *nouveaux Chrétiens* might be severely restricted, King Louis XIV issued a new series of *Lettres Patentes* in December 1656 which, although concerned specifically with the community in Bayonne, were applicable to the Bordeaux residents as well. In these *Lettres Patentes*, Louis confirmed the privileges of 1550 and 1574.[19] There was, however, a subtle difference between these decrees and those of 1550. The latter opened the whole realm of France to settlement by the *nouveaux Chrétiens;* the former lent itself to implicit confinement within the area of Guyenne.

The majority of the *marchands Portugais* had settled in Bordeaux and Bayonne or in smaller cities in the surrounding area. This geographical specificity created a *de facto* limitation of the *Lettres Patentes* which was further supported by their registration only by the *Parlement* of Bordeaux. In addition, while the *Lettres Patentes* of 1550 referred explicitly to all the cities of France, those of 1656 and subsequently of 1723 addressed themselves to Bordeaux and Bayonne and replaced "royaume" with the pronoun "y." "There" referred at most to the *Sénéchaussée* of Guyenne.[20]

That the passage of over one-hundred years had created only a minor change in the privileges of 1550 provided a certain amount of security for the *nouveaux Chrétiens,* who continued throughout this time to live within the frame of Catholicism. They were baptized, married, and buried according to the Catholic tradition and made no apparent attempts to reveal a Jewish heritage. They were repeating the history of the Marranos of Spain. Hiding to this extent their supposed religious faith and all that this faith required of them was the price they willingly paid for a temporarily secure existence.

Soon, however, this price ceased to have its former value, despite the almost irreproachable conduct of the *nouveaux Chrétiens* and their usefulness to the commerce of Bordeaux. Slowly the *marchands Portugais* began to be referred to as Jews, and the king and his advisors—including Madame de Maintenon, the strongly religious wife of the king—gave clear evidence that the future of these newly designated Jews was uncertain.

On November 20, 1684, by *arrêt* of Council, ninety-three Portuguese Jewish families who were not useful to the commerce of France were given one month to leave.[21] Although this is hardly a general expulsion order—the ninety-three, often called only by their first names, were exclusively the poorer Jews—the direction in which the government was heading was clear. For even Colbert, immune to the religious zeal motivating the king, had suggested the year before to the *intendant* of Bordeaux that eight or ten "Jewish" families be expelled each year. This procedure, Colbert reasoned, would permit the commerce of Bordeaux to pass into French hands.[22]

The royal government's change of heart, however, was not limited to the *nouveaux Chrétiens*. Louis' desire to establish one religion in his newly emerging state and to consolidate all power in the hands of the government led him to consider expelling all non-Catholics—Jews, crypto-Jews, and Protestants—from France. As the first step in this process, Louis revoked the Edict of Nantes on October 17, 1685.[23] Approximately two hundred thousand Huguenots, most of whom had been active among the commercial and industrial classes, migrated to Holland, Germany and America, while many more joined the Catholic Church as *nouveaux convertis*.

The economic effects of this revocation are not so clear as many historians assume.[24] Nevertheless, what was clear to most Frenchmen at the end of the 17th century was the retardation of the economic development of France; many began to blame the agricultural and industrial depressions, crop failures, famine, and bankruptcies on the exodus of the Huguenots.

Concern in Bordeaux about the impending expulsion of the *nouveaux Chrétiens* became greater as economic conditions worsened. With the maritime trade diminishing and credit and money scarce, M. de Bezons, *intendant* of Bordeaux, wrote in 1688 to the *Controleur général:*

It seems to me that trade has already diminished so much (because of the departure of new converts which occurs every day) that the government should not consider expelling the Portuguese from the realm at this time. They supply most of the money for bills of exchange here. I have long believed that nothing should be done about the Jews until new converts get over their desire to flee.[25]

The tensions between the desire to expel the *nouveaux Chrétiens* and the recognition of the practical consequences of this move were not easily resolved. The contemporary evaluation of the effects of the revocation, fear of further economic hardships and the declaration of war in 1688, however, led Louis to decide finally in favor of taxation rather than expulsion. That this tax, levied on February 9, 1700, was not allowed by the *Lettres Patentes* was no longer significant. That the tax was levied on *nouveaux Chrétiens* and not Jews was significant. The *marchands Portugais* were in a most precarious position vis-à-vis the king who, no longer choosing to believe politically in their Catholic camouflage, had begun to treat them as Jews. If ultimately viewed as Jews, however, the *nouveaux Chrétiens* would have no status.

The resolution was delayed for twenty-two years. An *arrêt* of Council dated February 21, 1722 ordered the *intendants* of Bordeaux and Auch to make a complete analysis of the Jews established there and the exact amount of their wealth. It ordered also that their property be seized and given to the king. Louis XV no longer hedged a categorical definition of the *marchands Portugais*. They were Jews, and as such could anticipate the same treatment as the Jews of Alsace, Metz, and Lorraine, for whom survival had never been a question of religious chameleonism but rather was dependent upon an ability to forego any financial roots or security and to pay exorbitant taxes for rights the *nouveaux Chrétiens* had always freely enjoyed.[26]

The *arrêt* was not left unchallenged, for the same differences of opinion which existed in 1688 continued to have influence in 1722. M. de Courson, *sous-intendant* of Bordeaux, took the defense of the *marchands Portugais*. In his *mémoire*, he explained that without the financial activities of the Jews, the commerce of Bordeaux (especially that of wine and liquor) and of the whole province would perish.[27]

The combination of an undeniable economic *utilité* on the part of the *nouveaux Chrétiens*, their capacity to pay a considerable sum of money to the government (100,000 *livres* and 2 *sols* per *livre*), and the lesson gained from the revoking of the Edict of Nantes were sufficiently influential to cause Louis XV to issue the *Lettres Patentes* of 1723. The *nouveaux Chrétiens* saw their privileges of 1550 and 1656 again confirmed, but with a most important addition. They were now officially recognized as Jews.[28]

The Bordeaux *Parlement* and *jurats*, as well as the royal *intendants*, had thus played no small part in convincing both Louis XIV and XV to permit the *nouveaux Chrétiens* to remain in France. What lay behind this continued support? Were the economic activities of the *marchands Portugais* in fact of major significance to the city of Bordeaux? The answer lies in the important transitional years of the close of the 17th and beginning of the 18th centuries. For it was then that Bordeaux experienced both the culmination of an economically sluggish century and the first stirrings of a commercial revitalization which was to make her the center of trade with the colonies and islands. The *marchands Portugais* were in a position to soften the effects of economic disasters, wars, and famines during the 17th century; the Jews consciously placed themselves in a position to take advantage of and aid in the commercial emergence of Bordeaux.

Seventeenth century Bordeaux represents a microcosm of the shortcomings of French commerce. Banking was rudimentary and almost nonexistent and the international trade (export of wine, resin products, cork, and various agricultural produce to England, Holland, the Hanseatic cities, and Scandinavia) was almost entirely in the hands of foreign merchants such as the Dutch, who resided in the city on a semipermanent basis. Bordelais ships were few and played a minor role in the activities of the port.[29] In addition to inferior naval power, political mistakes, and royal economic pressures, Bordeaux had a native bourgeoisie which, much to the chagrin of Colbert, was prudent, content with traditional practices and unwilling to become involved with the risks of shipping and colonial commerce. They preferred to remain in the secure position of middlemen, serving as liaisons for the foreign merchants.

The *marchands Portugais* evidenced the same economic timidity as the native Bordelais and appear to have played no part in the export of regional products to the northern markets, or in the exploration of the newly acquired European holdings in America. Instead, the majority devoted themselves to small and medium scale shopkeeping (with at least 10% of the community enjoying the privileges of a bourgeois status) as well as to the meager trade which existed between Bordeaux and Spain.[30] There were of course a few wealthy merchants who established the manufacturing of Moroccan leather and developed the silk manufacturing industry. But even these—the most wealthy— were more involved within the city of Bordeaux rather than in international trade.

The Sephardim did not limit themselves to economic pursuits alone. Continuing the diversity of earlier Spanish Jewish history, a considerable number entered the medical profession and served as doctors of the city of Bordeaux. Others became royal professors at the Faculty of Medicine.

The end of the 17th century brought one economic crisis after another to the previously complacent city of Bordeaux. Louis XIV's desire for territorial expansion led him to war with Holland in 1672, to the War of the League of Augsburg in 1688, and finally to the War of the Spanish Succession in 1702. In each instance, trade was disrupted, imports and exports were curtailed, and the city experienced the fiscal pressures of a king sorely in need of additional funds. In 1675, Bordeaux felt the king's wrath after an uprising in the city against an increase in royal taxes. Louis, always looking for ways to curtail local privileges, ordered the stationing of eighteen regiments in Bordeaux, the revocation of all the secular privileges of the bourgeoisie, including tax exemptions, and the transfer of all sovereign courts out of Bordeaux.[31]

The wars also led to a diminution of population which was exacerbated by the revocation of the Edict of Nantes. Finally, crop failures, famine, and severe winters (especially in 1672–74 and 1708–09) increased the suffering of the Bordelais. Wines were no longer sold, vineyards were abandoned, and the city of Bordeaux was soon required to pay the King 400,000 *livres* for the return of the *Parlement*, 200,000 for a gift, and 160,000 for the repurchase of posts. [32]

The 400 to 500 *nouveaux Chrétiens* were in a far better financial position than the majority of the Bordelais. Their retail trade had undoubtedly allowed them to accumulate a certain amount of savings which, rather than reinvest in land as their bourgeois status entitled them, they had retained as mobile wealth. Thus they were able to provide banking and credit services at a time when these services were at a premium and to obtain gold and silver (probably relying on Sephardic wealth in Amsterdam and England and Marrano wealth in the Iberian penisula) at a time when the shortage of specie was one of the central problems of the French economy.

From 1688 on, the wealthier Sephardim were able to impress both the local and central governments with their economic *utilité*. M. de Courson remarked that the "Jews" were the only ones who understood anything about banking. The vineyard owners, he wrote, find among the Portuguese Jews the sums they need for their agriculture, and the wholesale shippers the bills of exchange they need to fill their orders and to pay the king's revenues.[33] The local government was also impressed by the loyalty of the Sephardim when they loaned the city 30,000 *livres* in 1709, 100,000 in 1712, and another 100,000 in 1721.[34] The loans, advanced at a time of grain scarcity, were for the purpose of purchasing wheat.

We find then that as the 17th century came to a close, the *nouveaux Chrétiens* of Bordeaux were able to avoid expulsion by a happy coincidence of economic crisis and economic *utilité* and finally to be officially recognized as Jews in 1723. While economic considerations were behind their retention, what were the factors behind their emergence as self-avowed Jews? Certainly the king's reference to the *nouveaux Chrétiens* as Jews played a significant part. Nevertheless, this public recognition could never explain the subsequent development of a tightly organized Jewish community structure. We must turn to the Sephardim themselves for this explanation.

The stages by which the Portuguese merchants abandoned their "facade" of Catholicism may be easily traced. Between 1690 and 1700, the *nouveaux Chrétiens* ceased to baptize their children,[35] and by 1711 they were no longer having their marriages blessed in Church.[36] Instead the Bordelais curies had accepted the role, often accompanied by monetary gain, of civil agents who merely registered the marriages of the Jews.

As the Portuguese began to divest themselves of their Catholicism, they encountered pressures to convert which were aggravated by newly imposed economic and social restrictions. Notwithstanding the lax attitude on the part of many of the religious orders in Bordeaux and the willingness of the curies to act as civil agents, there was a significant number of Bordelais, as strongly attached to the Church as to the guilds, who sought to bring the Jews back into the Catholic fold.[37] In addition, there were those Jews who freely chose to convert to Catholicism, some because of their inability as Jews to practice medicine,[38] others either because of a low economic status or a romantic involvement with a non-Jew. For whatever reasons, conversion now held in its wake severe recrimination on the part of the newly emerged Jewish community and at times led to acts of physical violence.[39]

The definitive step came with the formal establishment of a Jewish communal structure. In 1693, the Portuguese merchants were taxed highly by the city of Bordeaux. The tax was in the form of a loan which no one expected to be paid back. The Bordelais, however, agreed to use the income from the loan for the poorhouse and to free the Portuguese merchants from their turn in filling the position of treasurer. This agreement not only removed the weighty financial burden from the Portuguese of making up the yearly deficits of the poorhouse, but it also paved the way for the creation of their own charitable organization.[40] By 1699, the *Société de Bienfaisance* or *Sedaca* was organized with a treasury to care for the indigent Sephardim of Bordeaux and with a syndic to oversee the operations.[41]

From the beginning, however, the *Sedaca* extended its activities beyond caring for the poor. In fact, the *Sedaca* quickly became synonymous with the Portuguese *nation*, and the syndic and deputies were invested with far reaching authority over the activities of all Sephardim. Numerous associations, each one with a different charitable mission, developed alongside the *Sedaca*, but clearly under its control.[42] Bakeries and kosher meat shops were established and overseen by the council of the *Sedaca*, and a rabbi, hired to care for the spiritual needs of the *nation*, was subject to the strict control of the syndic.[43] By 1711, all marriages had to have the approval of the syndic or his assistant. Such approval, inconsistent with traditional Jewish law which gave authority over marital matters to the father, was received only after the payment of a specified sum of money.[44] Control over the community was further strengthened by the retributive powers of the *Sedaca*. Anyone who chose not to pay his taxes was forbidden to attend any communal functions, excluded, in the case of the women, from the baths, and prevented from being buried or married by his fellow Jews.[45]

Thus, by the time the *Lettres Patentes* of 1723 recognized the *nouveaux Chrétiens* as Jews, they had established on their own a tightly organized Jewish community able to oversee and discipline the activities of its members.

We must return to the question of why the *marchands Protugais* chose to emerge as Jews and to establish such a community. The explanation is not a simple one, yet only with a further understanding of the reasons behind their emergence can we appreciate the role the Sephardim were to play both in Bordelais and French Jewish history.

One of the most often stated explanations is the ascendancy of a secular mercantilist outlook which prompted an official indifference to the religion of those who enriched France commercially.[46] According to this analysis, the *nouveaux Chrétiens*, having demonstrated their economic usefulness, were able to emerge as Jews without official hindrance.

There is no doubt that religious intolerance had little appeal to the 18th century Bordeaux bourgeoisie. Nevertheless, this diminution of Christian religious zeal did not create the Bordelais Jewish community. What is also assumed by this explanation, however, is the retention by the *nouveaux Chrétiens* of a crypto-Judaism which they would reveal as soon as circumstances permitted. This assumption is difficult to support factually and has long plagued those historians who seek to uncover the religious commitment of the Marranos.[47]

Some of the *nouveaux Chrétiens* who first arrived in Bordeaux apparently remained Christian and successfully fused into the French population. Claims of descent from the Portuguese merchants made by members of the *Parlement* substantiate this assertion. It appears likely, moreover, that many of those who came from Spain, where a greater assimilation had taken place between them and the Catholics, were in fact faithful Catholics.

By the end of the 17th century, however, a new wave of Portuguese emigrants arrived in Bordeaux as a result of Don Pedro's decision (1683) to expel all *cristãos novos* condemned by the Inquisition. These Marranos had once fled from Spain rather than convert to Catholicism; their conversion *en masse* in Portugal was not a result of an individual decision to embrace the dominant religion but rather was caused by the determination of the king to retain the wealth and economic sophistication these merchants brought to his realm. There is thus every reason to believe that those *nouveaux Chrétiens* who came to Bordeaux from Portugal, where the only normative Jewish community was ostensibly Catholic, would not only be prepared to live as Catholics but also would be the most likely to protect a potential Judaism. We might also conclude that Louis' reference to the *nouveaux*

Chrétiens as Jews was a reflection of the fact that these recent *émigrés* were indeed more Jewish.

Neither religious conviction nor public recognition, however, would have been sufficient to elicit their emergence as a corporate Jewish community had not the *nouveaux Chrétiens* also believed that by increasing their outward attachment to Judaism and seeking corporate status, they could become more secure. It may appear strange that at a time when they risked retaliation by a Catholic regime, the *nouveaux Chrétiens* would conclude that their security rested on their becoming more Jewish. Part of the explanation undoubtedly lies in the changes brought about by Louis XIV's death and the ascension of Louis XV. For under Louis XV and more significantly his regent, Philippe, duc d'Orléans, weighty financial concerns, a necessary reliance on an aristocratic revival, and a cynicism towards religion undermined the centralized absolutism of the past century. To emerge as a corporation in 18th century France was thus in fact a means of insuring stability, security, and official recognition.

Bordelais corporations represented a composite of both religious and commercial characteristics. Each one, placed under the patronage of a saint, participated in religious ceremonies and fulfilled municipal obligations. In return for a high taxation by the king, who saw himself as the dispenser of the right to work, they were allowed to limit their members and maintain an exclusive monopoly on their branch of industry. To emerge as a corporation was thus for the Sephardim not only a viable means of expressing their religious commitment, but also enabled them to retain their language and close association with other Sephardim and permitted them, at a time when their numbers were increasing, the right to regulate their own commercial and financial operations.

The commercial advantages must not be overlooked in seeking to explain the creation of the Portuguese *nation*. The *nouveaux Chrétiens* had entered France as a merchant group. Having already proven themselves in this capacity in Spain and Portugal, their usefulness to the economy was assumed. They had been protected largely because this was proven correct. Through the years, their financial resources and unusual commercial skills had saved them from expulsion. To assure their continued toleration was the prime concern of the Sephardim. It is understandable that they would choose the type of organization which could be integrated into French society and gain for them official recognition and a secure status while simultaneously allowing for control of the *raison d'être* (at least in the eyes of the non-Sephardim) of the group: their commercial usefulness.

The *nouveaux Chrétiens* emerged as Jews then not only because they retained a commitment to Judaism, but also because they believed that emergence would grant them the security that the *Lettres Patentes* no longer provided and the internal discipline that their increased population and economic interests required. Once incorporated, the Sephardim were in fact successful both in obtaining official recogni-tion for their tightly organized communal structure and in engaging fully in the economic development of Bordeaux. The commercial concerns of the *nation* moreover led (as happened generally in France) to an increasingly more secular outlook. This outlook was soon reflected in a Judaism which became for the *nation* a means of giving legitimacy and stability to the community, of mobilizing the emotional and spiritual support of the members, and of making it possible to finance and administer places of worship, welfare, education, and social activities all of which were used in the organization and administration of political and economic functions. As we examine the *nation*, first in its relation to Bordelais society, then in its internal development, we shall see this more exactly.

During the first half of the 18th century, the commerce of Bordeaux altered dramatically; by the close of the century, the city could boast a bourgeoisie whose standard of living was well above average, a thriving port, and an expectation that its commercial splendor would continue.[48] One of the main reasons for this economic change was the *Lettres Patentes* of 1717 which regulated commerce with the colonies. Authorized ports (including Bordeaux) were permitted to equip ships for the isles and colonies; these ships were automatically exempted from the customary fees of entering and leaving France. In addition, the king's council had declared that Bordeaux, along with Rouen, Nantes, and La Rochelle, had the exclusive rights of dealing with the Black trade in Africa. With these privileges, commerce began to blossom. Ships were built and outfitted, large sums of money were invested, exports rapidly began to exceed imports, and the population increased from 48,000 in 1710 to 108,000 by the end of the century (the Jewish population also increased threefold from 500 in 1713 to 1500 on the eve of the Revolution).[49]

The 18th century, however, was not lacking in economic hardships. Grain scarcities occurred throughout this period, and the wars during the middle of the century made commerce with England hazardous and eventually caused France to lose Canada and Louisiana. In addition, in the islands which remained—Martinique, Guadeloupe, Sainte Lucie, the Antilles—the English succeeded in underselling the French and the colonies chose to buy cheaply rather than patriotically.

Despite these hardships, active trade between Bordeaux and Northern Europe, the Isles, and even Spain continued. In fact, trade with Spain had a curious significance, for although it was not supported either by the French or Spanish governments until the last third of the century, it was continuous enough to play at least a secondary role in the commercial activity of the port. Imports, including iron bars, Spanish wool, and olive oil, were especially important and always exceeded the wheat and flour exported. During the Seven Years War, Spain became the center of a transit trade and Bordelais wine was shipped circuitously to England while Irish butter made the same trip back.[50]

The scarcity of documentary evidence makes it difficult to assess the various economic roles of the Sephardim during this period. We have found enough evidence, however, to convince us that although the Jews were not the most numerous group engaged in the commercial revitalization, their position as bankers, shippers, brokers, and merchants was significant.

The Gradis family is the one most often cited as illustrative of the involvement of the Sephardim in Bordelais commerce. Having begun as small merchants first in Toulouse and then in Bordeaux, the family soon amassed a considerable fortune. At the time of Abraham Gradis' death in 1780, his estate alone was estimated at 10 million *livres!* Relying upon family ties and personal contacts, the Gradis firm established connections with the Jews of London and Amsterdam and began trading with the French islands (especially Sainte Dominique and Martinique), where wine, alcohol, flour, and saltbeef were exported in return for sugar and indigo. In 1748, Gradis formed the *Société du Canada* which was responsible for equipping the colonies of Quebec and which, during the Seven Years War, involved itself in the chartering and arming of ships for the king—a costly venture which left the king indebted to the firm for many millions.[51]

Although the Gradis family was the most successful, there were numerous other Jewish families who took advantage not only of Bordeaux's favorable commercial position, but also of the personal contacts they had maintained with other European Sephardim. These latter were extremely helpful, since the unsophisticated banking methods, especially the *lettres de change* (bills of exchange), depended upon the honesty, integrity, and most important of all the accountability of the individuals involved.

In an incomplete list of the *négociants* of Bordeaux during the 18th century, the following three are among the 27 Sephardic families listed: David Lindo, *négociant* of wines and colonial products, whose extensive commercial correspondence covered Amsterdam, Spain, London, Hamburg, and various cities in France; Abraham Francia, a shipper who dealt exclusively with Sainte Dominique; Gabriel da

Silva, whose banking interests along with importing and exporting included Amsterdam, Spain, Curacao, London, Hamburg, Italy, and Antwerp. The representatives of these *négociants* in the various European cities were often (though never exclusively) Sephardic Jews. An exception, however, is found in the trade with Spain (usually overlooked as an area of Sephardic involvement), where Frenchmen were the liaison between the Sephardic Bordelais and the Spanish.[52]

Thus the Sephardim, benefiting from Bordeaux's commercial privileges and their own international contacts, successfully engaged in banking as well as in importing and exporting. To be sure, the *nation* was not exclusively comprised of these wealthy *négociants;* nevertheless, it is significant that, by 1785, 1.7% of the community was listed as *négociants* in contrast to .8% of the general Bordelais population.[53] In fact, as we further examine the composition of the *nation*, we find that its members are involved exclusively in commercial concerns, that many families belong to the bourgeois class,[54] and finally and most significantly that the *nation* as a whole is equivalent statistically to the bourgeoisie.

Although juridically defined, the bourgeoisie was a socially heterogeneous class to which wealthy *négociants*, lawyers, doctors, and professors as well as small merchants, shopkeepers, and tradesmen belonged. To become a member, one had to own a home in the city worth no less than 1,500 *livres* (a modest amount), live there at least five years, and have it be used as a normal residence. The benefits of the title were most often felt commercially, for example in the freedom to sell Bordeaux wines before the nonbourgeois and with the payment of only one-half of the usual taxes. Although the title carried with it privileges and a certain social status, it never implied a narrow socioeconomic group nor did it imply that all men of means were included. To describe the *nation* as a bourgeois body then is to assume the existence of varying degrees of wealth and commercial significance. It is also to assume that the *nation* stands for the most part economically above a minimum standard.

In a random selection of ten Bordelais bourgeois marriage contracts from 1782 to 1784, one finds that only one is greater than 25,600 *livres*.[55] In a comparable selection of Sephardic contracts, there is also only one contract greater than 25,600 *livres* (229,000) although one-half of the contracts involve 12,000 *livres* or more.[56] Marriage contracts reveal more, however, than financial means alone and the Sephardic contracts not only list the professions of the brides and grooms, but also specify the categories of wealth included in the dowries. All of the contracts involve Sephardic Jews marrying fellow Sephardim, some involve marriages within an extended family (for example cousins), all indicate professions of either tradesmen, merchants, brokers, bankers or *négociants,* and most reveal that family interests were strong in insuring economic stability. Thus we find that *lettres de change,* rents, property, and inherited titles (such as *courtier en la ville de Bordeaux*) are included in the dowries.

Investigation into inheritance statistics as well as the payments of the *capitation* and *vingtième* among both the Bordelais bourgeois and Sephardim further confirms the middle class composition of the *nation.* Among 45 Sephardic inheritance statements examined, more than one-half revealed assets of over 10,000 *francs,*[57] while one-third had property and capital worth more than 30,000 *francs.* Although there were a few Sephardim who died penniless, by far the vast majority had assets which would include them among the bourgeoisie.[58]

We shall soon pursue the composition of the *nation* more fully; nevertheless it is important for comparative purposes to understand the economic diversity within the community. In a *capitation* list of 1744, we find that the *nation,* taxed as a corporate group, paid 6,017.15 *livres,* that 25% of the Sephardim paid a *capitation* of 50 *livres* or more and 10% paid more than 100 *livres.*[59] These statistics not only compare favorably with the bourgeoisie, among whom 16% paid more than 50 *livres* and 25% paid between 10 and 50 *livres,* but also rank the *nation* an economic notch higher in equating it with the wealthiest merchant groups such as the *marchands de planches* (wood merchants).[60] What is not revealed by these statistics, however, is that only 158 out of 330 Jewish heads of family paid this *capitation.*[61] Undoubtedly there was in addition to the wealthy, a significant number of Sephardim judged too poor to pay any *capitation*—a situation explained in large part by the waves of immigration which continually brought new and often poor families to Bordeaux.

The amount and type of *vingtième* paid by the *nation* confirms even more clearly its bourgeois status. While this tax was divided into four parts, namely on land and houses, rents and loans, industrial and commercial undertakings, and duties and offices, it was the first part which was the most significant.[62] Originally designed as a tax to be paid by each individual regardless of class, the *vingtième* soon fell prey to the machinations surrounding any form of royal taxation. One might assume, nevertheless, that the Sephardim would have paid the various types of *vingtième* on an individual basis commensurate with their property and commercial assets. This was not the case, however, and instead the *nation* paid the *vingtième* of industry as a "community of Portuguese of the city," notwithstanding the fact that most payments were by individuals (sculptors, architects, *négociants . . .*). Only rarely, as in the case of the *marchands de planches* (500 *livres*) and the *marchands de poisson salé* (fish merchants—968 *livres*), was the tax paid by a group. Of these groups, the Jews paid by far the most—5610 *livres*. [63] The *nation* then, viewed officially as a commercial group, was taxed accordingly.

If commercial advantage was one of the motivating factors behind the creation of the *nation*, the expectations of the Sephardim were met. For as a corporate Jewish body, the *nation* prospered and acquired an economic status which further secured its presence in Bordeaux. Part of the success of the *nation* lay in its ability to control and regulate the economic as well as social, political, and spiritual activities of its members. For consistent with and reflecting its commercial role, the *nation* had developed a strong communal organization whose institutions were respected and supported on pragmatic grounds (especially by the wealthy who had the most to gain by keeping the group together) and were challenged and even discarded if found to be a hindrance to full economic assimilation.

Internally the *nation* divided itself into four categories, each of which occupied a clearly defined rung in the hierarchical ladder. The *anciens*, those taxpayers who had once been or were presently on the Council of the *Sedaca*, occupied the top rung. Following them in decreasing order of respectability and influence were the taxpayers, the poor who were provided for, and lastly the poor who were not provided for. [64] Financial success was the primary standard against which both the Christian and Jewish communities measured the worth of each Jew.

Notwithstanding the privileged position of the *nation*, the Sephardim were consistently burdened with high and varied tax obligations in the form of forced loans to the city of Bordeaux and the king and in the form of regular city and royal taxes, of which the two most significant were the *capitation* and the *vingtième*. [65] In addition, there were always the internal taxes of the *nation*.

Although these financial obligations were oppressive and often difficult to meet, they represented only part of the responsibility of the community. The *nation* also had to supervise the behavior of its members in order to prevent any difficulty with or inconvenience to the Bordelais population. Realizing that its security depended not only upon its role as a reliable source of revenue, but also upon its acceptability as a model bourgeois community, the *nation* could never afford to ignore the problems arising from an excess of poor Sephardim, illegal business activities of wealthy Sephardim, and competition and disgrace from Italian and Avignonese Jews.

From the very beginning the *Sedaca* strove to care for the poor among the Jewish community. Not only were there associations created for visiting, feeding, and burying the poor, but also the *nation* paid a doctor, surgeon, and pharmacist to treat the sick, and established a pension to be given to each indigent family.[66] In caring for its poor in this way, the *nation* hoped to avoid any disturbances they might create among the Bordelais. The tremendous increase in the Jewish population, however, soon made this type of surveillance-charity impossible and instead the *nation* began to restrict its concern and responsibility by providing for only ninety Sephardi families and finally by seeking the help of the royal *intendants* in expelling "vagabond" Jews.[67] Despite these measures, the *nation* was faced throughout the 18th century with the dilemma of protecting and regulating its poor (for example the poor were prevented from buying and selling old clothes) without increasing the already heavy tax burdens and thus risking a discipline problem among its other members.

If the *nation* was sensitive to the activities of its poor, it was also concerned that the wealthy *négociants* and bankers act in a respectable and irreproachable manner. An incident which occurred in 1750 confirmed the fears of the Sephardim that a misdemeanor among a few could jeopardize the position of the community. Danson and Verneuil were captains of two boats which had been provisioned by a Bordelais shipper, Dulorier, and lost at sea in 1750. The two boats and cargo were insured for 147,800 *livres* in the names of the shipper and five Sephardic *négociants*. The four insurance companies involved accused Dulorier and the *négociants* of having caused the loss of the ships and of having falsely described the cargo. In 1753, the *Parlement* of Bordeaux found the six to be guilty and condemned them to be hung in effigy until death.[68] The effects of this incident were not limited to the *Parlement*'s decision, however, for on June 6, 1751, the *intendant* of Bordeaux, M. de Tourny, ordered a census of the Bordelais Jews,[69] and on July 24, 1753, the *nation* found it expedient to expel a significant number of its poor.[70]

The activities of the few wealthy Sephardim had compromised the trustworthiness of the whole group; further restrictions and tighter controls were seen by the *nation* as necessary to avoid any further scandals which could have similar repercussions. Thus as a result of this incident as well as an increasing recalcitrance on the part of some Sephardim to pay taxes, assume the leadership of the *nation,* and obey the authority of the syndics and *anciens,* the *nation* sought and obtained official recognition for a rigid oligarchical organization with virtual dictatorial powers.[71]

On December 14, 1760, the *Règlement de la nation des Juifs Portugais de Bordeaux* was approved and authorized by the king. Article X, one of the most significant articles in the *Règlement,* permitted the *nation* by a two-thirds vote of the assembly (usually composed of former syndics) to expel any Jew whose conduct was found to be "irregular and reproachable."[72] The immediate effect of the royal sanction of this authority was an ordinance initiated by the *nation* and promulgated by the governor of Guyenne on September 17, 1761, in which one hundred and fifty-two Jews, mostly of Avignonese origin, were expelled from Bordeaux.[73]

The king continued to sanction the formalizing of the communal structure in his ordinance of May 13, 1763. This ordinance, necessitated by a disagreement within the Sephardic community over the power of taxation, decreed that the taxes of the *nation* were to be determined by the syndic, his two deputies, and four *anciens,* and that their decisions could be challenged before an assembly of 13 *anciens* with none of the initial seven participating.[74]

These two ordinances became the focal point for a conflict within the *nation* between the older "nobility" and the newer, less established, and often less wealthy families. Charges were hurled by the latter that the leaders of the community were almost all related to each other, that they overcharged the poorer members of the *nation,* and that they represented only the very wealthy—the bankers, shippers, and *négociants.* Everyone but the indigent and corrupt, the "rebels" declared, should be permitted to participate in communal affairs, including of course determining the tax rate. The rule of the few was henceforth to be eliminated.[75]

To counter these attacks, accusations were made that the dissidents included only those too old to understand and too easily led by the young, those involved in questionable economic activities, those too poor to be taxed, and finally those who had just arrived and were really unaware of the issues.[76]

The king was forced to intervene. After having consulted with M. Boutin, the *intendant* of Bordeaux in charge of hearing the views of the dissident members of the *nation,* he issued the definitive *arrêt* of Council on February 22, 1766. The *anciens* of the *nation* were to be defined as all those who previously had filled the position as syndic. In an attempt to appease the newer members of the community, however, two non-*anciens* were to join the syndic, the deputies, and the four *anciens* in matters of royal taxation; communal taxes were to be decided by thirteen *anciens.*[77]

The conflict within the *nation* had neither revolved about nor involved any substantial ideological issues. Clearly it was a struggle for control and the dissidents had to settle for what was in reality a worthless compromise. The two non-*anciens* were to be selected by the syndic and the *anciens*. The king, however, in realizing the significance of a well organized and financially dependable privileged group, had supported the compromise with his authority. This support enabled the *nation* to function unhindered by internal threats.

Thus throughout the first half of the 18th century, the *nation* had been faced with a multitude of problems which included an overabundance of poor, an influx of non-Sephardic Jews, and too few among the wealthy willing to assume responsibility as syndic. In addition, dismay increased among many (including as we shall soon see the rabbi himself) over the oligarchical nature of the community. Nevertheless, during this same time the *nation* successfully defined itself as a tightly organized community directed by the wealthy and responsive at all times to the expectations of the Bordeaux community and the central government.

These expectations, however, were neither so clear nor so consistent as the Sephardim would have liked. The hiatus between the *Lettres Patentes* of 1723 and those of 1776 saw a continuation of the struggle on the part of the *nation*, supported by the *intendant* of Bordeaux, to uphold both the distinction between Sephardic and Ashkenazic Jews and the privileges which supported the autonomous existence of the *nation*.

For the Jews of Spanish and Portuguese descent, there had long existed an unbridgeable gap between themselves and all other Jews—a gap which reflected not only the very real cultural differences, but also an assumed racial superiority on the part of the Sephardim.[78] Identification with the Ashkenazic Jews of France, who chose to remain culturally estranged from their environment, to dress and live in accordance with traditional Jewish practice, and who, in addition, were subject to humiliating economic, social, and political restrictions, was unthinkable.[79] The most that the Jews of Bordeaux could envision was tolerance. This tolerance, however, was dependent upon an official acknowledgment of the separateness of the communities—an acknowledgment which the Sephardim often found difficult to elicit.

On May 5, 1731, the Counselor of State, in a letter to the *intendant* of Bordeaux, M. de Boucher, declared that the Jews of Bordeaux ought to pay the same amount of protection taxes as the Ashkenazic Jews. This had just been fixed at forty *livres* annually for each head of family. M. de Boucher came to the defense of the Sephardim and reminded the Counselor that the Portuguese merchants, as contrasted to the Jews of the Northeast, who were merely tolerated, enjoyed the same privileges and fiscal obligations as the other inhabitants of Bordeaux.[80] Not content with M. de Boucher's reply, the Counselor then requested an explanation of the differences between the Portuguese and Avignonese Jews. Again M. de Boucher defended the Sephardim and carefully distinguished them from the "poor and miserable Avignonese" whom the Sephardim "scorned" and with whom they had no commercial connections.[81]

Although the *intendant* of Bordeaux stated that the Portuguese had the same privileges as other Bordelais, both he and the Sephardim knew this to be an exaggeration. The Jews, restricted to commercial activities, were prevented from participating in the Chamber of Commerce, excluded from the guilds and municipal functions and, with the help of the *intendant* himself, threatened with expulsion if they did not curtail their religious practices. The same M. de Boucher who was willing to support the distinctions between the Ashkenazim and Sephardim and to prevent the *nation* from being burdened by additional royal taxation, was also willing to suggest a number of ways in which the king could prohibit the Jews from practicing their religion. The Jewish *nation*, he wrote in a letter to M. le Chancelier d'Aguesseau in February 1734, is fearful and always in alarm concerning the orders from the court. Far from being loved by the Christians, the Jews are abhorred by them and, if they continue with success, it is only that certain influential persons derive benefits from their presence. The *intendant* then continued with suggestions for the king:

The king can, without difficulty, order the synagogues to be destroyed, and prohibit Jews of any tribe from reestablishing them. Consequently, Jews will no longer be permitted to assemble for prayer, regardless of pretext, without facing expulsion from the kingdom, confiscation of their possessions, and even corporal punishment.

Prohibit them from having rabbis or other specially appointed persons for their ceremonies; seize the ornaments and sacred vases and dispose of them as the king orders; prohibit them from closing their shops except on those days ordered by the Church. . . .[82]

M. de Boucher's position was not unique among the *intendants* of Bordeaux; twenty years later, on March 6, 1753, M. de Tourny wrote that one ought to recognize and suffer only the *marchands Portugais* and not the Jews. No open synagogues, he declared, no day of Sabbath, and no public ceremonies should be allowed.[83] Both *intendants* sought to focus on the economic character of the *nation* and at the same time to restrict its religious activities, thereby preventing any further discomfort to the king and his advisors from the Judaism of their subjects. Notwithstanding the fact that these stringent measures were never enforced, the Sephardim could not ignore the conclusion that their Judaism allowed for a confusion with the Ashkenazim and provided the basis for discriminatory legislation. All this was to change, however, when the king recognized the *nation* in the *Règlements* of 1760 and 1763.[84] From then on it was assumed that not only did the *nation* have the power to police itself, but also it had implicitly received official sanction for its Judaism.[85]

By the middle of the 18th century, the Sephardim were thus well aware of both the advantages and the risks which their corporate status entailed. As a Jewish *nation*, they were able to consolidate, organize, and ultimately legitimize their community.[86] As a Jewish *nation*, however, they were also committed to a religious faith and tradition which was alien to the Catholicism of their country and which associated them with a people almost universally despised. As we follow the Sephardim on the eve of the Revolution and during the struggle for enfranchisement and emancipation, we shall see how the *nation* took advantage of its corporate status and minimized or eschewed any potentially negative features of its religious commitment. For the present, however, we shall focus on the nature and quality of the Sephardic commitment to Judaism.

While we have a number of different sources which together enable us to describe in detail the institutional expressions of the *nation*'s commitment to Judaism, there are few sources which allow us to penetrate the minds and hearts of the Sephardim. Their personal spiritual lives remain obscure.[87]

The report in which M. de Boucher recommended curbing the religious practices of the Jews also included a detailed description of the Jewish community written by the *intendant*'s staff assistant, M. de Puddefer. The most illuminating passages of this report are worth citing:

Five or six of these families trade in arms and goods with America, others are bankers. Their trade is quite considerable; they have the money of the principal townspeople . . . ; several are brokers in paper and commodities, others trade in calico, chocolate, tea, coffee, and porcelain. Among the Avignonese (the tribe of Benjamin), some trade in cloth, but the majority peddle old gold and silver braidings throughout the town or trade in second-hand clothes.

Five or six years ago, the Jews still carried their children into our churches to receive baptism; but since then they publicly circumcize the children in a rabbi's presence. The rabbis perform marriages as publicly as the Christians.

They close their shops on Saturday and carry publicly in their hands their prayer books, as well as their white veils and other ornaments. Sometimes they go to the synagogue barefooted, slippers for shoes, and ungartered, with the borders of their hats pulled down over their eyes. All of this is done openly and in full view of Christians. Their main holidays are in September for the

Tabernacles and March at the full moon for their Easter; at certain times they wear a *tala,* and carry *cecis* with the ends of white wool hanging down. They sing and pray out loud. They use a horn called a *sosopha* to invoke the angel in the desert. The Jews have acquired over the past two or three years certain lands along the walls of Saint-Julien parish. Here they have put the sepultures of their dead; they bury their dead openly, and often even during the day.[88]

From M. de Puddefer's investigation, undertaken according to M. de Boucher with circumspection and secrecy, we learn that not only did the Sephardim have a number of synagogues (the services were actually held in private homes) where they publicly celebrated their marriages and circumcisions,[89] but also they celebrated Yom Kippur ("the slippered feet") and Sukkoth and observed the traditional blowing of the *shofar*.[90]

In addition, we find from the minutes of the community that the *nation* observed the Sabbath and punished with fines those who did not, had monopolies which took care of baking matzo as well as preparing and selling kosher meat memorialized its dead during Yom Kippur and Passover, and convened a *Bet Din* (Jewish court of law), composed of the rabbi and two lay members, to consider the legality of issues such as engagements and marriages. Lastly, the *nation* established a *Talmud Torah* (an elementary Jewish school maintained primarily for the poor), although its continuous existence is questionable.[91]

Was this Judaism which emerged and which permeated the lives of the Sephardim a reflection of the religious commitment of the *nation*'s leaders? Events will indicate that often this was not the case. Nevertheless, as the *nation* became manifestly Jewish and as a greater number of Portuguese *émigrés* arrived in Bordeaux, the activities and responsibilities of the community reinforced its moral as well as institutional commitment to Judaism. *Sheluhim* ("envoys") from Safed, Jerusalem, Tiberias, and Hebron journeyed to Bordeaux and succeeded in obtaining financial assistance for the Sephardic communities of Palestine. The *nation* responded, moreover, to the distress of the communities of Smyrna and Bosnia, found it necessary to consult with the Sephardim of Amsterdam, and soon became responsible for insuring the *kashrut* of the wines of Bordeaux shipped to the Ashkenazim of Germany and the Jews of England and Holland.[92] The role of the rabbi (the first and probably most influential being Joseph Falcon from Jerusalem) in reawakening the *nation*'s ties to traditional Judaism must also be emphasized.

It is perhaps in the status of the rabbi as well as in the absence of traditional Jewish education that we are best able to perceive the limitations of the *nation*'s Judaism. As in many 18th century Jewish communities, the lay leaders of the *nation* were more powerful than their rabbi. But the rabbi of Bordeaux was not only less powerful than the lay leaders (he had no civil jurisdiction), his authority in religious matters as well was subject to the dictates of an oligarchy jealous of its ubiquitous control. Thus, in addition to decreeing that the syndic must confirm any marriage or engagement for it to be legal,[93] the leaders of the *nation* made it painfully clear to the rabbi, in a series of regulations, where his authority, or lack of it, lay. The rabbi, they decreed, was to care for the spiritual functions (which always remained rather vague) of the community while refraining from imposing any penalties, publishing any decisions, or marrying any couples without the permission of the syndic. On the other hand the rabbi (on pain of being fired) was to publish everything given him by the syndic, deputies, and *anciens*. Commensurate with this rather limited role was the rabbi's salary which was raised to 300 *livres* in 1743, 900 *livres* in 1775, and 1200 *livres* in 1786.[94]

Apparently one of the three rabbis employed by the *nation* during the 18th century (Joseph Falcon, Jacob Athias, or David Athias) attempted to improve his position. In a letter awkward both in its demands and its French style, this rabbi begged the *intendant* of Bordeaux to intervene to gain him the respect of his community.

> [If] His Grace the Intendant would be so kind as to take the trouble to make a small reprimand to the heads of the Portuguese nation about the lack of respect and deference that they have for their rabbi. All and sundry would be all the more thankful for his kindness in view of the resulting law and order.
>
> Since the light of His Greatness is far above that of the suppliant, he will know what means to take and what pretext to use without making the reprimand appear to have been solicited.[95]

The rabbis appear to have had equally little control over the *Talmud Torah* which the *nation* reestablished in 1760. There had been one in existence in 1731 but sometime between then and the middle of the century it appears to have disappeared. Administered by a committee responsible to the leaders of the *nation*, the *Talmud Torah* was funded by an annual allotment by the *nation*, individual contributions and when both quickly proved to be insufficient by a surcharge on the existing meat tax.[96] The curriculum of December 25, 1760, designed to teach the young Hebrew grammar, an appreciation of the Psalms and Prophets, and a knowledge of the prayer book—all of which would lead to "a fear of God and the development of honest men"—conscientiously excluded any study of the Talmud and replaced Yid-

dish with Spanish as the language into which the verses were translated.[97] Anticipating the educational reforms of the *Maskilim*
(enlightened Jews) of Germany, the Sephardim stressed decorum,
orderliness, and tranquillity; prohibited the use of the rod, which
they viewed as retarding the educational process; and most significantly introduced French and arithmetic into the revised curriculum
of March 20, 1774.[98]

By rejecting the Talmud and Midrash and stressing the Bible as the
exclusive source of divine truth, the Sephardim developed a Judaism
which was compatible with 18th century rationalism. The *nation* was
bound neither by the ancient laws and customs nor the religious-
political heritage and destiny which united Jewish communities
throughout the world. One looks in vain, moreover, for indications of
a profound religiosity and spirituality in the life of the *nation*. Never,
for example, is there mention of a religious debate; never is there a
development of religious heterodoxy; never in fact is there any indication of a spiritual or intellectual crisis. None of this denies that individual Sephardim may have had a deep personal commitment to their
religion. Nevertheless, the absence of an intense religious environment, the profound break with tradition represented by the inclusion
of non-Jewish standards and values, and the denationalization of the
Jewish faith reveal the extent to which the Judaism of the *nation* was
transformed and, as we shall see, explain the ease with which the
Sephardim were to emerge as French citizens.

Despite official support for its structure and religion obtained with
the *Règlements* of 1760 and 63, the *nation* continued to seek areas in
which it could increase its influence and fortify its privileges. Thus, in
addition to giving the government money to help purchase ships in
times of war, the Sephardim maintained contact with their influential
agent in Paris, Jacob Rodrigues Péreire, who advised when and to
whom they should lend rather significant sums of money.[99] With the
help of Péreire, who received 2400 *livres* in gratitude, the most generous of all *Lettres Patentes* were finally promulgated in June 1776. For
the first time since 1550, the Jews of Bordeaux were explicitly free to
dwell wherever they chose.[100]

All the *Lettres Patentes* to the contrary, the Sephardim remained, as
Lopes-Dubec demonstrated in his autobiographical *mémoire*,
privileged only within the limits defined by the usefulness of their
position.

I was born on the 28th of April. I was taught to read French and Hebrew, to
write, to do arithmetic, and finance. That was the only instruction which was
given to Israelite children who, finding themselves excluded by the country's

laws from all the professions (even the arts and crafts for which it was necessary to be of the Catholic faith), were destined to practise commerce.[101]

Nevertheless, their privileges were far more extensive than those enjoyed either by the Northeastern Jews or the Southwestern Protestants and thus elicited from the *nation* support for the monarchy and a commitment to retaining intact the societal structures of the *ancien régime*.[102]

Intellectually, the *nation* as a whole had remained relatively silent. To be sure there were the famous defenses of the Sephardic Jews written by Péreire (who resided in Paris) and Isaac de Pinto (who spent most of his life in Holland) as well as the noted accomplishments of these two in the fields of linguistics and economics.[103] Louis Francia de Beaufleury and David Gradis were prominent Bordelais "intellectuals," although neither made any significant or enduring contributions. What was blatantly lacking, however, was any serious confrontation with Judaism (as we had in the Amsterdam community) or any profound philosophical framework within which the Sephardim as Jews and as Frenchmen could give meaning to their lives. For the most part the men of the *nation* had directed their energies to the commercial field; where they entered the intellectual field at all, it was more as Frenchmen than as Jews.

Proud, pragmatic, and strongly committed to the *modus vivendi*, the Jews of Bordeaux had integrated themselves into the French community. The compromises which they had made with traditional Judaism had come without significant conflict; they had assimilated the French standards for acceptability (derived from the increasingly more secularized bourgeois world in which they were living) simultaneously with their emergence as Jews. Thus assimilation and emergence went hand in hand and, as we shall see, fused to become the single thread in the psychological development of the *nation*.

2

The Malesherbes "Commission"
and the
Portuguese NATION

Having attained a privileged status which was viewed as satisfactory, the *nation* would have been content merely to enjoy that status. In 1787, however, an edict was promulgated concerning the status of non-Catholics. The possible application of this edict to the Jews of France and the consequent examination of their status now spurred the Sephardim to reenter the political arena. Called upon to explain the position of the French Jews and to justify the existence of separate Ashkenazic and Sephardic communities, the men of the *nation* expressed publicly for the first time their antipathy to the Jews of the Northeast, their commitment to their corporative status, and their willingness to assimilate to the society in which they lived. Unanticipated events would soon render this position obsolete. Nevertheless, it is well worth our while to capture the intentions of both the Jews of Bordeaux and the French ministers as they strove on the eve of the Revolution to redefine and ameliorate the condition of French Jewry.

The 1787 edict was the direct result of a concern on the part of the king and his ministers with the plight of the French Protestants.[1] Primarily the work of Chrétien Guillaume de Lamoignon de Malesherbes, the edict reflected the significant ideological changes which had occurred in 18th century France. For the first time a non-Catholic minority group was to enjoy civil rights. While the influence of the Church in France was not to be threatened, it could no longer limit the granting of civil rights to those professing the Catholic faith.[2]

Immediately after its promulgation, the edict caused a stir among the Ashkenazic Jews and the Jews of the Papal provinces. Did the edict, as its title might imply, concern all those who did not practice Catholicism or was it in fact limited to the Protestants? There was room for either interpretation, since the edict never explicitly omitted the Jews from its terms. Although the Protestants were specified in the Introduction, one could not overlook the more generalized phrasing of many of the articles.[3]

The Jews of Avignon, Carpentras, Cavaillon, and L'Isle-sur-Sorgue, believing that they too would benefit from the edict, made plans to leave their homes for new ones in France. The Ashkenazic Jews of France began to test the applicability of the edict by registering Jewish births, marriages, and deaths in the registries recently opened to Protestants for that purpose. The Sephardic Jews, however, remained silent, for they realized that their position was perhaps preferable to that which would be theirs under the new edict. Although they did not enjoy a secular état-civil, they had obtained official recognition for their marriages, births, and deaths and suffered no significant hindrances in matters of inheritance. The edict did allow for the free practicing of the arts and professions, privileges which the Sephardic Jews did not enjoy, but there would be inevitably a lapse of time between the issuance of these rights and their realization. In addition, article 3 of the edict, which prohibited non-Catholics from forming a group, community, or particular society, if literally enforced, would destroy the autonomy which the nation had struggled to attain and would struggle even harder to retain.[4]

The ambiguity of the edict was short lived. Within a year after its promulgation, "the edict concerning those who do not profess the Catholic religion" was interpreted almost universally as applying exclusively to the Protestants. Nevertheless, some Jews continued in their attempts to benefit from a secular état-civil.[5] The authorities, however, began to turn their attention towards uncovering the nature of French Jewish existence. The educated and privileged Sephardic Jews, choosing to remain in the background, found themselves instead the designated spokesmen.

On March 22, 1788, in answer to a letter from M. Dupré de Saint-Maur, past intendant of Bordeaux, Moyse Gradis congratulated the government on its proposed treatment of the Jews.[6] He did not hesitate to add, however, that the Sephardic Jews, by virtue of their moral and charitable conduct, merited the favorable intentions of the government, while the other Jews of France would be proven worthy in the future. Two weeks later, on April 8, Gradis wrote a second letter in which he answered Saint-Maur's detailed questions concerning divorce, cultivation of the land, admission to the guilds, registering of births, marriages, and deaths, and the essence of the distinction between the Sephardic Jews and other Jews of France. The answers which Gradis gave were significant, for they provided the outline for future positions taken by the Sephardic Jews. These positions, more rigidly defined in the mémoire presented to Malesherbes in 1788, were maintained until the Revolution destroyed the structure upon which they rested.

Divorce, wrote Gradis, was allowed for reasons of adultery and mutual consent of the married couple. Polygamy, although tradition-ally permitted, was not practiced by the Sephardic Jews and ought to be prohibited among all Jews of France. Cultivation of the land was held in high esteem by the Bordelais Jews, who often bought landed properties. Treading delicately on a sensitive issue, Gradis acknowl-edged the ancient distinction between the Ashkenazim and the more privileged Sephardic Jews, but he attributed that distinction to their different historical environments. Despite the "justifiable" chasm between the Bordelais Jews and all others, Gradis did not preclude the integration of the Northeastern Jews into the French community. This "generous" prediction for the future regeneration of the Ashkenazic Jews, however, would fade from the *nation's* concern when its own position was threatened by that of these potential citizens.[7]

On behalf of the *nation*, Gradis pleaded for acceptance into the guilds and, for those qualified, membership in the chamber of com-merce and participation in municipal meetings. Although the *nation* kept its own registries, Gradis was willing to conform to the new laws because, as he explained, "it has always been one of our principles to assimilate to other citizens of France."[8]

Gradis was correct when he added rather gratuitously, although not solely for tactical purposes, that the *nation* had always maintained assimilation as one of its principles. He was equally correct, moreover, when he implied—by asking Saint-Maur to abrogate article 3 of the edict which contradicted French laws concerning the Sephardic Jews—that the *nation* saw this assimilation as obtainable only if its position as a privileged corporate body was retained.[9] The Sephardim wanted to live as other Frenchmen, with the same rights, respon-sibilities, and privileges; they did not want, however, to be confused with the Ashkenazic and Avignonese Jews or to lose the commercial advantages of their autonomy. They were unwilling therefore to abandon their particularity and to fuse into the general population, not because assimilation was ideologically and emotionally distaste-ful, but rather because they saw it as identifying them with the rest of the Jews of France and depriving them of their commercial signifi-cance. In exchange, they would be offered an equality, questionable because of the existing institutions of France, and unlikely both be-cause of the juridical bases upon which the Jews had been accepted into France and the social and economic realities of the relations between them and non-Jews.

If assimilation was not rejected in theory, was it in fact accepted, as

Gradis maintained, or was the extent to which the Sephardim were willing to live as Frenchmen based solely on advantage and pragmatics? Historically, there is no doubt that as *nouveaux Chrétiens* the Portuguese merchants were required to live as French Catholics. Subsequently, as a Sephardic *nation* it was advantageous to live according to French laws in those areas, primarily commercial, which involved Jew and Christian. While the pragmatic benefits of assimilation may have been the initial impetus, however, if not for Gradis himself, at least for many of the younger Sephardim, a genuine interest in living as Frenchmen first and only secondarily as Jews soon developed.

Having stated the position of the *nation* as clearly as he could, Gradis announced to Saint-Maur that two deputies from Bordeaux, MM. Lopes-Dubec and Abraham Furtado, and one deputy from Bayonne, M. Fonseca neveu, were on their way to Paris to continue the dialogue.[10]

Furtado and Lopes-Dubec left Bordeaux on April 8, 1788. The task set before these two wealthy and articulate Sephardic Jews was complex, for they were not in a position to discuss French Jewry freely. They were representatives of the *nation* and as such were subject to its rigid control.[11] The syndics, faithful to traditional political patterns, preferred that Lopes-Dubec and Furtado quietly approach Saint-Maur and Malesherbes and make the wishes of the Bordelais Jews known without causing any public reaction. In as unobtrusive a manner as possible, the leaders of the *nation* hoped to achieve both an extension of their privileges consistent with the new rights granted to non-Catholics, and a retention of their separate and unique status.

From the beginning, however, it was clear that the two deputies in Paris would be uncomfortable in confining themselves to what they quickly felt to be the myopia of the Bordeaux leadership. Soon after their arrival, Lopes-Dubec and Furtado were officially and publicly received by Saint-Maur. The syndics immediately registered their disapproval and the deputies, barely hiding their frustration, wrote back that the demand for secrecy was either unwise or insufficiently explained.[12]

More significant than the differences arising out of the titular capacity of the two deputies were the differences between the intentions of the government as Furtado and Lopes-Dubec perceived them, and the desires of the *nation*. Apparently Malesherbes had decided to prepare an edict for the Jews comparable in many ways to that of 1787. This would mean, Furtado wrote, that Jewish corporations—Sephardic, Avignonese and Ashkenazic—would be abolished, that all Jews would be known as Jews or Hebrews and that each Jew would be classified according to his trade or profession along with other Frenchmen. For religious purposes, of course, the Jews would be free to form suitable associations. [13]

Furtado and Lopes-Dubec were well aware of the Sephardic commitment to maintain the corporate distinctions between themselves and the Ashkenazim and thus had no illusions concerning the reaction of the syndics. They understood, however, as the syndics did not, that the Parisian rationalists viewed erasing distinctions between Jews and Frenchmen and maintaining distinctions between Sephardim and Ashkenazim as incompatible and logically inconsistent.

The syndics' response was clear and unequivocal. The distinction between the Sephardic and Ashkenazic Jews had to be maintained. Furtado and Lopes-Dubec were advised to make this position clear to Saint-Maur and, without depreciating the Ashkenazic Jews more than was necessary, to give him the reasons which lay behind the demanded separation. [14]

The deputies were thus required to support a position which they understood to be incompatible with the reforms proposed by the French government. They agreed, nevertheless, to follow their instructions from Bordeaux and soon succeeded in eliciting from the sympathetic Saint-Maur the promise that he would do all that he could to maintain the privileges of the Sephardic Jews, while at the same time assuring to all the Jews of France the civil rights granted to other Frenchmen.

Furtado and Lopes-Dubec had been asked to prepare a study on the history of the Jewish people, their situation in France, and the type of constitution which they would most desire. For this task they had obtained the help of the Jewish historian L. Francia de Beaufleury. Together they completed the one-hundred fifty-one page *mémoire* which was presented to the government on June 15. [15] The *mémoire* is significant, for it provides us with a panoramic view of the Sephardic position on the eve of the French Revolution.

In their introduction, Furtado and Lopes-Dubec stated that, not wishing to afflict sensitive hearts with a detailed account of privations, they would limit themselves to what had been favorable in the history of Jews in other states. We need not examine in detail the various historical accounts, which, though limited and rarely up to date, are nevertheless accurate. More important, however, is the way in which the Sephardic Jews chose to use these accounts to emphasize and justify their own position.

In discussing the Jews of Holland, for example, Furtado and Lopes-Dubec drew an analogy to what they would hope to see in France. The Dutch Jews, they wrote, are divided into two separate bodies and, although they each have their own synagogues and cemeteries, they enjoy rights and privileges common to both. While the Ashkenazic Dutch Jews dress and behave in a manner which distinguishes them from all others, the Portuguese have adopted the customs and ways of the Dutch. The social and cultural barriers between these two Jewish communities, insurmountable in Holland as elsewhere, do not prevent the government from viewing both groups equally without involving itself in the reasons for the separation. Furtado and Lopes-Dubec continued their description with a striking commentary:

A Portuguese Jew is English in England and French in France, but a German Jew is German everywhere because of his customs from which he deviates rarely; thus one can look at the English and the Germans as brothers who, although sharing the same mother, have nevertheless developed characteristics which are absolutely different, nay even incompatible.[16]

Austria, where the Jews had recently been granted the opportunity to enter the arts, professions, universities, and political associations, provided the Sephardim with a positive example. Rather than examine the motivations and subtleties underlying the famous Edict of Toleration, Furtado and Lopes-Dubec concentrated instead on the "advantages" inherent in Joseph's forced assimilation.[17]

Interestingly, this first chapter of the *mémoire* does not rely upon any philosophical foundation for the granting of extensive privileges; no attempt is made to construct a synthesis between Judaism and European culture or to harmonize the Jewish religion with the religion of reason. Consistent with the past perspective of the Sephardim, the justifications for better treatment of the Jews are limited to *utilité* and more specifically to the commercial benefits to the various states.

Chapter II of the *mémoire* concentrates exclusively on the development of the Jewish communities in France. As in the first chapter, the accounts are accurate and often reveal what the *nation* felt were the motivations underlying the actions of both the government and the Jews. As in the first chapter, there is also a determined omission of certain significant facts.[18] Having felt confident, nevertheless, that their presentation had done justice to the official character of French Jewish existence and to the necessity for maintaining the carefully described distinctions between the different communities, Furtado and Lopes-Dubec accepted "without pain" the impending legislation of the government.[19]

Chapter III of the *mémoire*, divided into section I which answers Malesherbes' twelve questions and section II which answers the thirteenth question concerning the type of constitution the Jews wished to have, is the most significant and demands a more detailed examination. Not until Napoleon was to convoke the Assembly of Notables were the Jews to define so precisely the character and essentials of their faith. 1788 sees the beginning of what was to become in 1806 a clear distinction between religious faith and daily life. In 1788, as in 1806, the Marrano heritage of the Sephardic Jews helped provide the ease with which this chasm was created.

Since the first three questions posed by Malesherbes concerning the situation of European and French Jews had already been answered in the beginning chapters of the *mémoire*, Furtado and Lopes-Dubec addressed themselves to question four. This question, concerning the rights of Jews to possess land and homes, was briefly answered. Many Jews had these rights; reason and politics demanded that the Alsatian Jews also enjoy them.[20]

Questions five and six dealt with the possibilities of freely practicing the arts and professions. Did the Jews then have the right to do so, and would they choose to also in the future? The Sephardic answers to these questions were unequivocal. The Jews should be admitted freely to the different guilds and professions. In addition, they should be permitted to practice medicine and to attend public schools, universities, and academies. There would be no inconvenience arising from the Jewish Sabbath. The Jews would not work on Saturday; they would work and do business on Sunday, however, only with their stores closed. In this manner they would respect the sanctity of the Christian Sabbath. The Sephardim were so confident in the future significance of these privileges that they could add:

If these happy revolutions take place in France, one will see that what is so improperly and so unjustly called the moral character of the Jews is only a prejudice and an illusion.[21]

Question seven is important enough to quote in full.

Could not one hope for them that they try to incorporate themselves more with the other inhabitants of the country, and that they retain only those differences which belong so essentially to their religion, and which would be impossible to destroy?[22]

Here Malesherbes and the government were revealing that "incorporation" was the practical, if not ideal, solution to the Jewish problem. Incorporation, however, need not imply any abandonment of particularity on the part of the Jews; we shall soon see that assimilation was more precisely what Malesherbes intended and what the

Sephardic deputies understood. The *nation*, Furtado and Lopes-Dubec answered, was no less desirous of facilitating this incorporation and anticipated its *natural* and *gradual* (italics mine) occurrence once the Jews were relieved of the constant anguish of fear. And if, they continued, we are to have the full freedom to incorporate, there can be no reason for excluding us from the chambers of commerce and the municipal councils.[23]

Consistent with Malesherbes' intention to bring the Jews into the mainstream of French life was his concern, nourished by the Physiocrats' emphasis on cultivation of the land, with the Jews' avoidance of all agricultural pursuits. Why, he asked, had this situation occurred and could the Jews, in continuing to practice their faith, successfully devote themselves to the land? The answers offered in the *mémoire* would reappear often in the next decade as Furtado would be called upon to defend the Jews' estrangement from agriculture and to prove that its cause was rooted in the continually reinforced precariousness of Jewish survival. The Jews, the deputies explained, were not inherently alienated from the land; rather, persecutions, expulsions, and confiscations caused them to lose interest in an occupation which demanded above all a permanent status.[24] The inconveniences to the Jews arising from the Christian Sabbath, they added, were minor. As in commercial pursuits, the Jews could work on Sunday only when and where it would not be disruptive.

Question 11 specifically concerned the Northeastern Jews. Would not these Jews, who presently lived as "a people apart," prefer to be treated like all others and to follow the established laws pertaining to buying, selling, and inheritance?[25] Furtado and Lopes-Dubec were convinced that the Ashkenazic Jews would not only not welcome this radical change, having always directed matters of inheritance according to the laws of Moses, but also would be extremely sensitive to any innovation in the area. It is precisely this difference, they concluded, which made impossible any *"réunion"* with the Ashkenazic Jews.[26]

Malesherbes questioned last the arrangements necessary to insure that the Jews would fulfill the military responsibilities consistent with their rights as citizens. The Jews, as all others, can and should fulfill their military service, Furtado and Lopes-Dubec affirmed, but they too should be permitted to seek replacements.[27]

With all twelve questions answered, the remaining task of the Sephardic deputies was to describe the type of constitution which they would most desire to have in France. Although much of what the *nation* desired had already been discussed in previous sections of the *mémoire*, Furtado and Lopes-Dubec outlined in twenty points the ideal system in which the Jews would choose to live.

Predictably, the first requirement was that the Sephardim be permitted to retain all the privileges granted them in 1550, that they remain in their corporation with the same *règlements* governing their internal police, and that the privileges granted all other Jews as well as their particular status be maintained.[28] With this corporate autonomy as a foundation, the deputies were able to specify the additional rights which they desired. These rights were often phrased exactly as they had been in the 1787 edict for the Protestants.

The Jews, the *mémoire* stated, should be permitted to live wherever they chose, to marry and to divorce according to Jewish law (polygamy was to be prohibited and engagement carefully regulated), to practice all professions and arts, to be admitted into the public colleges and universities, and finally to own and cultivate their property. They were to continue to have their synagogues, rabbis, schools and colleges, to pay royal taxes as well as their own taxes in their respective "corporations" and to resolve civil and criminal disputes involving only Jews. In addition, no Jew was to settle in a French city or village without a two-thirds vote of approval by the Jewish Assembly of that area. Since the Sephardic Jews followed the laws of the realm in matters of inheritance, the Germans and other Jews were to declare at the registering of their marriage which law they chose to follow. If they were to follow the laws of Moses, their inheritance would be regulated as it was in Metz and similar places.[29]

Ten days after a marriage, birth, or death, the Jews would be required, as were the Protestants, to declare the facts before the first officer of Justice, either royal or seignorial. Punishment for failure to comply would be left to the Jewish community.[30] Here we find a revealing contrast to the requirement of the 1787 edict. While punishment and control of the Protestants resided in the hands of French authorities, the *nation* chose to retain its exclusive right to discipline Jews. In addition, for the Jews the declaration before the judge was of a *fait accompli*, while for the Protestants it became the *fait* itself. For example, the Jews were to be recognized as married according to the laws of Moses and subsequently it would be only a question of making the marriage official. Protestant marriages, on the other hand, had no validity whatsoever until they were made official. Intent upon retaining exclusive control over the community, the *nation* overlooked the potential significance of these differences. Rights had been extended to the Protestants as Frenchmen, not as Protestants; the rights and privileges of the Sephardim, however, continued to rest on their status as Jews.

The differences and similarities between the constitution for the Jews as outlined in the *mémoire*, and the various provisions of the 1787 edict reflect the exact extent to which the Sephardic Jews wished to be a part of the French community. The distinctions within the constitution between Sephardic and Ashkenazic Jews indicate the type of "equality" which the *nation* wished to see among all Jews. Indeed, as we have seen, the *nation* neither trusted the French fully nor identified with other Jews. Its corporate integrity acted as a buffer against mistreatment by the former and confusion with the latter.

With the presentation of the *mémoire* and the assurances of Saint-Maur, the work of the deputies was largely completed. Having been informed that the Council of State would be unable to address itself immediately to the situation of the Jews, Furtado and Lopes-Dubec took leave of Malesherbes and Saint-Maur, and on July 3, 1788 they returned to Bordeaux.[31] The syndics were pleased with the accomplishments of their representatives and were still confident that the France of the future, while auguring an improved status for all French Jews, would be so designed as to incorporate a Sephardic Jewish *nation* composed of Frenchmen and German Jewish *corps* composed of Jews.

An important question is left unanswered despite our understanding of both the desires of the *nation* and the observations of the two deputies. What in fact did Malesherbes visualize for the Jews of France? In his *Second Mémoire sur le Mariage des Protestans*, Malesherbes stated:

It would be desirable if the horror towards the Jewish nation would diminish, and if the Christians would content themselves with detesting only the religion of the Jews.

1. Because the indelible mark of being originally from a Jewish family is a large obstacle to their conversion, nothing is more sure to double their attachment to their religion than knowing that if they leave it, they will be looked at in horror by their whole nation and will be eternally despised among Christians:

2. Because, finding themselves excluded almost everywhere from most of the professions, they are obliged to turn to speculation and usury; because, not enjoying anywhere the support of those laws common to all citizens, they are in the necessity of following their own laws. . . .

If one were interested in this nation, one could apply to it many of the established principles in these two memoirs, for if during the length of the Edict of Nantes, the P.R.'s (Protestants) were in France an *Imperium in Imperio* the Jews are in the entire universe an *Imperium in Imperiis*. It is not within the limits of the sovereign's power to destroy in a short time this horror towards the Jewish nation, which is surely carried too far. But I think that the edict which, without naming them, will permit them to proceed in their acts and to appear in the Tribunals, without losing the qualification of their religion, could contribute in bringing some of them closer to Christianity.[32]

Historians have concluded from this passage that Malesherbes' desires for reform were mainly means to lead to the conversion of the Jews.[33] We cannot rest, however, with this conclusion, for not only does it simplify the intention of the edict and contradict the reception and promises which Malesherbes himself gave to Furtado and Lopes-Dubec, but also and more significantly it overlooks Malesherbes' sensitivity both to the complexity of the Jewish question and the currents of 18th century enlightenment.

Let us look more closely at the 1787 edict (which Malesherbes probably intended to apply also to the Jews) and Malesherbes' views on the Jewish question. The introduction to the edict states the dilemma in which the French Government had found itself. Political, social, and economic ostracism had failed to convert non-Catholics to Catholicism; instead Protestants, having been stripped of any legal existence, had either profaned the sacraments by false conversions or compromised the status of their children. The solution, therefore, lay in acknowledging as fictitious that there were only Catholics in France and in officially recognizing those of different religions. The unique position of the Catholic church would, of course, be maintained.[34]

When the edict had definitively been interpreted as applying solely to the Protestants, Malesherbes and two other French statesmen, Lacretelle and Roederer, were advised to address themselves to the Jewish question. As we have shown, the Sephardic Jews became the spokesmen for the Jewish position. (There is record that the Ashkenazic Jews were also represented in Paris, although there is no evidence of any reports made by them.) After Furtado and Lopes-Dubec met with Malesherbes, they immediately wrote a letter to Bordeaux (May 2, 1788) in which they recounted both the Minister's warm reception and his promise to retain the privileges of the *nation* while simultaneously granting all Jews extended rights and liberties.[35] Was Malesherbes merely playing politics with the Sephardic deputies? It appears more likely that he had been convinced by Furtado and Lopes-Dubec that they and the Sephardic Jews shared both his concerns over the Jews of France and his evaluation of the position of the Ashkenazim. The *nation* was as disturbed as he by the nonassimilable practices of the Jews of the Northeast and also attributed much of the negative characteristics of Jewish life there to the treatment which the Jews received. Malesherbes could thus see the Sephardim of Bordeaux as demonstrating the "perfectibility" of the Jews; perhaps also he believed that they would be able to provide both the impetus and the justification for the changes he hoped would occur among French Jews.

Malesherbes would not have easily agreed to the retention of the privileges of the *nation*. Not only was he well aware of and antagonistic to the commercial reasons which had allowed the protection of a few Jews in the face of general intolerance, but also he was against any form of Jewish communal autonomy which he felt prevented the Jews from becoming members of the French community. Specifically, he was against those practices such as the Sabbath, dietary regulations, and refusal to engage in agriculture which legal autonomy appeared to reinforce.[36]

If Malesherbes intended then to retain the privileges of the *nation*, even if only temporarily, it was probably because the Bordelais Jews, who engaged in agriculture, dined at the same table with their non-Jewish friends, and overcame the two days of "laziness" which the Jewish Sabbath seemed to necessitate, convinced the minister that they successfully and productively lived as Frenchmen while remaining Jews.

Malesherbes viewed the Jews as representing not only an *"imperium in imperio"* (state within a state), as the Protestants had, but also an *"imperium in imperiis"* (nation within all nations).[37] For Malesherbes, and this was not at all original with him, the emergence of modern states made the autonomous existence of religious, social, or ethnic communities obsolete. Was conversion to Catholicism then his key to the solution of this anachronism? That Malesherbes sought to destroy the *imperium* of the Jews is indisputable. That he saw this accomplished, however, only by converting the Jews to Catholicism is questionable, especially since he had laid the groundwork in the 1787 edict for a secularization of certain basic human rights. Although there was not yet a secular nation-state to which the Jews and Protestants could belong as citizens, the process of secularization had begun and with it was developing an alternative to conversion— assimilation.

Malesherbes' solution was not unique. There had already been a significant amount of public discussion concerning the Jewish problem, and statesmen such as Dohm, Roederer, and Grégoire had proposed comparable means of ameliorating the position of the French Jews.[38] They shared with Malesherbes, in addition to the delicate balance of Christian and secular concern, the views that the Jews were in a lowly and unproductive state, that the government was largely responsible for this, that both the government and to a lesser extent the Jews must take the responsibility for change and finally that Judaism, especially Talmudic Judaism, must be substantially reformed as well as refined. They also shared the belief that the Jews were entitled to the human rights which they had so long been denied. These rights they viewed as attainable, however, only in a transformed society where transformed Jews ceased in most ways to be Jews. The Sephardim of Bordeaux, by their compromises with traditional Judaism and their strict alienation from other Jews, justified these attitudes.

3

Revolution and Emancipation

Whatever might have been Malesherbes' solution for the Jews of France, it was destined to be stillborn. Strong and ill comprehended currents had begun to threaten the medieval stability of 18th century France. The nobles, increasingly blind to their fundamental dependence upon the monarchy, challenged the king by attempting to increase their strength in the central and local governments. The bourgeois, disturbed by their social and political weakness and demanding more influence in economic affairs, were willing to support their king but unwilling to accede to the dominance of the nobility. The peasants, although inarticulate and still unaware of the power of their numbers, were being led to the brink of an economic crisis to which they would respond violently. The king was besieged by the nobility on the one hand and the peasantry and middle class on the other. Attempting to placate all his subjects, he eventually succeeded only in exacerbating those spiraling currents of unrest.

The first call for the Estates General, a consequence of direct aristocratic pressure on the weakened bankrupt monarchy, was made in 1787. The definitive call did not occur until Louis XVI issued his *lettres patentes* of January 24, 1789, which included a *règlement,* based on the electoral procedure of 1614, for the convocation of the various assemblies.[1] This summoning of the Estates General, and the procedure followed to choose electors and to compose the *cahiers de doléance,* represented the last significant action of the *ancien régime.* From the first meeting on May 5, 1789, the discontented among the three estates began the struggle which quickly and somewhat unintentionally led to the emergence of a French citizenry and the declaration of the nationhood of France. The Jews of France, whose status had depended on the now crumbling structures of medieval corporate society, were to find themselves prevented from either entering the new order or returning to the old.

The events of the Revolution have been told and retold, always with an attempt to discover the forces behind such a cataclysmic explosion. The history of the Jews during this period has also been carefully examined, for it has become clear to many that the experience of the modern Jew began in earnest with his suspended existence during the early years of the Revolution.[2] What has not been sufficiently examined, however, is the part which the Sephardic Jews played during these formative years.

On February 25, 1789, a letter of convocation for the nomination of deputies to the Estates General was sent from the municipal officers to the syndic of the Portuguese Jews of Bordeaux. A comparable letter was addressed to the Avignonese Jews of Bordeaux.[3] The procedures to be followed were the same for all those comprising the third estate. The Jews were to meet in their corporations and choose the deputies which their numbers permitted. These deputies would then participate in the election of the ninety delegates to the *Sénéchaussée* of Guyenne. Among the ninety, four would be chosen to represent the third estate in Paris. For the Sephardic and Avignonese Jews, their automatic inclusion in the elections became a definitive statement on their status within the French community.

Despite the use to which participation in the elections to the National Assembly was put, the Jews of Bordeaux were not received unanimously by the rest of the population. On February 28, 1789, two letters were sent from the Mayor, Lieutenant Mayor, and *Jurat* of Bordeaux. One was addressed to M. Necker and the other to M. de Villedeuil. The first, after announcing that all the arrangements for the ensuing elections had been completed, stated that the corporations were against admitting the Portuguese Jews who had, by virtue of their letters of naturalization, the right to participate.[4] The second letter, devoted specifically to the problem with the Jews, made it clear that many Bordelais wished to retract the invitations sent to the two Jewish corporations.[5]

The Bordelais corporations were not successful, however, in preventing the Jews from participating. On March 2, 1789, the minutes of the Sephardic *nation* mention that MM. Azevedo aîné, David Gradis, Lopes-Dubec, and Abraham Furtado were nominated as representatives of the Portuguese Jews of Bordeaux to the Assembly of the third estate.[6]

Each corporation was to write its own *cahier de doléance*, after which the various *cahiers* would be integrated into one *cahier* for each of the three estates. The Jews of Bordeaux did not take advantage, as they had previously in their exhaustive memorandum to Malesherbes, of this opportunity to state their wishes. Their decision, maintained throughout the following months, was to avoid calling particular attention to themselves as Jews, to refrain from any public complaints or requests, and to assume inclusion in any significant economic, political, or social changes.

On March 8, the third estate of Bordeaux chose its ninety electors, among whom were two of the most prominent Sephardic Jews, David Gradis and Abraham Furtado.[7] Gradis missed becoming one of the four deputies to the Estates General by only a few votes.[8] Subsequently, the ninety electors were to become the municipal government of Bordeaux.

Despite the fact that the corporations wished to prevent the Jews from participating in the elections to the third estate, there is no complaint regarding the Jews in any of the printed *cahiers*. The clergy, nobles, third estate, and the various corporations were surprisingly silent on this question.[9] The clergy did, however, bemoan the situation created by the edict for non-Catholics and demanded both that Catholicism be made the only true and official religion, and that the privileges granted to non-Catholics be rescinded.[10] It is highly probable that the clergy was not speaking of the Bordelais Jews, since they had been excluded from the 1787 edict. Nevertheless, there is little doubt that the position of the Jews would have been challenged had the wishes of the clergy prevailed.

The *cahiers* of the clergy, as well as those of the other estates, were written with an intention to restore the glorious past, rather than with a view towards revolutionary changes. Each group, while proclaiming the natural rights of all men, attempted in fact to recapture their lost privileges.[11] Even in their silence the Jews of Bordeaux were no different from the rest of the population; they desired not to change their status, but rather to retain it as they had in the past.

The Jews of Saint-Esprit-de-Bayonne, never as assimilated as the Jews of Bordeaux, were not admitted to the elections as easily or as successfully. The *Sénéchaussée* of Tartas, having been overlooked in the general rule of January 24, was treated separately in the decree of February 19, 1789. According to this decree, the inhabitants of Saint-Esprit were to elect their deputies directly rather than in corporations. It was decided, however, to convene the Jews separately instead of including them with the rest of the third estate. The Christian population, having elected ten deputies, then announced that they alone were entitled to send their deputies to the Assembly. The Jews answered by stating that they represented the Jewish community which had the right to a particular deputation. The *Sénéchal*, rather than referring to the letters concerning the convoking of the Jewish community which were in favor of the Jewish position, brought about a compromise in which two of the four Jewish representatives, MM. Silveyra and Fonseca, were permitted to join the ten Christian deputies. [12]

Despite the obstacles which were placed in their path, the Sephardim succeeded in participating with the French in the general elections for the Estates General. Whatever doubts were raised concerning their status as *étrangers* (aliens) were for the time being resolved in favor of their being treated as *régnicoles* (natives). The Jews residing in Alsace, Metz, and Lorraine, however, were excluded from the general convocation. Their exclusion supported and reinforced the Sephardic thesis that identification with the Northeastern Jews ought to be avoided.

The Ashkenazic Jews were unwilling to remain silent. They requested that they be allowed to group together, discuss their interests, and then ask one or more deputies to the Estates General to make known their demands. Permission was granted, and they assembled and subsequently wrote their own *cahier* which was presented to Cerf Berr in Paris. Berr, through an intermediary, presented the Jewish *mémoire* to the king. Thus, while these Jews were excluded from the general elections of deputies to the Estates General and from making known their interests in the *cahiers* of the general population, they did succeed in obtaining an official though particular convocation. [13]

The *cahier* which was drawn up by the Jews of Alsace, Metz, and Lorraine in April 1789 has been lost. Fortunately, there still exists a complete analysis of it by the Abbé Grégoire. One is thus able to discover the essence of the demands made by the Ashkenazic Jews as a whole, and the particular demands made by those living in Alsace, Metz, and Lorraine.

Of prime importance to the Ashkenazic Jews was the wish to be exempted from having to pay both the king and the nobles for the right of protection. They also asked that they be permitted to practice the arts and the professions, to acquire property, to cultivate the land, and to establish themselves in all the provinces without being forced to live in separate quarters. In addition, they wished to practice their religion and to retain their rabbis, syndics, and communities. [14]

The leaders of the Jewish communities of Northeastern France were asking to be considered a part of the general population for economic purposes; simultaneously they sought to retain their juridical autonomy. What they were demanding was in essence what Dohm and Mirabeau had advocated and what the Sephardic Jews to a great extent already enjoyed. [15] If what the Sephardim and Ashkenazim desired, however, revealed no apparent differences, the tactics they employed and the underlying issues motivating their choice of tactics did.

Political circumstances provide a partial explanation for the differing approaches. The Ashkenazic Jews had nothing to lose in overtly demanding the rights which they now felt were theirs. They could anticipate no tacit acceptance by their fellow countrymen for whom they had become the most obvious scapegoat.[16] There had never been, nor did there appear to be in the future, a point at which the Jews of Northeastern France could assume the benefits of any political or social reforms. The Sephardim, on the other hand, had nothing to gain from calling attention to their particular situation. Silence was as politically justifiable as was political agitation among the Northeastern Jews. Implicit in this silence, nevertheless, was also an historically conditioned lack of concern for and involvement with the Ashkenazic Jews of France.

Not only was there little rapport between the Ashkenazic and Sephardic Jews, but also there was a comparably small degree of knowledge of each other's situation. A letter from Zalkind Hourwitz, the only Jew to win the prize from the Metz Academy and a most likely person to be acquainted with the affairs of the *nation*, dated September 8, 1788 and addressed to Abraham Furtado, reveals the extent to which the Jews of Northeastern and Southwestern France were knowledgeable about each other's situation. "Would you kindly tell me," Hourwitz asked, "if you pay the *capitation* as a community or individually each in his own parish."[17] Despite this ignorance concerning the taxpaying procedures of the *nation*, Hourwitz had succeeded in meeting Saloma, a Bordelais Avignonese Jew, who advised him to seek the help of Furtado in publishing the award winning *mémoire*.

In addition to Furtado and Saloma, moreover, Hourwitz was also in contact with Lopes-Dubec who, after having read the three winning *mémoires*, wrote Hourwitz a significantly critical letter. Although Lopes-Dubec admired the desire to ameliorate the condition of the Jews, he was greatly disturbed by the detailed descriptions of their many vices. By focussing on these vices, he warned Hourwitz, one succeeds only in demeaning the Jews and exacerbating the already pervasive prejudices felt towards them.[18]

Communication between the Jews of France, while rare and limited to those few individuals who actively sought it, was nevertheless increasing by the end of the 18th century. This communication, however, did not necessarily reflect mutual involvement. While preparations were being made for the first meeting of the Estates General, David Gradis wrote a letter to M. Dupré de Saint-Maur on April 18, 1789, in which he told him of the *nation's* success in participating in the recent elections. The Jews of Bordeaux and Bayonne, Gradis announced, are fully incorporated into the state and have been permitted to enjoy not only all the benefits of the 1787 edict but also those additional privileges granted them in the past. The Jews are satisfied and seek nothing more from the government. This satisfaction, however, depended on a continued separation from the less privileged Ashkenazic Jews; Saint-Maur was asked to remind Malesherbes that the Sephardim were to be excluded from any new law in favor of the Jews of Alsace and Lorraine.[19]

The *nation's* concern was rapidly overshadowed by events in Paris. On June 17, 1789, the third estate of the Estates General proclaimed itself a National Assembly and took an oath not to separate until it had drawn up a written constitution for France. The nobles and clergy, unable to avoid the course of events, joined the third estate, and together they began the task of demolishing the old and building the new. The first major step taken by the National Assembly was its Declaration of the Rights of Man and the Citizen, which was provisionally adopted on August 26, 1789.[20] This declaration destroyed any remaining feudal categories and proclaimed in their place the juridical unity of all of France. The consequences of this alone necessitated a restructuring of the bases of French society. The question of the place of the Jews in this new society could not and would not be overlooked.

The Jews themselves resolved to present petitions to the National Assembly. They did not unite, however, in their presentations; instead they were motivated as in the past to act separately and in a counterproductive manner.

On August 14, 1789, the Sephardim wrote a letter to the Abbé Grégoire, who had been recognized as the protagonist in the struggle for Jewish reform. They did not wish to see Grégoire, as they had not wished to see Saint-Maur and Malesherbes, make special pleas for the emancipation[21] of the Jews. Their desired course of action was to assume tacitly that all the Jews, or at least the Sephardic Jews, were included in the August Declaration. The position of the Sephardim had not changed; they still feared that any separate action on behalf of the Jews would identify them with their disavowed Ashkenazic brethren and could result in at least temporary disabilities which they did not have then.[22]

The Ashkenazic Jews, however, needed not only to be included explicitly in the Declaration and the new Constitution, but also to be officially freed from their disabilities. Their address, dated August 31, 1789, was written probably by Berr Isaac Berr, the syndic of the Jewish community of Nancy (Lorraine). The main difference between this new address and the lost *cahier* was in the request for civil rights. The rest was a reiteration of previous demands, namely freedom of residence and work, equality of taxation, and conservation of communal status.[23] In requesting simultaneously civil rights and communal autonomy, Berr Isaac Berr was expressing his belief that not only was there no contradiction between the two, but also the continuation of communal autonomy would help the Jews to be better citizens. Although the National Assembly had not yet dissolved the corporations, the August declaration had made it clear that communal autonomy, certainly juridical autonomy, would be incompatible with the new society. This demand of the Ashkenazim for retention of their autonomy would succeed only in adding grist to the mill of those who believed that the Jews were inherently a nation within a nation.

The Sephardic Jews had not abandoned their corporate status, but their silence on this issue was useful. When the time came, they quickly dissolved the *nation* and professed surprise and indignation that the Ashkenazic Jews still wished to live apart. In fact, for a long time the leaders of the Northeast were willing to sacrifice their enjoyment of active citizenry for a retention of autonomy.[24] To Berr Isaac Berr and many other Ashkenazic spokesmen, more important than participating in public offices was a feared disintegration of Judaism in the wake of the destruction of the community. In addition, they saw the probable repercussions among the many Christian creditors if the Jewish community, which was indebted to these creditors, were to be dissolved.

The Jews of Paris, with no privileges to protect and few prejudices to resist, could afford to be most radical in their response to the Declaration.[25] In July and August, 1789, they formed a committee to take in hand the cause of the Jews and to demand for them the rights of citizens. These Parisian Jews, as did the Sephardic Jews, wished to accept the decisions made by the National Assembly; unlike the Sephardic Jews, they demanded that it be explicitly stated that the Jews were included in these decisions. The Jews residing in Paris would not have been implicitly included in the decisions made by the National Assembly. In addition, however, the Jews of Paris were keenly aware both of the drastic changes which France was undergoing and the equally drastic price which the Jews would have to pay to benefit from these changes. Thus the Parisian Jews, in their address of August 26, 1789, to the National Assembly, asked to be subject to the same juridical and administrative bodies as all other Frenchmen; in return, while retaining the right to remain faithful to their religion, they renounced explicitly the privileges of a corporate existence.[26]

The actions of the Parisian Jews changed neither the silence of the Sephardim nor the demands of the Ashkenazim. The latter made two attempts to appeal to the National Assembly. They were unsuccessful on October 4, but they were received on October 14 and were promised prompt consideration. The Sephardim began to involve themselves in the affairs of the Bordeaux community, to whom they presented an extravagant gift in October, and to act as if their inclusion in the August Declaration was undebatable. For the present, they were finding little animosity in their relations with the Bordelais community.[27] On August 22, 1789, the bureau of commerce of Bordeaux had appointed a committee to organize their instructions to M. M. Peret, deputy to the National Assembly. The deliberations of this committee reveals neither any mention of the Jews nor any desire to restrict their commerce.[28] Since many of the Sephardic Jews were in fact influential bourgeois of the city, their interests undoubtedly coincided with those of the rest of the bourgeois population.[29]

There were, nevertheless, minor incidents in Bordeaux. One of these, involving some Jews who came to register in the National Guard and an irate curé, was recounted by Pierre Bernadau, a highly controversial personality who recorded many details of the revolutionary years in Bordeaux. On August 6, 1789, Bernadau tells us, the curé of Saint-Eloi,

. . . having observed in his church many Jews who hurried to place themselves under their parish flags, gathered around him a circle of devout people whom he invited to pray to God for the enemies of his cult, who had that very day profaned his sanctuary and scandalized the true believers, by presenting themselves in front of the altar of the Son of Man whom they had crucified.[30]

One senses, Bernadau concludes, all that this scene offered of the ridiculous and intolerant.

Had the Jews of France been assumed to be included in the Declaration of the Rights of Man, the Bordelais Jews would have found few obstacles to their enjoyment of this equality. A general law alone, however, would have been insufficient to abolish prejudicial restrictions in the lives of the Northeastern Jews. Still, the fall of 1789 left the implications of the Declaration unspecified, and thus susceptible to various interpretations. This was especially true after the proposition that no one was to be molested even for his religious views was adopted on August 23 (Article X). By the following winter, however, despite the ardent anticipations of the Sephardim, it had become clear that neither the Jews nor the Protestants were to be included automatically in the practical consequences of the Declaration. When it became a question of participating in public office, regardless of religious persuasion, a special law specifying Protestants and Jews was found to be necessary.

The events of December 23 and 24 have become by now infamous; nevertheless we shall review the major thrusts of these debates, for to understand the future actions of the French Jews is to understand the implications of the vote taken in the assembly on December 24th in which 408 voted against and 403 voted for Jewish emancipation. The discussion in the Assembly began with M. de Clermont-Tonnerre's motion that all active citizens, be they Protestants or Jews, were to be admitted to public office. For the first time, the question of the Jews was publicly aired, and many took the opportunity to state explicitly their reaction to the inclusion of the Jews in the nationhood of France. The two main arguments presented against the Jews, namely that they formed a nation within a nation and were thereby inherently unassimilable,[31] and that their emancipation would impel the Christian population of Alsace to destroy them, were such as to touch the core of the Jewish problem. These arguments were in fact precisely what the Sephardic Jews were subtly attacking in their attempts to prove that they as Frenchmen were fully accepted by their Christian neighbors.

The Jews, the Abbé Maury declared, represent a people living and wishing to live in isolation, and this isolation precludes their participating in the agricultural and military pursuits of France. Reubell, the only ultra-revolutionist who spoke against Jewish emancipation, predicted that in Alsace the decree which would grant the Jews citizenship would also be their death sentence.[32] Robespierre, challenging both Reubell and the Abbé Maury, eloquently defended the Jews; with a logic which was to be used often in defense of emancipation, he accused the French of having both created and exaggerated the vices of the Jews.[33]

The Assembly, unable to decide for or against the inclusion of the Jews, reduced its problem to one of immediate exclusion or adjournment until the question had been studied more thoroughly. Despite the attempts by Reubell, Barnave, and Target to dispose of the Jews definitively, the Assembly decreed on December 24, 1789 that non-Catholics were to be eligible for civil and military office, but that this had no relation to the Jews, "on whose status the Assembly reserves the right to withhold judgment."[34]

Thus the Jews of Bordeaux, who were in fact actively participating in municipal politics, found themselves doing so contrary to the decision of the Assembly. To be sure, the major arguments had been directed against the Ashkenazic Jews, but there had been no distinctions made between them and the Jews of Southwestern France. All the Jews of France were to await future legislation and until then were to remain poised between exclusion from and inclusion in the emerging nation-state.

The time had come when silence was no longer profitable. The Sephardim of Bordeaux and Bayonne would now have to prove what for a long time they had hoped was assumed, namely that their past status and present intentions were acceptable to and compatible with the new order. If necessary, their proof would be offered regardless of its effect on the emancipation of the Ashkenazic Jews.

On December 30, 1789, the General Assembly of the *nation* met and decided to send a number of deputies to Paris. Gradis, Dacosta, Raba junior, Lopes-Dubec, George, and Salom left for Paris, arriving on January 4, 1790. The rest of the delegates arrived on January 7.[35] Interestingly, the first visit which was made on January 4 was to the Jewish deputies of Alsace and Lorraine. For a brief moment, the Ashkenazic and Sephardic Jews were united in their mutual desire to be recognized as citizens. In a letter dated January 5, which Lopes-Dubec and the others sent to the syndic of Bordeaux, they described in happy terms the mutuality of interests which they observed among themselves and the Ashkenazim.[36] The union, however, was on tenuous ground from the start, for the conditions of its cohesiveness were that the rights of the Sephardic Jews would remain undiminished by any involvement with the rest of the Jews of France. The Jews of Bordeaux continued to see their primary allegiance to be to themselves; any assistance offered to the other Jews would have to leave that allegiance unchallenged.[37]

It did not take long for the Sephardim to be disillusioned. On January 8, they again met with the Ashkenazim, but this time the deputies from the *nation* felt that the Jews of Alsace and Lorraine were willing to settle for less than they, notwithstanding the fact that their spokesman Cerf Berr was asking for full citizenship. The fear that at the critical moment the Northeastern Jews would settle for the rights to acquire and sell their property, exercise their commerce, arts and professions, and dwell where they chose—rights which the Sephardim already enjoyed—at the price of full participation in the administration of the country was enough for the Sephardic Jews to decide to follow a course independent of the other Jews. That the Bordelais Jews were right in their fears was substantiated by the Ashkenazic deputies who admitted their willingness to compromise.[38]

After January 8, the Jews of Bordeaux, accustomed to sophisticated lobbying, directed their energies toward meeting with as many deputies to the Assembly as was possible and convincing them of the injustices inherent in the December 24th decision. In addition, they wrote a petition which, having been received favorably, they decided to publish on January 17.[39] The petition contains the reasons why the members of the *nation* found it necessary to address the National Assembly, proof (based on a rather one-sided account) of the past privileges enjoyed by the Sephardim, and a list of documents attesting to their participation as active citizens.[40]

Convinced that the present situation would not have occurred had the Jews of Alsace, Lorraine, and the Trois-Evêches not created a confusion of "ideas," the Sephardim expressed in the petition their disapproval of the separatist intentions of the Ashkenazim.

Although we do not have access to the public papers, they must seem quite extraordinary, since these Jews aspire to live in France under a particular regime, to retain their own laws, and to constitute a class of citizens separated from all the others. If it is true that this claim has been made, we must attribute it to the effervescence of a misunderstood religious zeal. We assume that when they become more rational, they will appreciate better the value and advantage of the honorable rights attached to the quality of French citizenship . . .[41]

Could these demands, they asked, deprive us of the rights which we have always enjoyed?

Among the privileges which the Bordeaux Jews described were their right to acquire and sell property, their admission as bourgeois of the city, their payment of all royal taxes on the same level as the French, and their participation in public assemblies. The *nation,* they declared, has no special laws, tribunals, or officers, and since 1550 its members have enjoyed all the rights of naturalized Frenchmen (an exaggeration which the Sephardim themselves would later have cause to refute). The petition concluded with a list of those documents which supported the status of the Bordeaux Sephardim as French citizens, among which were letters of convocation to the Assemblies of Bordeaux and letters establishing that even on Saturdays the Jews fulfilled their service in the patriotic regiments.[42]

The Jews of Bayonne, intentionally excluded from the Bordeaux petition, presented their own to the National Assembly in which they pleaded for themselves and the Portuguese Jews dwelling in Paris, Marseilles, and Lyon. After recounting the unique history of the Sephardim since their sojourn in Babylonia, the Bayonnais Jews asserted that the Portuguese and Spanish Jews living in France were exclusively French.[43]

The Sephardim were aware that Cerf Berr and the other Ashkenazic representatives were far from pleased not only with the two petitions, but also with the fact that the fate of the Ashkenazic Jews was quickly being separated from that of the Sephardim. This was in no small degree a result of the activities of the seven deputies from Bordeaux.

On January 26th, these deputies recorded confidently that M. Barère de Vieuzac had stated that he, along with many other deputies, intended to separate and postpone the question of the Ashkenazic Jews. That same day the Bordelais deputies dined rather uncomfortably with Cerf Berr, Roederer, and the Abbé Grégoire. They had hoped to postpone the decision concerning the Sephardim until a petition on behalf of the Northeastern Jews could also be presented. Godard, a lawyer and one of the leading Parisian liberals, was author of the yet unfinished petition.[44]

The night before the *comité de constitution* (constitutional committee), to whom the petition of the Bordeaux Sephardim had been brought, was to make its definitive report, there was a gathering in Paris of French and Jewish spokesmen. The Sephardic Jews addressed the assembled deputies and brought attention to the uniqueness of their position. Thiery, a friend of the Ashkenazic Jews, attempted to defend them by denying the distinctions which the Jews of Bordeaux sought to uphold. If full citizenship cannot be granted to all Jews, Thiery proclaimed, it must be withheld from the Sephardim. While his intentions were to support the Ashkenazim, Thiery's tactics were the same as those who fought against Jewish emancipation. The Jews of Bordeaux, keenly aware of the danger of equating their cause with that of the Jews of the Northeast, attacked Thiery's "sophistic" position.[45]

The next day, January 28, 1790, at 2:00 in the afternoon, Talleyrand, Evêque d'Autun, spoke in the name of the *comité de constitution.* Without prejudicing the situation of the Jews as a whole, Talleyrand stated, the *comité* felt that it was just to decree that the Jews of Bordeaux, who had previously enjoyed the quality of citizenship, should continue to do so as active citizens.[46] Le Chapelier, agreeing with Talleyrand's report, added:

There is no connection whatsoever between the status of the Jews of Bordeaux and those of Alsace. It is a question of conserving the status of the former and giving to the latter what they do not yet possess. I conclude by asking that priority be given to the decree proposed by the Committee.[47]

After a prolonged and heated discussion which continued until the evening, the Assembly, now numbering only two-thirds of its members, decreed by a vote of 374–224 that

All the Portuguese, Spanish, and Avignonese Jews will continue to enjoy those rights which they have enjoyed up until now, and which are sanctioned in their favour by the *Lettres Patentes;* consequently they will enjoy the rights of active citizens, when they fulfill the conditions required by the Assembly's decrees.[48]

News traveled fast, and the Bordelais population soon learned of the January 28th decree. A report of the morning meeting of February 9th of the National Assembly reveals that there had been a minor disturbance in Bordeaux. A number of young Bordelais gathered at the Bourse, the financial hub of the city, and demonstrated during the day and evening against the Jews. Had this occurred in Alsace, Lorraine, or the Trois-Evêches, there would have resulted a general and volatile upheaval of the majority of the population. In Bordeaux, however, the demonstration was limited to a day. Apologies were made to the Jews and a counter-demonstration was staged in order to express sympathy with the decisions of the National Assembly.[49]

The Jews of Bordeaux had been successful. They had convinced the French patriots that they were worthy of participation in the new order. The tactics used by the men of the *nation* were not new; on the contrary their responses to the vote of December 24th were much more a continuation of centuries of petitioning for special consideration. That they chose to act independently of the Ashkenazim was consistent both with their self-perception and their political assessments as well as with their ideological priorities. That they chose also to act independently of the other Sephardim of the Southwest—for it had been Grégoire who demanded the extension of rights to all the Jews of Southwestern France—was indicative of the extent to which they would separate themselves from any group capable of threatening their position.

The Bordeaux Sephardim were not the only ones to rely on past privileges. Those deputies of the Assembly who accepted the arguments of these privileged Jews (there were many among the clergy and aristocracy who rejected the enfranchisement of any Jews), did so by choosing to ignore the Declaration of the Rights of Man and by relying instead on a prerevolutionary status documented by the various *lettres patentes*.

A significant degree of political and social assimilation and a respected economic position, however, were the real and compelling forces behind the January 28th decision. The *lettres patentes* were used as a device. They were also used to separate the Ashkenazim from the Sephardim.

One might be reluctant to view this enfranchisement of the Jews of the Southwest as the first instance of Jewish emancipation. For if emancipation is to be defined as the culmination of a struggle based on programmatic ideological grounds and implying that natural rights had been withheld from the Jews, then surely neither the Sephardim nor the National Assembly were supporting emancipation. If the decree of January 28th, however, did not emancipate the Jews of the

Southwest, the implications of that decree significantly affected the emancipation of the Jews of the Northeast. In making of themselves the prototype of the assimilated and therefore acceptable Jews, the Sephardim had validated the standards to which the Ashkenazim would eventually have to conform.

One of the conditions which the Sephardim were required to fulfill was that of dissolution of their *nation*. Corporate privileges had been abolished by the acts of the National Assembly, and the Jews of Bordeaux understood that their citizenship was incompatible with a separate communal existence.[50] On February 18, 1790, the *nation* met to dissolve itself. Corporate autonomy had served the Sephardim well. It had enabled them to secure an official and privileged status, to control and limit the number of their members, and to consolidate and regulate their economic, political, and social functions. Most recently, it had become the basis for their full enfranchisement. Now, not only was corporateness abolished, but also for the Jews of Bordeaux the political and economic need for it had lessened with the attainment of citizenship and the ascendancy of a newly enfranchised bourgeoisie. Citizenship and broader economic opportunities, nevertheless, were insufficient guarantees against any further inappropriate and embarrassing activities on the part of the Sephardim. They were also inadequate substitutes for the former social and religious cohesiveness of the *nation*. Thus the Jews of Bordeaux created an *Association de Bienfaisance* which was to continue the charitable activities of the former *nation*.

In their struggle for recognition, the Sephardim had abandoned both the Jews of the Northeast and those of Paris. Having successfully obtained their goal, they again resorted to silence and left the rest of the Jews of France to undertake the final struggle for emancipation.

On the morning of January 28, Godard had delivered a fiery speech before the General Assembly of the Paris Commune, in which he had urged the Parisian revolutionaries to take upon themselves the struggle for obtaining equality for all the Jews of France. You will have the sweet satisfaction, he predicted, of serving not only the cause of the Jews of Paris but also that of all the Jews of the kingdom and thus of ensuring the happiness of fifty thousand individuals.[51] As a result of this scene before the Paris Commune, on January 29, 1790, the Jews of Paris obtained a certificate from the Carmelite section testifying to their excellent reputation and demanding equal rights for them. This was followed by supporting statements from almost all the city districts of Paris. With the resolutions of the sections as well as with a memorandum adopted on February 24th by the whole commune, a deputation presented itself to the National Assembly. The Assembly, still unwilling to deal with the question of civil rights for the Jews, decided to postpone the discussion indefinitely.

Godard had also prepared a petition signed by the leaders of the Northeastern Jews which he presented to the Assembly the day the Sephardim were enfranchised.[52] The significance of the petition, which pleaded for the full emancipation of the Jews of France, lies in its striking contrasts to the various *mémoires* and statements of the Sephardim.

Godard begins by eloquently restating those principles of the Revolution which necessitated granting the Jews equality. The Jews are either men and therefore included in the Rights of Man, he proclaimed, or they are an unidentifiable entity. The aims of the Revolution allow for no other conclusion in regard to this segment of the population which has not yet benefited from the distinctions between religious principles and civil rights.

Total conformity to the rest of the population is represented by Godard as neither a positive value nor a requirement for emancipation. Is it really necessary, Godard asks, that all Frenchmen serve in the army? Certainly, if the religion of the Jews prevents their full participation in this area, there are many other professions which they can freely and profitably enter. Their different eating habits, moreover, offer no justification for withholding civil rights.

Godard treads a delicate and subtle line when he declares that while the Jews would be discernible by their practices, it is as citizens that they should be viewed. Of what importance is their concentration in Alsace, he asks, unless one continues to separate the quality of Jew from that of citizen. Will one see the Jew everywhere, and the citizen nowhere?

No, it would not be a Jewish colony but a citizens' colony which would be established in Alsace. . . . Therefore, as citizens the Jews will be able, without inconvenience, to be more numerous here than there, to have more properties in one place than in another, in exactly the same way that the Protestants have been able, without inconvenience, to be more numerous and wealthy in the Languedoc region than in the other provinces. . . . the names of the sects mean nothing, and it is only with the title of citizen that the individuals of the same empire should approach one another. . . .[53]

Godard does not overlook the economic implications of emancipation. He, like the Sephardim, recounts the economic benefits accruing from the presence of Jews, but in a departure from the usual adds that if continually oppressed, the Jews will not only become an economic and political burden but also will be justified in avenging their discrimination.[54]

The differences between Godard's petition and the Sephardic position lie in the former's reliance on the revolutionary logic of universal human equality as the basis for granting equal rights. The Sephardim based their argument on the degree to which French culture, values, and economic institutions were accepted among their people. Equally significant is the positive evaluation of Jewish tradition found in Godard's petition. An example of this is his assertion that the Jews should be allowed to continue their practice of *kashrut*. In contrast is the Sephardic determination to prove that Jewish tradition is secondary to patriotic allegiance. Thus they focus on the willingness of the Jews of Bordeaux to violate the Sabbath in order to serve in their regiments.

The similarities between the two positions are also significant. The Sephardim and subsequently the Ashkenazim were willing to accept the price to be paid for enfranchisement and emancipation. Citizenship for both groups meant the end of corporate autonomy and subjection to the juridical, political, and police powers of a non-Jewish nation-state.

"Hasten the time of your justice," Godard concludes, "for the unfortunates are impatient." The Assembly, however, did not hasten its decision, but rather continued to postpone it indefinitely. On April 18, 1790, however, it did pass the Law of Protection for Alsatian Jews which explicitly stated that the Alsatian Jews were under the protection of the laws of France. On July 20, 1790, the Assembly remitted without indemnification the taxes paid by the Jews of France.[55]

Just before the National Assembly was to dissolve itself to make way for a more revolutionary body (without having decided anything about the Jews), Duport, a member of the Jacobin club, arose and stated that he believed that freedom of worship implied that no distinction be made in the political rights of citizens on account of their creed. The Assembly, silencing the objections made, adopted Duport's proposal to grant civil rights to the Jews. On September 27, 1791, it formulated the law that all exceptional regulations against Jews be abrogated and that the German Jews be admitted to the oath of citizenship. The National Assembly was dissolved on September 29, and on November 13, 1791, Louis XVI confirmed the full equality of the French Jews.[56]

Ideological consistency expressed by a more revolutionary body of deputies finally emancipated the Jews of France. They were granted the freedom to participate in the new political structure on an equal footing with all other Frenchmen. In return, they were required to renounce under oath all particular privileges.[57]

The Jews of France were now French citizens. The conditions for this citizenship, or more precisely the conditions of emancipation, were for the first time made explicit and legally binding. With the Declaration of the Rights of Man, the revolutionaries had made religious commitment a private affair; with the Civil Constitution of the Clergy, enacted on July 12, 1790, they had subordinated the Catholic Church to the state. For the Jews to be emancipated necessitated their redefinition of Judaism in such a way as to make it compatible with these changes. The Jews would have to enter society as individuals whose religious beliefs were both private and politically innocuous.

Both Frenchman and Jew would soon acknowledge the compelling and realistic motives behind Sephardic enfranchisement. Godard's arguments were undoubtedly indispensable to the emancipation of the unassimilated and generally despised Ashkenazim. The Sephardic Jews, however, were both pragmatic and prophetic when they ignored revolutionary ideology in favor of assimilation. Their fellow Jews of the Northeast would soon discover that complete conformity to French life, in contrast to Godard's revolutionary idealism, would be required to translate their legal right into a social and political reality.

Significantly, Sephardic compromises with traditional Talmudic Judaism were equally prophetic. The Jews of Bordeaux, perhaps as no other group of Jews, had intuited the bifurcation between personal religious belief and public conduct now demanded by the French nation-state and soon to be demanded of all who chose to embrace modernity.

The most obvious change among the Ashkenazim after the emancipation decree was in their participation in the political life of France. Although the number who participated actively was limited, there were those both in the Northeast and in the former papal provinces who joined the political clubs, participated in elections, and volunteered for service in the army.[58]

While most of those Jews who were politically involved favored the Revolution, there were a number who openly favored the *ancien régime*. Among them was Berr Isaac Berr, who signed a petition of the aristocrats of Nancy against the destruction of the monument of Louis XV in the city's Place Royale. There was also a significant number of Ashkenazic Jews on the list of emigrants from France. This list, however, must be examined closely since some Jews listed never left France at all, some fell victim to invading armies, while others left in order to avoid being drafted or to avoid paying debts. Notwithstanding the various motives, there is no doubt that a number of Ashkenazic Jews were political emigrants from France.[59]

The professions of the Jews of Northeastern France and the papal provinces did not change dramatically in the early years of the Revolution. This is easily understandable since the Jews knew no other professions than the ones which they had practiced for generations. In addition, in the early years of the Revolution, the Jews did not yet feel themselves a part of the French nation, and this estrangement permitted them to continue their occupations of money-lending and speculation, regardless of the political implications. Thus, there were Jews who were speculating with *assignats*, Jews who were aiding the counter-revolutionaries, and Jews who were buying nationalized property in order to sell it in small pieces to the land-hungry peasants. These diverse economic activities served to exacerbate the traditional prejudices felt towards the Jews and to introduce new reasons for their lack of respect. For example, the Jacobins distrusted the Jews for their lack of patriotism and their willingness to become involved with counter-revolutionaries; the latter distrusted them for their direct involvement in the parcelling of the land which the aristocrats held so dear.[60]

The emancipation decrees spoke not only of a new political position for the Jews, but also of a new social status. There was to be no discrimination of any kind on the basis of distinctions considered irrelevant by the revolutionaries. In spite of the determination of these revolutionaries to remain faithful to their principles, the majority of the people continued to think and act in terms of the old social and religious differences. The Ashkenazim, viewed and treated as Jews by their Gentile neighbors, in turn continued to think in terms of Christian and Jew. The continued existence of tight communal regulation, even after 1791, necessitated by the large debts which Northeastern and Avignonese Jews owed their Christian creditors, further impeded any rapid development of social interaction between the two groups.

In contrast to the Ashkenazim, the Sephardim drew closer to the non-Jewish population. The Bordelais Jews were active in the *Société des Sciences, Belles-Lettres et Arts,* in the *Musée,* and also in the *Société des Amis de la Constitution.* Some joined the army and many participated in the National Guard. A few were elected as municipal officers of the commune of Bordeaux, thereby playing an influential role in the early revolutionary years.[61]

The wealthy Sephardim, along with the Bordelais bourgeois, purchased a significant amount of nationalized property. Often this property was located in the few areas where the Jews formed the majority of the population.[62] The Jews of Bordeaux, however, were not involved in speculative purchases, as were the Northeastern Jews; most of the property which they bought not only was acquired for themselves, but also was purchased during the early years when buying was stable and speculation minimal.[63]

The anticipated ease with which the Bordelais Jews saw themselves entering French society was hardly illusory. The wealthy and increasingly more politically oriented Sephardim met no prejudicial obstacles in their attempts to live as Frenchmen. The poorer members of the Jewish community, however, were unable to afford the luxuries of assimilation. Although far more successful than their Ashkenazic counterparts, the less fortunate Jews of Bordeaux were neither so accepted nor so involved as their wealthy spokesmen. There were, in fact, a few minor incidents in which these Jews were criticized for a lack of patriotism.

One such incident occurred when a group of Jews was accused of fabricating false *assignats*. The municipality of Bordeaux, in which there were some Jewish officers, investigated the case and found that the correspondence concerning the venture was in Hebrew. Any involvement on the part of the prominent and established Sephardic Jews, notoriously ignorant of the Hebrew language, was highly unlikely.[64] A more general charge against the Jews occurred on June 15, 1793, when the 23rd section of Bordeaux declared that while the Jews were the ones most favored by the Revolution, they were seeking to cause desolation among the citizens, rather than contributing to the success of the Republic. The section, complaining that the Jews were monopolizing merchandise and causing prices to rise exorbitantly, decided to join with the other sections of the city to demand that the municipality put a brake to these activities.[65]

The Jews of Bordeaux continued throughout the Revolution to rely almost exclusively on commerce and trade. By the spring of 1794, however, Bordeaux had suffered severe economic losses. The slaves had revolted in the colonies, war had reduced commerce with other nations, and restrictive legislation had made relations with neutral countries difficult. A commercial agency was established in Bordeaux on March 31, 1794 by the *Comité de Salut public* (committee of public safety) in order to stimulate the citizens to take part in exporting goods, to make known to the *Commission des Subsistances* the obstacles and difficulties which were retarding commerce, and also to renounce those who by lack of patriotism and indifference were impeding commercial success. The agency, which held its first meeting on April 21, 1794, soon counted among its members *négociants* whose participation reflected in part an honest desire to revitalize the commerce of Bordeaux and in part the necessity to prove their patriotism to the suspicious Jacobins. Furtado and Lopes-Dubec, having both been associated with the Girondists, were among those who successfully devoted their talents to this agency.[66]

There is no evidence to indicate that the Sephardim were active as a community during the Revolution. Predictably, the wealthy identified themselves both economically and politically with the bourgeois of Bordeaux and thus were most active during the early years of the Revolution; some of the poorer Jews participated in the Jacobin rule of 1793–4.[67] A Jewish section, number 19, existed, but this was more a result of geographic circumstances than a decision to unite politically. Although the *Société de Bienfaisance* continued to play a role in caring for the poor and sick, supervising funerals, and assuring the propriety of the Jewish community, its influence was inconsequential compared to that of the dissolved *nation*.[68] Many Sephardim, having acquired all the rights and duties of French citizens, chose to exercise these rights along their individual political, economic, and social commitments. For them the Jewish Community ceased to play a significant role.

Abraham Furtado, deputy to the Malesherbes "Commission" in 1787 and future President of the Jewish Assembly of Notables in 1806, typifies the young, wealthy, and assimilated Sephardi for whom the fate of the Jews was subsumed in the more "immediate" and "significant" question of the fate of France.

Furtado had not accompanied the Sephardic deputies to Paris.[69] He may have been unsympathetic to their willingness to press for enfranchisement separately from the Ashkenazim; more likely, however, his political commitments in Bordeaux prevented him from leaving. By the summer of 1789, he had been chosen one of the ninety electors to the *Sénéchaussée* of Guyenne and subsequently had become a member of the new municipal government composed of these electors.

The focus of Furtado's concern was no longer the Jewish community. With the lawyers Vergniaud and Gensonné, future Girondist leaders, he had emerged as an active participant in the revolutionary vanguard of Bordeaux. Armed with the hedonistic critical humanitarianism of Voltaire and the democratic romanticism of Rousseau, he now sought to translate the dreams and passions of his generation into political realities. Along with other Sephardim such as Lopes-Dubec, Péreyre, Azevedo, and Lopes-Dias, he became a founder of the *Société des Amis de la Constitution*, the least demagogic of the three most popular clubs in Bordeaux, and with them dedicated himself to support the decisions of the National Assembly and the Constitution.[70]

In 1783, under the patronage of Saint-Maur, *intendant* of Bordeaux, the *Musée* had been formed. Composed of a cross-section of the intellectual and financial bourgeoisie of Bordeaux, including

Catholics, Protestants, and Jews, this group adopted the insignia of the Freemasons—liberty, equality and fraternity—and devoted itself to social and political questions as well as philanthropy.[71] On January 15, 1791, Furtado, joined by Vergniaud, Ducos fils, and Fonfrede aîné, created a political furor by resigning from the *Musée* because of the aristocratic leanings of the society. The *Comité des Quatre*, as the four were called, publicized their resignations with letters and pamphlets and soon succeeded in attracting almost all the future Girondists to their cause.

Furtado's resignation elicited the first political statement calling attention to his being a Jew. "Perhaps you will ask yourself," Granié, *commissaire* of the *Musée*, wrote, "how a citizen, whom the *Musée* had adopted before the Constitution had taken him from the debasement where an unjust prejudice held him, would be able to fail to acknowledge this recognition."[72] Apparently Furtado felt no reciprocal obligation for his early acceptance by the *Musé*.

On January 12, 1793, Furtado was elected municipal officer to the General Council of the commune of Bordeaux.[73] His activities became more numerous and often his name appears in the minutes of the municipality.[74] As a municipal officer he also became involved with the sections of Bordeaux, and on April 8, 1793, headed a delegation from the 23rd section to search out and disarm suspect persons.[75]

Intellectually, Furtado was no less committed to the Revolution. "Enlighten mankind," he had written in a treatise entitled *Folie de Jeunesse*.[76] "Banish from its midst error and superstition and those whose interest it is to propagate them and let us see thereafter if man is less unfortunate and better."[77] Furtado believed along with Voltaire and Diderot that there was a clear connection between the unenlightened condition of man and the existence of traditional religious beliefs and institutions. But he proceeded one step beyond what these *philosophes* would have advocated. Furtado was seeking to demonstrate that the Revolution could finally destroy the power of the Church, facilitate the spread of rational and just laws, and ultimately free man from his self-estrangement (a phrase apparently coined by himself). Because of monstrous opinions and lies, dressed in religious beliefs and doctrines, mankind had become a stranger to itself, socially divided, morally corrupt, politically vicious, and intellectually stagnant.[78]

Furtado's desire to combat the influence of religion was not motivated specifically by any anti-Jewish feelings. On the contrary, it was invariably the Catholic Church, its priests, and its doctrines which bore the brunt of his biting criticism.[79] There were in his words, nevertheless, a general distrust of all religions (which of necessity included his own), a belief that progress implied an abandonment of specific religious practices, and perhaps most significantly of all a sense of possible release from a marginality and estrangement which had become unbearable.

Furtado's enthusiastic embracing of the revolutionary dream was matched by his disillusion with the events of 1793–4. Man was finally to be given the opportunity to create a just and harmonious society in which all unnatural divisions would cease to exist. Yet instead of greater freedom, greater security, and more widespread enlightenment, Furtado witnessed a society at war with its neighbors and a people led to unimagined cruelties not by pernicious religious beliefs but rather by an excess and distortion of the very principles on which he had placed such confidence. He witnessed this, moreover, as an accused traitor to his country, for he had been proscribed by the National Convention's Jacobin leadership along with all those Bordelais who had participated in the ill-fated Girondist *Commission Populaire*.[80]

The years of the Terror saw Furtado abandoning the intellectual friends of his youth (Rousseau and Voltaire), renouncing his faith in a revolutionary idealism, and reconstructing for himself a meaningful approach to the philosophical, psychological, and political complexities which his youthful arrogance had so easily dismissed.[81] Through the influence of Montesquieu and Locke, he was led to appreciate the role of historical experience, to reevaluate the essential bulwarks of society, and ultimately as we shall see to reconsider the legitimacy of traditional institutions including those of his own religion.

The only issue during the revolutionary years to involve all the French Jewish communities and to elicit a unified response from the Sephardim was that of nationalizing the Jewish debt. Both the Sephardim and Ashkenazim sought to gain from the decisions concerning nationalization, but as in the past what was beneficial to the former would become a burden to the latter.

Although all the communities of the Northeast and the former papal provinces were in debt, those of Metz, Avignon, Carpentras, and L'Isle-sur-Sorgue were indebted to Christian creditors. It was the hope of these four communities, notwithstanding their separate actions, that the decrees of June 14 and July 30, 1791, and August 15, 1793, which nationalized the debts of all those corporations dissolved by the decree of October 1790, would also be applied to them, since they too had been dissolved by the decree of September 27, 1791.

The expectations of these communities were not fulfilled, despite the fact that there were many Christians as well as Jews who felt that the Jewish debts should be nationalized. On December 6, 1797, the Council of Five Hundred, after having received reports from three different commissions (all of which were in favor of nationalizing the Jewish debt), decided that the Jewish communities were not included in the dissolution order which nationalized the debts of the corporations and religious communities. The decision of the Council of Five Hundred was based on the outcome of the debate concerning the status of a foreigner, *aubain,* and its application to the Jews living in Northeastern France and the former papal provinces. In the opinion of the Council of Five Hundred, the Jews did not form a community of French inhabitants but rather they were a group of strangers tolerated by the state.[82] Since the Jews were officially recognized as strangers in France before they were emancipated, the Council reasoned, they could not have been and were not included in the dissolution order. The fact that there had been a question of the status of the Jews before the Revolution gave the Council the leeway to make this finding.

While this was the explicit argument against nationalizing the Jewish debt, there appears to be little doubt that anti-Jewish as well as economic motives played a significant part in influencing the final decisions of the Council. The Christian creditors of the Jews were against the nationalization of the Jewish debt because they saw either themselves deprived of their due or the French nation deprived of a considerable sum of money. The Committee of Finances, in stating that nationalization of Jewish debts would be ruinous to the Republic's finances, further justified the already strong fears of the Christian creditors.

An ironic consequence of the failure to nationalize the debts was that the Ashkenazic communities were compelled, notwithstanding their official dissolution, to remain organized in order to collect the taxes necessary to pay these debts. In addition, these communities, in paying their Christian creditors, suffered severe economic losses.[83]

The Sephardic Jews of Bordeaux, having had no need to become indebted to the Christian population, viewed nationalizing Jewish property and debts from an entirely different perspective. For them nationalization had only one effect, namely to allow Jewish communal property to be purchased by non-Jews. The arguments concerning nationalizing their property, based primarily on whether the Sephardic Jews had ever formed a corporation, were no less heated than those involving nationalizing the Ashkenazic debts.

The Bordelais Jews would undoubtedly have remained silent during the debates in the Council of Five Hundred had there not occurred a public confrontation concerning their cemetery of Sablonat. Two citizens of Bordeaux, Despiau and Pujos, had succeeded in depositing one half of the price for the Jewish cemetery which had been offered for sale as part of the *biens nationaux*. The Jews immediately obtained a suspension of the transaction on the grounds that their property could not be nationalized, since they had never formed a corporation, but rather had been organized as a *Société de Bienfaisance*. Unlike the national property of the Catholic Church, the Jews maintained that their cemetery was private property which they had purchased for their own particular customs.

The Jews of Bordeaux obtained a departmental *arrêt* on the 11th Messidor, Year IV(1796) in which their claims to be a *Société* were upheld. The following year, the Minister of Finance gave his opinions which, while in accord with the conclusions of the *arrêt*, were opposed to the reasons offered by the *départment*. Since the existence of the *Société* is uncertain, the Minister wrote, it is more accurate to state that the property belonged to certain individuals of the Jewish sect.[84] Two *mémoires* had been presented by the Jews and two by Pujos and Despiau, all of which attempted to refute the assertions of the opposite party. We shall not review these *mémoires* in detail, but rather we shall attempt to seize upon the main points of each.

For Pujos and Despiau, the positions of the Jews and those of the Department and Minister of Finance were totally unjustifiable. Are the Jews now to be regarded as a class separated from all other Frenchmen, Despiau and Pujos asked? They were in fact organized as a *corps* before the Revolution and in turn they must be treated as such in regard to their property. To support their argument, Despiau and Pujos described the corporations as they had existed in the *ancien régime*, and declared that the *nation's* ordinance of 1763, rather than describing a loose organization of those who voluntarily chose to belong, in fact represented a corporative *règlement* which forced obedience to the established statutes.[85]

The Jews of Bordeaux answered Despiau and Pujos by declaring that they had never been organized as a corporation nor were they ever permitted to belong to one. For the first time, the Sephardim dwelt upon both the disabilities which they had endured during the *ancien régime* and the similarities of their status to that of the Jews of Metz, Alsace, and Lorraine. According to them neither the Jews of Bordeaux nor those of the Northeast had ever enjoyed the privileges and dignity of a corporative status. In fact, the Sephardim continued, we cannot understand how the Jews of Metz in good faith could have asserted the contrary.[86]

Both Despiau and Pujos and the Bordelais Jews were involved in much more than a definitional controversy. The former feared a severe economic loss if, after having paid a significant sum, they were denied the right to the cemetery, and the latter feared that they would be required subsequently to repurchase the ashes of their ancestors. As we have seen, the government was also more involved with the practical consequences of the problem than with the justice of either position.

The Sephardim succeeded in keeping their cemetery and the Ashkenazim continued to pay their burdensome debts. Although finally united as French citizens of the Jewish religion, there was neither equality nor unity among the Jews of France. General confusion during the first decade of the Revolution allowed for a continued avoidance of any of the practical consequences of emancipation. Not until 1806 would the French Jews be required actively to face and resolve their unified emergence into a modern nation-state.

4

Napoleon
and the
Assembly of Notables

The end of the revolutionary decade found the French weary of up-heaval and ready to accept a rule of peace and order at the expense of achieving the highest hopes of 1789. They found their "surveillance infatigable" in Napoleon Bonaparte who, with a brilliance unequalled by other European "despots," rapidly transformed the chaos of op-posing political and religious factions into a "socially bourgeois, legally equalitarian, and administratively bureaucratic" state.

Napoleon is often viewed as the popular general who brought the French internal peace (and for a short time international peace) while simultaneously preserving for them the accomplishments of their revolution. Paradoxically Napoleon must also be viewed as the First Consul and Emperor who abandoned the Republic along with the ideal of equality and who thus laid the foundations for the July Monarchy. "We do not have a Republic and we will not have one unless we sow some blocks of granite on the soil of France," Napoleon had said to his Council of State.[1] His blocks of granite, however, were comparable to the corporate bodies of the *ancien régime*, revived not to compete with a monarchy but to be subjected to a modern state and to be used to assure the obedience of the masses. The assemblies, the Legion of Honor, the electoral colleges, and eventually the Jews were so many blocks set in the "grains of sand" Napoleon called his nation.

Intent upon reuniting the clergy of France, making peace with the Holy See, and obtaining papal recognition for the Revolution, Napo-leon signed a concordat with the Vatican on the 26th Messidor, an IX (1801). The Pope received the right to depose French bishops and agreed to raise no question over the former tithes and Church lands. Publicity of Catholic worship was again allowed, Napoleon stated that Catholicism was the religion of the majority of the Frenchmen, and the state was henceforth required to pay the salaries of the clergy. Napoleon had not agreed, however, to establish Catholicism as the religion of the state. In order to make this clear, he issued a decree on the 18th Germinal, an X (1802), according to which Protestant ministers of all denominations were also to be paid by the state.

Either out of indifference or ignorance (perhaps both), Napoleon ignored the Jews of his empire. Free to practice their religion publicly, they were left on their own to pay their rabbis, organize their communities, and resolve any contradictions between their political status and religious commitments.

Despite the successful emergence of the Sephardim as French citizens, there remained certain civil ambiguities, such as matters of marriage and divorce, which had never been resolved. On May 14, 1792, the tribunal of Bordeaux had decided that the Jews were to remain subject to their own laws and customs in matters of marriage because the Assembly had not yet fixed the forms of union for non-Catholics.[2] During the Empire, when the Napoleonic codes, five in all dealing with civil, commercial, and criminal procedures, made France legally and juridically uniform, the Sephardim continued to marry and divorce according to the laws of Moses.[3] Since there was little if any significant conflict between them and the rest of the population, they would have undoubtedly resolved the relation between the laws of Moses and the laws of the country by accepting civil marriage and divorce. This was not to occur; instead the Jews of the Northeast were to bring to the attention of Napoleon the anomalous position of all French Jews.

Emancipation had dealt a severe blow to the discipline and organization of the Ashkenazic communities, and the leaders, unable to control the threatening anarchy and seeking a reinforcement of their authority, appealed to the government to intervene on their behalf. Specifically, they wished to see the Jews organized officially and included along with the Protestants in the decree of 1802.[4] Jean Etienne Marie Portalis, Minister of Cults, studied the complaints of both the Northeastern Jews and those prefects involved in settling the increasingly more numerous disturbances.[5] After first expressing his opposition to governmental intervention, Portalis finally agreed to find a means of bringing order and peace to the communities of Alsace, Metz, and Lorraine.[6]

At the same time that Berr Isaac Berr and others were petitioning the government to recognize an official Jewish leadership, the non-Jews were increasing both their verbal and physical attacks upon the Jews. The residents of Alsace and Lorraine accused the Ashkenazim of usury and feared that soon all their property would be mortgaged to these "enemies" of the Church. Municipal councils began to suggest measures which would reduce the credits owed the Jews, and the debtors began to take the situation into their own hands.[7]

Continuous complaints by the general councils of Haut- and Bas-Rhin, along with the increase in violent outbreaks in the summer and fall of 1805, finally prompted the Minister of Justice to examine the problem. Although specifically denouncing the usury of the Jews, he advised, nevertheless, a general remedy which would no longer permit the rate of interest to be established by the parties involved.[8]

Neither the projects of Portalis nor those of the Minister of Justice were realized; not until Napoleon addressed himself to the Jewish problem were the dual issues of internal organization and usurious practices joined together. The results—an arbitrary infringement of the economic freedom of the Northeastern Jews, a resolution of all questions concerning the relation of Jewish and French law, and the union of all the Jews of France in one centrally controlled organization—were consistent with Napoleon's decision both to consolidate the accomplishments of the Revolution and to reconstruct subservient intermediary bodies. In obtaining these results, however, Napoleon was to reverse the process by which the Revolution had emancipated the Jews. The issue of citizenship and the worthiness of the Jews were again questioned, and doctrinal as well as concrete economic proofs of their intentions were demanded.

Although he had been aware of the Jews' petitions to the government and the Alsatians' desire to curtail the economic activities of their non-Christian population, Napoleon did not address himself personally to the problem until after he had stopped in Strasbourg on January 23 and 24, 1806.[9] As a result of this visit, during which he undoubtedly heard at first hand the complaints against the "usurious" Jews, Napoleon directed both the Ministers of Interior and of Justice to draw up acceptable programs.

The Minister of Justice, now asked to prepare a second report, no longer relied upon general reforms, but rather suggested measures specifically directed against the Jews. In his report, sent by Napoleon on March 6 to the Council of State, the Minister advised the departments of Legislation and of the Interior to prepare legislation which would annul the mortgages taken by Jews, prevent them from taking any additional mortgages, revoke their rights of citizenship, and subject nonpropertied Jews to a special license in addition to that required by all Frenchmen. The Minister of Interior, Jean Baptiste Champagny, rejected these anti-Jewish measures and proposed to delay any legal action against the Jews.[10]

The atmosphere in Paris was far from neutral when the Council of State received the proposals of the Ministers of Justice and the Interi-

or. Louis Gabriel Bonald, a Catholic writer passionately hostile to the
Jews, had already published his infamous article in the February 8th
edition of *Le Moniteur*. For Bonald, the problem was easily solved. The
Jews were not able to be and never would be citizens under Christianity without becoming Christians.[11] Bonald's thesis, debated in government circles as well as throughout the country, elicited in defense
of the Jews Grégoire's *Observations nouvelles sur les Juifs et spécialement
sur ceux d'Allemagne*, as well as a printed pamphlet by Moyse P[xxxxx]
and, it is reported, an unpublished response by Furtado.[12] All of these
defenses, however, came too late to affect the course of events.

The Council of State was an extremely important political body,
since the Ministers never met together and Napoleon had silenced the
Legislative body and the Tribunal. Each question brought to the
Council was first examined by the competent sections (departments)
under the leadership of an auditor (official in charge of preparing the
reports) and then presented to the whole assembly by a report of a
councillor. Thus the Jewish question was duly assigned by Regnaud
de Saint-Jean-d'Angély, president of the section of the Interior, to
Louis-Mathieu Molé, a young auditor whom Napleon had recently
appointed. Molé's report, which differed little from the suggestions of
the Minister of Justice and showed an obvious reliance on Bonald's
article, was received with surprise and disagreement by the other
members of the section.[13]

Regnaud presented the almost unanimous opinion of the section of
the Interior at the first meeting of the Council of State at which
Napoleon was absent. Claude Beugnot, a recently appointed councillor, spoke in support of his section's position and characterized the
proposed restrictions against the Jews as "illegal" and "unjust."
Everyone in the Council, except Molé, was impressed by Beugnot's
speech and advised him to present his opinion to Napoleon at the next
meeting to take place at St. Cloud on April 30th.[14]

Although Beugnot had presented his defense to the first meeting of
the Council in a rational and logical manner, his second presentation
before Napoleon, more "emphatique" and "prétentieux," succeeded
in enraging the unsympathetic Emperor.[15] After accusing Beugnot of
sacrificing reality for abstractions, Napoleon ordered the publication
of Molé's report, which had not yet been presented. Obviously aware
of the contents of this report, Napoleon then expressed his own views,
which were strikingly similar to those presented to the National
Assembly by the Abbé Maury and Reubell on December 23 and 24,
1789.

It is necessary to consider the Jews as a nation and not as a sect, for they are a nation within a nation. I would like to prevent them, at least for a certain length of time, from taking mortgages; it is too humiliating for the French nation to find itself at the mercy of the vilest of all nations.[16]

Regnaud and the Comte de Ségur, both old friends of the Jews, spoke out on their behalf; the meeting ended with a resolution to investigate the situation of the Jews in France and specifically their habits concerning usury.

A third and final meeting took place on May 7, when a less emotional Napoleon declared himself an enemy of any arbitrary and violent measures which would be disapproved of by posterity. While he still considered specific legislation against the Jews necessary, he had been convinced that the Jews were perfectible and should participate in their regeneration. A convocation of an Assembly of Jewish Notables appealed to him as the best means to achieve this regeneration.[17]

The decree concerning the Jews which was prepared by Regnaud, who attempted to justify the economic restrictions, and abridged by Napoleon, who felt no need for justification, was finally promulgated on May 30, 1806. In essence, there was a temporary moratorium placed on all debts owed the Jews by the non-commercial farmers of the Northeast.[18] In addition to granting this reprieve to the overburdened peasants, the decree also ordered the convocation in Paris on July 15 (it was delayed until July 26) of an Assembly of Jews. The prefects were to choose the deputies from among the rabbis, landowners, and other Jews who were distinguished by their "integrity" and "intelligence." Attached to the decree was a table listing the number of deputies which each of fourteen departments was permitted to send. A general provision, however, declared that there was to be one deputy for every one-hundred to five-hundred Jews, and thus any area in which there were at least that many was authorized to send deputies.[19]

Napoleon had charged the Minister of the Interior with the execution of the provisions of the May 30th decree. Unhappy with this assignment, Champagny requested that he no longer be responsible for the affairs of the Jews and suggested as his replacement Portalis, the Minister of Cults. Without agreeing to discharge Champagny, Napoleon named Molé, Joseph Portalis, the son of the Minister, and Etienne-Denis Pasquier as the Commissioners who would be directly responsible for all matters pertaining to the Jews. They were required, however, to communicate directly with the Minister of Interior.[20] M. Molé, Pasquier wrote, being the first in the order of nomination, was unanimously elected President of the Commission.[21] Molé was not only the first to be nominated but also, and much more important for future events, the most sympathetic of the three to Napoleon's intentions.[22]

The distribution of deputies indicated in the decree bore little if any resemblance to the true proportion of Jews. The government had estimated 6,513 Jews in the department of Vosges where there were only 250; 6,883 in Meurthe instead of 3,000 and 600 instead of 2,131 in the Gironde.[23] The government's ignorance, moreover, worked to its disadvantage, for a note attached to the May 30th decree had stated that one deputy had been chosen for every 1,000 in the North and for every 500 in the South where there were fewer but more enlightened Jews. The unequal representation was necessary, the government had reasoned, "pour pouvoir composer les opinions."[24] Napoleon had ordered, at the second meeting of the Council of State, a full statistical report on the French Jews; the information had not been available, however, when he signed the decree.

It was not until June 18 that the prefect of the Gironde was asked to furnish information concerning the number of Jews, their profession, the percent of interest they charged, their synagogues, public education, views on conscription, and finally the manner in which they observed the civil law.[25] On June 27th, the prefect responded with a seven-point report in which the Jews of Bordeaux, numbering 1,800, were shown to be no different from the rest of the population:

1st, that the existence of Jews living in the Gironde region is the same as that of other citizens, that several have filled and are filling public functions; 2nd, that their approximate number is about 1,800 divided into 460 families; 3rd, that 200 of these families own houses and that several figure among the most highly taxed; 4th, that they engage in the professions of money-changers, bankers, merchants, retailers; that there are few workers among them; 5th, that the interest rate stipulated by them in their transactions follows the market rate and that no complaint, such as those which have been so strongly articulated against the Jews in Alsace, has been made against those in Bordeaux; 6th, that they have no synagogues organized according to their law, but only rooms where they unite for prayer; that their children are sent to the usual public schools, such as the primary, secondary, and imperial lycée; that the Hebrew language is taught to some by private tutors; 7th, finally, that they obey the civil laws and especially the one of 19th Floréal (6th year) on conscription, exactly as do all other citizens, and that no complaint has been raised against them.[26]

The Minister of Interior, unsatisfied with the prefect's report, asked for a more detailed and precise statement on the Bordelais Jews. This time the prefect asked the help of the *Société de Bienfaisance* whose President was Lopes-Dubec. The report of the *Société* as well as additional information provided by the prefect were sent to the Minister of Interior on November 10 and December 5 and 11.[27] In this new report, the number of Jews was stated to be 2,131 among whom 144 were Avignonese and 336 German, and the number of synagogues, established in private homes, to be nine. There is only one rabbi, the report continued, who is limited to casuistry and enjoys no religious authority. Any well mannered Jew who knows Hebrew is entitled to lead the prayers and deliver sermons. There are no beggars, for their *Société de Bienfaisance* cares for their sick and poor.[28]

There is official record only of the reports sent by the prefect to the Minister of Interior; nevertheless, a *mémoire* written by Abraham Furtado and modelled in almost every detail after the one presented to Malesherbes, may have also been submitted for the edification of the French ministers.[29]

In his introduction, Furtado explains that the *mémoire* is divided into four sections, the first recounting the history of the French Jews until their expulsion in 1394, the second describing their establishment in France, the third reviewing the effects of legislation upon the moral character of the Jews, and the fourth, missing from the manuscript, indicating both the means of ameliorating the condition of the Jews and the obstacles which the government would have to surmount.[30] The first two sections, quoted almost exactly from the 1788 *mémoire*, differ from the latter not in what is presented, but rather most strikingly in what is omitted. Both the polemics concerning the superiority of the Sephardic Jews and their unique descent from the house of Judah as well as all references to the establishment of the *nation* are missing in this revision. Although the facts themselves speak of the particular treatment which the Portuguese Jews received, Furtado dwells neither on this nor on any aspect of communal organization which would show a separation of the Jews from the rest of the population.

The third and last section, unrelated to anything which appeared in the earlier *mémoire*, vividly illustrates Furtado's analysis of and remedies for French Jewry. Having developed a firm belief in the power and influence of prevailing laws, Furtado blames, as did those early revolutionaries who were committed to the emancipation of the Jews, the variable and oppressive laws under which the Alsatian Jews were forced to live for their present character and occupations.[31] It is not at all natural, he explains, that men would consider themselves a part of the nation in which they lived when that nation treated them as enemies.[32] If the Jews of the Gironde had witnessed the same oppression as the Jews of the North, perhaps they too would have evidenced the same degradation. They are better only because they have been less unhappy.[33] In fact, Furtado adds, if one pauses to reflect on the matter, one should be surprised not that there are some ignorant and superstitious Jews in the North, but that there are so few.[34] Furtado did not yet suspect that his acceptance of the Ashkenazim not as they were but as they could become reinforced, despite his moral indignation, the ambivalent and potentially discriminatory attitudes of even the more enlightened among the French statesmen.

In a biting tone which will reappear in his battles against the May 30 and March 17 decrees, Furtado addresses the Alsatians and describes in detail the "perverse climate" in which they expected the Jews to reform. You treat the Jews of your country as slaves and reproach them for not having noble and elevated sentiments. You deprive them of all means of instruction and wish them to be educated. You ostracize them from society, prohibit their involvement in agriculture and the arts, and then reproach their estrangement from the land and their artistic ineptitude. The Jews are men; treat them as such and do not debase them in order to give yourselves the barbarous pleasure of despising them.[35] Do you answer that their religion is unsociable, that their observances are ridiculous and perpetuate ignorance and superstition? Do you not see, Furtado responds with a logic both alien and hostile to traditional Judaism, that a continuation of persecutions will succeed only in eliciting a deeper attachment to their religion, their rites, and their sect. This religion, moreover, against which so many assertions are made, and concerning which so little is actually known, can be reduced in its entirety to a few words:

To believe in the existence of a God, in His unity, in His spirituality, to believe that prayers and adoration have no need of intermediaries; that God revealed Himself to men and that His revelation is true; that Moses is the greatest of the prophets; that our religion is eternal; that God knows the thoughts and actions of men; that God recompenses the good and punishes the wicked; etc.[36]

Even to those Ashkenazim who realized the significance of enlightened culture and *mores,* this abridged and typically Bordelais Sephardic exposition of the Jewish faith would be unacceptable. Missing were the Talmudic dictates and the interpretations of the rabbis; missing was a Judaism of legislation. One cannot help but conclude from Furtado's definition, however (and this is precisely what he intended), that given the opportunity, all the Jews could and would choose to live as Frenchmen committed to a "purified" and somewhat anemic expression of Judaism.

Exclusive of the faulty statistics, the prefects were given no practical instructions concerning the manner in which they were to select the deputies. Aware, however, of the government's desire to have men favorable to its intentions, they named the deputies accordingly. The prefects have chosen, Pasquier recalled, those Jews who are not only respected but also accommodating. It is principally among those of Bordeaux that one hopes to find both the most enlightened and influential and those whom one can use with the most confidence.[37]

On Saturday, July 26, 1806, after having assembled for prayers in the Parisian synagogues of the "rue Sainte Avoye" and the "rue du Chaume," the deputies from France and Italy gathered together at the *Hôtel de Ville* to name their officers. Abraham Furtado, receiving sixty-two votes against thirty-two for Berr Isaac Berr, was elected President. Isaac Samuel Avigdor (Nice) and Rodriques fils (Seine) were elected Secretaries; the auditors were Orly Hayem Worms (Seine), Theodore Cerf Berr (Seine) and Emilie Vitta (Italy).

By choosing Furtado as their President and in limiting their other choices to men from Italy, Paris, and the South of France, the Assembly gave the first indication of its willingness to make the Jews useful citizens, conciliate their beliefs with the duties of Frenchmen, and remove from them any reproaches. Such were the government's objectives, made clear by Champagny in a letter sent to each of the deputies upon his arrival in Paris.[38]

Furtado was well known to the deputies both for his participation in the Malesherbes "Commission" and his leadership of the Bordeaux community. Equally known was his primary concern with the civil rather than religious life of the Jews. What was less well known, although perhaps intuited by some, was his intense involvement and subsequent disillusion with the events and ideals of the Revolution. In many respects he was the first example of a modern Jew who sought to embrace an utopian solution to end his marginality and who, disillusioned with the excesses of that solution, realized its inevitable failure.

By accepting his election as President, Furtado returned to the Jewish community. His primary allegiance was still to France. More politically conservative and less optimistic than in 1789, however, he more readily acknowledged the need for communal participation in assimilating the Jews to French institutions.

As the Assembly was to become more involved with the details of making the Jews "useful citizens," Furtado's secular attitude would cause suspicion among those deputies for whom Judaism was at least as essential as the demands made by the government.[39] Notwithstanding the lessened respect felt for him by the more traditional deputies, there is little doubt that as spokesman for both Emperor and Jew, Furtado played a significant role in directing the discussions of

the Assembly and in influencing the answers which were subsequently sanctioned by the Sanhedrin. There is equally little doubt,
moreover, that he, more than any other individual, legitimized and
institutionalized the inescapable bifurcation of modern Jewish life.

From the minutes published soon after, we are able to follow closely
the proceedings both of the Assembly and the Sanhedin.[40] These
minutes, however, have been edited by Furtado and the Imperial
Commissioners and reflect an official rather than precise picture of the
debates which took place.[41] Rarely if ever is the name of a speaker
given ("un rabbin dit . . .") and often the tumult within the Assembly
is reproduced merely by a declaration to that effect. That the minutes
do not contradict what took place may be assumed; that they omit
particulars and reduce the controversies to a minimum is illustrated
by Furtado's personal letters and notes.

The Assembly met a second time on July 29. The Imperial Commissioners were present and Molé, speaking on behalf of the government,
addressed the assembled Jews. Reminding them that they had been
called together from different parts of the Empire because of the
"justifiable" complaints against many of them, he revealed that they
would be presented with twelve questions.[42] Your task, he warned in
a tone which revealed his lack of respect and sympathy, is to answer
each question honestly, for to do otherwise is to render yourselves
both guilty and blind to your true interests.[43]

Molé followed his unconcealed threat with a list of the twelve
questions, which dealt with marriage and divorce, the commitments
of the Jews to France and the Frenchmen, and the internal regulations
of the Jewish community in regard to their organization and their
economic transactions.[44] Despite the "unanimous" feeling on the part
of the deputies that the questions implied a lack of attachment on the
part of the Jews to France and their fellow Frenchmen (a response
which was justified merely by the fact that such questions were
asked), Furtado replied to Molé's presentation by praising the genius
who had finally put an end to the anarchy within France and the
ambitious enemies outside of France, and who now had taken upon
himself the immediate regeneration of the Jews.[45]

After following the Commissioners' departure with cries of "Long
live the Emperor," the Assembly formed, on the basis of Furtado's
eclectic selection, a Commission of twelve deputies. The Commission,
composed of Rabbis Sinzheim (Bas-Rhin), Segre (Italy) and Andrade
(Landes) and MM. Berr Isaac Berr, Jacob Lazard, Jacob Goudechaux
Berr, Moses Levy, Rodrigues, Samuel Jacob Guediglia, Michel Berr,
Baruch Cerf Berr and Lyon Marx and representing the Jews of the
Northeast, Southwest and Italy, was to prepare the groundwork for

the proceeding discussions.

By the third meeting of the Assembly on August 4, the Commission of twelve had prepared a draft of the answers to the first three questions. Each answer was to be read to the deputies in French, translated into German by M. Lyon Marx and Italian by M. Avigdor, and then opened for discussion. The first two questions, eliciting no discussion, were quickly adopted; the first, outlawing polygamy, almost unanimously and without any alteration and the second, invalidating divorce if not previously pronounced under the French code, unanimously.[46]

The answer proposed by the Commission to the third question pertaining to intermarriage immediately caused a rift between the rabbis and traditionalists on the one hand and the secularists on the other. Although the exact answer which the Commission proposed is unknown, we can approximate it by the succeeding discussions and the compromise solution which was finally accepted. Apparently the Commission stated that the Bible forbade Jews to marry idolators only and that the Talmud declared formally that modern nations, who worshipped the God of heaven and earth, were not to be considered as such. Although the natural conclusion, that there was thus no interdiction of mixed marriage between Jew and Christian, was logically sound, the results were contrary to the traditional Jewish position.

After the prepared answer was read, a rabbi proposed that in any theological question the rabbis should be consulted separately and their opinions given greater weight. Furtado then reminded the Assembly that the principle of majority of votes was inherent to the nature of every deliberation. The rabbis, half-heartedly accepting Furtado's observations, continued to express their dissatisfaction with the answer and their desire to see all mixed marriages prohibited. One of the deputies, very likely from the Southwest, answered the rabbis by emphasizing the political advantages of intermarriage.

They have tried to dwell on the domestic inconveniences that these marriages could entail, but have they said a word about the great political advantages that they present? If one had to balance the one against the other, how would it be possible to doubt the superiority of the latter? No, it is necessary to be content with the Commission's answer, which contains the whole truth.[47]

This opinion, the minutes stated, was strongly supported by many members.

Unable to resolve the controversy and faced with an increase of "tumult," Furtado suspended the discussion and a new answer was prepared with the assistance of all the rabbis and the twelve members of the Commission. Less than an hour later, the revised answer was adopted almost unanimously. The compromises arrived at included the Commission's statements that the Talmud did not consider modern nations to be idolators but extended the answer to include the rabbis' opinion that notwithstanding this position, the Jewish religion did not permit mixed marriages. The rabbis added, however (perhaps at the instigation of the more radical notables), that a Jew who married a Christian woman did not cease to be considered a Jew any more than if he had married a Jewess civilly and not religiously.[48]

At the next meeting of the Assembly, on August 7, there was again disagreement which this time centered on the response proposed to the fourth question. In answer to whether Frenchmen were considered as brethren or strangers by the Jews, the Commission had provided a detailed reply which included a reference to the difference between the Portuguese and German Jews. Both the length and content of the answer were criticized by the deputies. After defending the controversial paragraph by explaining that the distinctions between the Jews of the North and South were included to show that the latter had made more progress only because they were less unhappy, Furtado finally agreed to submit only the first part of the answer to a vote. The revised answer, which stated unequivocally that Jews considered Frenchmen as their brethren, was adopted unanimously.[49]

The answers to both the fifth and sixth questions, each affirming that the Jews regarded themselves as Frenchmen both in rights and responsibilities, were quickly adopted by a unanimous vote, and the answer to the seventh question, explaining that the rabbis were designated most often, although not uniformly, by the leaders of the community was slightly altered and adopted by the majority.[50] The eighth answer, however, dealing with the jurisdiction and judicial power of the rabbis, was unacceptable. Characterizing it as insufficiently explicit, the Assembly returned it to the Commission for revision.

On August 12, the Assembly adopted the answers to the remaining five questions.[51] The revised answer to the eighth question, which declared that since the Revolution the rabbis exercised neither police jurisdiction nor judicial powers, was accepted almost unanimously as was the ninth answer, which again denied the police-judicial jurisdiction of the rabbis.[52] In both instances the dissident votes were probably those of the rabbis. The tenth answer, declaring that there were no professions which the law of the Jews forbade, was quickly and unanimously adopted.[53]

Considering the continuous complaints against the economic activities of the Jews, the specific situation in Bas- and Haut-Rhin and the decree of May 30, which ostensibly sought to help the peasants but in fact punished the Jews, the answers to the eleventh and twelfth questions, concerning the legality of "usurious" interest between Jews and between Jew and non-Jew, were the most likely to have practical influence on any future legislation.

The response of the Assembly to these crucial questions was long and filled with Biblical quotations and Talmudic references.[54] Modern historians have felt that the deputies, already defensive because of the assumptions underlying the questions, avoided describing the economic practices common among the Jews.[55] Fortunately, we have not only the minutes and printed response, but also Furtado's draft of the answers.[56] These combined sources indicate that the Jewish position was neither as defensive nor as evasive as has been previously assumed.

Both the Assembly's reply and Furtado's draft present essentially the same answers to the questions, and derive their exegetical comments from Deuteronomy, Chapter XXIII, vs. 19: "Thou shall not lend upon usury (so translated in the Christian Bible) to thy brother, usury of money, usury of victuals, usury of anything that is lent upon usury." Both concluded that the Hebrew word *neshekh* meant interest and not usury, that taking interest had been permitted only from strangers not dwelling in the midst of the Jews, that brother implied fellow countryman, and that this precept, established with the view of retaining a primitive equality, was no longer applicable. Since their dispersion, the Jews were allowed to take interest from Jew as well as non-Jew, and in neither circumstance was there a question of condonation of usury. On the contrary, usurious practices were to be condemned.[57]

The deputies, after debating the literal translation of *ahikha*, with some interpreting it as brother, others as fellow countryman, requested that the answer be read three times, after which it was adopted almost unanimously.

The answer not only stated the points already indicated but also embellished them with detailed descriptions of preexilic times, with a reference to Maimonides' position (make profit of the stranger) and its rejection by Talmudists, and finally with numerous supportive quotes from the Bible. Furtado's draft, on the other hand, which answers both questions together (in the printed response there are two separate answers) relies for its persuasiveness not on Biblical and Talmudic references, but rather on a logical argument based primarily on economic considerations. Included in the Assembly's reply were two brief statements, the one defining usury and interest—Is not usury an interest above the legal interest, above the rate fixed by law?—and the

other establishing the absence in Biblical texts of any term of comparison for these practices—*Neshekh* could not have implied usury, for
usury is an expression relative to, and compared with, another and
lawful interest. It is these two arguments which Furtado carefully
develops in his draft and which he uses both to establish the translation of *Neshekh* and the clarification of ancient economic practices as
well as to citicize Christian interpretation and by implication contemporary economic policies.

Usury, Furtado states, may be defined in two different ways, the
first very simply by an excess of interest in comparison to a fixed rate
and the second, far from simply, by a rate above the commercial price.
If one considers the latter definition, Furtado continues, one must take
into account not only the different economic times, but also the individuals who are lending and borrowing and the risks involved in the
various transactions.[58] We believe, Furtado concludes, that it is impossible to have a clear and precise idea of usury before the laws
(which in fact had not yet been promulgated) establish a fixed rate of
interest. To substantiate this, Furtado refers to Montesquieu's *L'Esprit
des lois*, Chapter 22, in which usury and interest among ancient
peoples are shown to have had the same meaning. Returning to the
quotation from Deuteronomy, which undoubtedly was used in an
accusatory manner by non-Jews, Furtado then explains how the mis-
translation of *neshekh* occurred. The Christian casuists, in whose eyes
even the most modest interest implied usury, and who confused the
one with the other in their moral code, translated the term by the
French word "usure." Hardly in an apologetic manner, Furtado dem-
onstrates that these casuists had no other alternative without resorting
to a contradiction of their principles.[59]

The Assembly had been placed in a defensive position both by the
existing decree of May 30 and by the manner in which the questions
had been presented. Neither Furtado's answer, however, nor the
responses adopted by the deputies, can be considered as attempts to
apologize for the economic activities of the Jews. On the contrary, they
emphasized the reasonableness of lending on interest, the unreason-
ableness of the Christian interpretation, and finally the obvious
necessity of establishing laws to distinguish usury from interest.

The responses provided by the Assembly to these last questions,
however, had a significance which went far beyond the explanations
offered and which was understood by those deputies who questioned
the interpretation of *ahikha*. Both the medieval Jews and Christians
had interacted socially, politically, and economically on the basis of
their differing religious identities. While there were isolated instances of an attempt to see the Christian as a brother and to interpret

scriptural and halachic dictates accordingly, for example David de Pomi, 1525–93?, maintained that the Jew did not take interest from the Christian as if he were an alien, but acted instead under the veil of some agreement, the traditional view allowed for and often demanded an essential distinction between Jew and non-Jew.[60] That one would lend money to a Gentile and expect a profit was unchallengeable, not so much because lending money was necessitated, but because the borrower was a Gentile.

The existence of a moral and ethical code unique to the Jews was abolished by the Assembly's decisions. Despite the fact that there were deputies who wished to translate *ahikha* as fellow Jew, the majority, by extending the traditional interpretation, adopted the view that Frenchmen, because they were geographically united, were brothers.

Geographic boundaries, however, were not the exclusive basis for the fraternity which the Assembly extended. In fact the answers to the questions concerning the relationship between Jew and non-Jew indicate that many of the deputies were still thinking in religious rather than secular terms.[61] Since the French as Christians observe the seven Noahide commandments, the fourth answer explained, the Jews are commanded by their Talmud to love them as brothers.

The answers to the twelve questions indicate the differences of approach and intention among the deputies. Biblical quotes, always more acceptable to the enlightened, are interwoven with Talmudic precepts; common denominators of religious morality are reinforced by common geographic boundaries, political institutions, and a common humanity. Both the secular and the sacred are intermingled and compromises between the two are often the result.

Despite the confusion within the Assembly and the disagreement among the deputies, there was no group for whom emancipation was undesirable or French citizenship deniable. The deputies were united in their attempts to make Judaism and the Jews completely compatible with France and the Frenchmen. They were deeply divided, however, over the significance of the preservation of Jewry and Judaism, as the controversy concerning intermarriage and the never unanimous votes on the functions of the rabbis indicate. These conflicts, made more complex by the differing attitudes towards the essence of Judaism, were the most profound and the most enduring and influenced all future divisions within the Assembly.

The Imperial Commissioners had informed the Minister of Interior of the progress of the Assembly in reports dated August 5 and 11, 1806.[62] Champagny, in his role as liaison, reported to Napoleon on July 30 and August 20. The Assembly, this Minister concluded after reviewing the answers adopted, had responded sincerely to the questions; had the deputies gone any further they would have derogated from their sacred principles. The examination of Jewish doctrines, moreover, did not reveal any commandment which prescribed what the French code prohibited. Judaism in no way contradicted the commitment of the Jews to become "sujets fidèles et soumis."[63]

Despite Champagny's favorable conclusions, the official newspapers were unsympathetic to the work of the Assembly.[64] Both the *Moniteur,* in its July 25 article written by Molé, and the *Journal de l'Empire,* in its July 26 edition, represented the Assembly's task as one of determining if the Jews ought to be admitted as Frenchmen. On August 21, the *Moniteur* and on August 30 the *Publiciste* both implied that the Commission of twelve prepared the answers to the questions *with* the Imperial Commissioners, *before* reporting them to the Assembly. Although on September 7 and 8 these two newspapers rectified their "error," the independence and integrity of the Commission of twelve has continued to be questioned until today.[65]

Throughout the sessions, the newspapers were intent upon diminishing the work of the Assembly in the eyes of the public. On September 16, the *Gazette de France* printed the answers to the third and sixth questions. (The same article subsequently appeared in the *Publiciste.*) In reviewing the decision concerning intermarriage, the paper explained that the exceptions made in favor of the French were because the laws of Moses did not specifically name them and hardly because the French were not to be considered "immonde." While the Assembly showed itself prepared to defend its country, the rabbis obviously had scruples and it would be interesting, the article concluded, to see how defense of the country would be adhered to without renouncing the belief in the coming of the Messiah and the return to the Holy Land. Apparently the author of the article had not understood the subtleties of the Assembly's answer to the fourth question which stated that the Jews regarded their incorporation into the "Great Nation" as a privilege and as political redemption. The belief in the coming of the Messiah, although not renounced, was in the process of being relegated to the realm of eschatology.

Napoleon was rarely "unaware" of the official presentation of events; nevertheless his next instructions concerning the Jews, sent to Champagny on August 23, were far from critical of the decisions adopted by the Assembly.[66] On the contrary, Napoleon decided that the only way to give an effective force to the responses was to present them on an equal footing with the Talmud, to be articles of faith and principles of religious legislation. To this effect, he ordered the convocation of the "Great Sanhedrin" whose task would be to convert the answers into binding theological decisions, which, while remaining faithful to the essential character of the laws of Moses, would be adapted to the present morals and customs.

In the same letter, Napoleon reviewed the twelve questions, outlined the answers already provided by the Assembly, and added three significant comments. Concerning intermarriage, he indicated that the Sanhedrin was to recommend such unions as a means of "protection and convenience" for the Jewish people. In addition, he decided that only half the Jews drafted could buy themselves free of service each year; the others were to serve personally. Most significant for the future legislation, however, was his reaction to the eleventh and twelfth answers. Napoleon was willing to accept the Assembly's interpretation that the French were considered brothers and that the Jews, under no circumstances, were to take illicit profit from them. He revealed, however, that after this decision was enacted by the Sanhedrin, he would reexamine the situation to discover if there were effective means to restrain and check the disposition towards financial speculation and the organization of fraud and usury. Finally, Napoleon advised his Commissioners to have a Committee of nine chosen from among the most enlightened members of the Assembly with whom they could work and produce "great results."

Molé, Portalis, and Pasquier immediately began to acquaint themselves with the composition and details of the ancient Sanhedrin. Aware of the requirement that at least two-thirds of the members be rabbis, they decided to call thirty rabbis from France, Italy, Spain, Portugal, and Germany and to invite fifteen rabbis already in Paris to join them. Napoleon disagreed with this plan. He saw in the dissolution of the Assembly and the presence of thirty rabbis, whose commitments were unknown, a possible abandoning of the certain for the uncertain. Instead he chose to prolong the Assembly's existence for the purpose of encouraging the timid rabbis and threatening the fanatical with expulsion of the Jewish people if they would not conform.[67]

On September 11, Champagny informed the Commissioners that they were now able to communicate the news of the Sanhedrin to the Assembly and to invite that body to convene the necessary number of rabbis.[68] Two days later, Molé sent a declaration to Champagny, signed by seventeen rabbis from the Assembly, in which these men declared themselves accepting of the principles of the twelve responses and ready to participate in a new edition of these responses.[69]

On September 18, the three Commissioners appeared before the Assembly; Molé was again designated as spokesman. The Jews, he stated, have continuously born the brunt of their sovereign's avarice.

Their customs and practices have isolated them from society which in its turn has pushed them away. Even today they explain the antipathy on the part of some to agriculture and the professions by a lack of confidence in a future whose existence has always depended on the spirit of the moment.[70] From now on, he declared, unable to complain, you will thus be unable to justify yourselves. And to be sure that no excuse remains, His Majesty asks from you a religious guarantee of the principles announced in your answers.[71]

The religious guarantee was to be the formation of the Sanhedrin whose responses would acquire in the eyes of the Jews of all the countries and for all the centuries "la plus grande autorité possible." Molé concluded by asking the deputies to form a committee of three Portuguese, three Italian, and three German deputies, and to announce to all the synagogues of Europe the advent of the Sanhedrin.

Furtado, who had been aware of the government's plans since at least September 11, applauded Napoleon's decision and promised that this great and beneficent ruler would live to see millions of useful citizens.[72] The Assembly then prepared a resolution in which they expressed their loyalty to Napoleon, their decision to invite twenty-five deputies of the Assembly to participate in the Sanhedrin, their acceptance of the government's intention to include twenty-nine rabbis from France and Italy, and finally their willingness to remain in existence until the Great Sanhedrin had terminated its sittings.[73]

The deputies never suspected that they would remain in Paris until the spring.[74] In a personal letter written on September 11 to his friend Pery in Bordeaux, Furtado predicted hopefully that he would stay only another two months.[75] Feeling himself free to describe to Pery how he viewed the events around him, Furtado complained of his committee (the Commission of twelve) whose noise and gossip were deafening and of the Assembly, none of whose members were more worthy than he. One is able to say of us, Furtado admits, what we say of so many others; from afar it is something and from within it is nothing.[76]

Despite his position as President of the Assembly, Furtado continued to feel little identification with and respect for his fellow deputies. Oh how I have need of you and your excellent Ferrère.[77] Tell me, he asked Pery, what both of you think of the responses to the first questions?[78] It appears, he confided, that the Emperor has great plans for us. No longer is it a question of revealing in what ways our religion accords with and differs from the French and Italian code of laws, but rather how we can give to the decisions of our assembly the solemnity and force of the decisions of a synod or an ecumenical council.[79]

Wary of this new and even more demanding task, Furtado asked Pery to comment on the speech he planned to deliver when the

Assembly was presented to Napoleon.[80] With his usual eloquence, Furtado intended to use this opportunity to praise the Emperor, to explain the causes (while discrediting the results) of the present situation of the Northeastern Jews as distinct from those of the Southwest, and finally to assure Napoleon that the distinctions between the Jews and those of other religions would soon disappear.[81]

Despite his complaints to Pery concerning the composition and atmosphere of the Assembly and the tasks yet awaiting the deputies, Furtado's life in Paris could hardly be considered dreary. Hoping to convince his friend to join him, Furtado described the nonofficial side of his stay. We are six deputies living together, he wrote, all of us "bon vivans," who frequently journey to the country and to charming homes with even more charming hosts. I will introduce you, he promised Pery, to the most distinguished men of letters and you will dine with Suart and Delisle.[82]

Few of the deputies could claim such pleasant diversions. On the contrary, most of them were facing financial ruin caused by their absence from their homes and few had sufficient funds to sustain them during the winter months. In spite of the legitimate assumption (shared by most of the communal leaders) that the government's "invitation" to participate included a promise for reimbursement, the deputies voted on September 24, to have the Jewish communities pay for their expenses.

After first preparing a letter, which Champagny immediately vetoed, to the prefects to see to this matter, Furtado then composed a statement to the Jews of France requesting that they assume the responsibility of paying their deputies.[83] A circular was subsequently sent to the prefects on October 4 in which they were asked not to exercise their formal authority, but rather to influence the Jews by persuasion. After many departments sent nothing and after it became clear that neither the members of the Assembly nor the rabbis who were asked to participate in the Sanhedrin could afford to support themselves, Champagny suggested to Napoleon that the authorities should intervene. On November 29, 1806, Napoleon approved the decree to make a contribution for the expenses obligatory.[84]

The Assembly, at its December 23 meeting, at first manifested its willingness to form a general assessment which would include all the Jews of France and Italy. It was decided, however, on the basis of several members' assertions that they were perfectly satisfied with the departments that sent them, that those deputies who had claims to make should inform the President who in his turn would communicate them to the Minister of the Interior. This Furtado did in his letter to Champagny dated January, 1807. Reminding the Minister that the deputies had been chosen not because they were the wealthiest, but rather because they were the most honest, Furtado declared that most of the deputies, unable to afford their stay any longer, would have to leave Paris. Although sincerely concerned with these problems, Furtado did not hesitate to convey to Champagny the unwillingness on the part of the Sephardic Jews to help pay the expenses of the other deputies. The Jews of the South will say, he explained, that it is neither their present nor their past conduct which has necessitated the convocation of this Assembly, that it is enough for them to have supported the expenses of two deputies without having to cooperate in the expenses of those of the North with whom they have nothing in common except a religious belief which establishes no solidarity between them.[85]

Champagny must have found this letter surprising. How different was its tone from Furtado's numerous statements concerning the desirability of uniting all Frenchmen and preventing any religious group from separating into "sects" whose existence would threaten the order and peace of the country.[86] The Minister, unswayed by the Southern deputies' refusal to pay, answered Furtado's letter by stating that the general expenses of the Assembly must be paid by the Jews of Gironde as well as the others.[87]

The problem was hardly solved by Champagny's decision to have all the departments cover the expenses. Although he fixed the amount owed on a fictitious number of deputies, the complex procedures necessary to collect the money doomed the operation from the beginning. In addition, many of the deputies were unsatisfied with what they considered to be a meager (200 *francs*) monthly allowance. Despite the numerous letters and meetings between Furtado and Champagny and the circulars sent by the latter, the deputies were never paid satisfactorily and some were actually ruined financially.[88] Compelled to find a means of at least temporarily relieving the problem, Furtado finally gained the help of the wealthy Orly Hayem Worms (Romilly) who agreed not only to receive and distribute the funds from the departments but also to make advances, often without being reimbursed for many months.[89]

At the same time that Furtado was seeking a solution to the financial problems of the deputies, he and his Committee of nine were busily preparing a *règlement* for the French Jews. Unfortunately, despite the numerous letters from Molé to Furtado, we know little about the meetings of the Committee, which apparently continued through September, October, and November, except that the deputies were often pressured by Molé and conciliated by the other two Commissioners.[90] What we do know, however, are the contents of the *règle-*

ment, approved by the Imperial Commissioners and proposed by the Committee to the Assembly, the controversies excited by certain of the articles, and Furtado's extreme dissatisfaction with those members of the Committee who publicly announced their disapproval.

On December 9, the Committee of nine presented its plan for the organization of the "Mosaic worship" to the Assembly. Furtado introduced the *règlement* by emphasizing the fact that the Jews were to be organized in a manner which would solve their internal difficulties but would in no way distinguish them from the rest of the French citizens. As if to impress upon the deputies the significance of the proposed organization, the Committee had included in their preface that the Assembly had unanimously adopted the following articles, a prediction which would be far from realized.

In essence the plan established the consistories of France and outlined the functions of the departmental consistories, the central consistory, and the rabbis. A synagogue and consistory was to be established in every department which contained two-thousand individuals professing the religion of Moses. Under no circumstances, however, was there to be more than one consistory for each department. The consistorial synagogue, moreover, had to sanction any additional synagogues established in the department. For each consistory, twenty-five notables would be selected by a competent authority and these notables, all of whom were to be men of means, would in turn choose the Grand Rabbi and the three other "Israelites" who would head the consistorial organization. According to Article X, no one could be a member of the consistory who was not thirty years of age, had been bankrupt (unless he honorably paid afterwards), and had been known to be a usurer.

The functions of the consistories were fourfold; to oversee that the rabbis acted in accordance with the decisions of the Assembly and Sanhedrin, to maintain order within the synagogues, to encourage Jews to engage in useful occupations and report those without any means of existence, and to inform the authorities of the number of Jewish conscripts each year. The central consistory of Paris was to correspond with the local consistories, oversee compliance with consistorial regulations, denounce to the competent authority any infractions of those regulations, and finally to confirm the nomination of rabbis and propose, when necessary, the removal of any member of the consistory. The rabbis were to teach religion, inculcate doctrines contained in the decisions of the Sanhedrin, preach obedience to the laws and especially those relating to the defense of the country, and celebrate marriages and pronounce divorces, after their sanction by the civil authority. The consistories were to be responsible for paying, with sums levied on each district, the expenses of the rabbis as well as other expenses of worship.

The Committee of nine had attached an *arrêt* to the end of the regulations in which they added certain observations to be communicated to the Emperor, namely that the government might contribute something to the salary of the rabbis and that the local authorities should be directed to work with the consistories to insure obedience to the laws of conscription.[91]

Shortly after the reading of the plan, a member of the Committee of nine declared that he felt it incumbent upon him to renew his objections to several clauses of the *règlement* which he considered "unbecoming, inefficient, and inadmissible." This member, whom we know from Furtado's notes to be Marc Foi, "négociant" from the Basses-Pyrénées, and whom we find subsequently listed among those converted to Catholicism, objected to the Jews' accusing themselves of usury, making policemen of their religious dignitaries, setting up a system of espionage for the government to check into the affairs of the community, casting doubt on the devotion of the Jews to France, and finally drawing the attention of the government to one class of individuals who professed the same faith, which was tantamount to establishing a civil difference based on religious differences.[92]

To counteract the accusations made by Foi, another member of the Committee (Berr Isaac Berr?) defended the proposed regulations. He observed that those members who found fault with the *règlement* were viewing the Jews not as they really were but as they ought to be. In addition, he maintained that many of the discredited articles were unlikely to produce the effects which he had attributed to them. The Jews, this deputy concluded, were being unjustifiably fearful.

A number of notables, wary of establishing a distinction between the Jews and the rest of society, spoke in support of all or some of the objections which Foi had made. It was finally agreed, however, to put the regulations to a vote (they were adopted only by the majority) and to include an abstract, to be written by Furtado, which would inform the government of the principal objections made by the deputies. In a forceful and convincing manner, Furtado focused on Article X of the *règlement* (No one may be a member of the consistory . . .) which he characterized as unnecessary and unjust in its implied connection between Jew and usurer. This could only hurt the honest, he explained, without changing the manners of the dishonest. Towards these last, Furtado added somewhat gratuitously, restrictive measures of quite another nature must be adopted.[93]

On December 11, the Assembly met again, this time to discuss the *arrêt*. Two days had passed since the adoption of the regulations, however, and many of the deputies found themselves dissatisfied both with the way in which the deliberations had been resolved and the accuracy of the voting by show of hands. That a number of notables were far from happy with the *règlement,* independent of the accused irregularity of the deliberations, is quite clear. The Commissioners, on their part, were aware of this and, in their communications to Champagny, informed the Minister of the conflicts within the Assembly. The Assembly has voted the project, they wrote (the vote of December 9 was confirmed on December 11 by a majority of forty-five out of sixty-one), in spite of the opposition of the rabbis and the almost invincible repugnance of the nonbelieving Jews. The former, they explained, dread governmental authority to which they have never before been subjected; the latter fear that an organization, which by its very nature could not be considered purely religious, would isolate them once again from the French people.[94]

Although the minutes only allude to the atmosphere in the Assembly during these sessions, Furtado's personal reflections, written after the meeting of December 11, reveal the extent to which there was disagreement among the deputies and mounting frustration on the part of their President. These reflections deserve full recording.

The Secretary who had long voiced his opinion against the project, takes charge of the drawing up of the report, first impropriety. He writes in great detail all the opinions against the project, and doesn't mention their refutation, second impropriety. The minutes of the Assembly never mentioned the name of persons who have held such and such opinion, and on this occasion for the first time, they name the persons, third impropriety. An uneducated and unenlightened man maintains against his own conviction that the decision taken at the session the day before yesterday is irregular and asks that it be revoked. A M. Foy had the impudence to make this affront publicly to the Assembly . . . fourth impropriety. He maintains that there had been amendments which should have been put to the vote before the adoption of the project, while in fact there had only been contradictory and opposing propositions, impossible to separate from the project, fifth impropriety. This same impudent man, seeing that the report of the project could not take place as he had asked, upholds audaciously that a roll call had been demanded, and that the president had refused to put it to the vote while he knows as everyone does that the president had begun the roll call and that one of the four disturbers of the assembly protested against it by shouting like a madman that it was a list of proscription, sixth impropriety. But what is at the height of imprudence and dishonesty is that after nine meetings of the full committee, where everything had been examined, discussed, and reconciled, where everything had been settled ahead of time to adopt the project, four or five disturbers come and repeat all that had been said and refuted and make a truly revolting public scandal, seventh impropriety. Finally four individuals, with no knowledge whatsoever dare to want to preach the law to the Assembly, questioning what had already been decided, and the Assembly had the inconceivable feebleness to tolerate this outrage and to condescend to decide a second time what had been decided a first time. An excess of outrage from one side, of unqualified apathy and cowardice on the other. This is what the Assembly of the Jews at Paris is like. . . .[95]

Contrary to what has generally been maintained, the Assembly was hardly a docile body. In addition to expressing their disagreements concerning various articles of the *règlement*, the deputies went even further by objecting to the proposed *arrêt*. As with the consistorial plan, however, the *arrêt* was finally adopted by the majority on December 18. Significantly, its adoption was followed by the creation of an enlarged Commission (composed of the nine together with deputies representing the eight Northeastern departments) which, in protest against the May 30 decree, would determine the means to prevent its further extension.[96]

We have yet to pursue the resolution of the May 30 decree, the accomplishments of the Sanhedrin, and the concluding decisions of the Assembly. Before this, however, it is worthwhile to pause and consider the composition of the Assembly and the nature of the divisions which were expressed in the discussions surrounding both the twelve answers and organizational plan.

The traditional characterization of the Assembly maintains that there were four distinct ideological groups, namely the enlightened Jews of the Mendelssohn school, outright reformers holding deistic beliefs, old-type German rabbis, and tolerant traditionalists.[97] The French Jewish historian, Robert Anchel, after rejecting the fact that there were parties in the Assembly, opposing tendencies which were unaware of their role, or even that the deputies from the South were more advanced than others, concludes that the only true difference between the deputies was their financial situation. The richest, Anchel maintains, were the most willing to satisfy the demands of the government and sacrifice their religious principles; the poorer members were more respectful of cultural matters.[98]

There were in fact both clear ideological tendencies among the deputies and obvious financial dissimilarities which were heightened by the extended existence of the Assembly. There were also, and perhaps herein lies the most striking and influential division, differences between the Sephardim and the Ashkenazim which no shared financial status or tolerant and humanitarian attitudes could bridge. The Jews of the Southwest consistently and vociferously defended their rights as Frenchmen; unwilling to compromise their citizenship, they were more than willing to minimize their Judaism. The Jews of the Northeast, as committed to their Judaism as to their citizenship, were concerned lest they compromise their tradition in those areas essential both theologically and for the survival of their communities.

Ironically, the fears of both the Sephardim and the Ashkenazim were realized in the consistorial plan and this accounts for the difficulties Furtado had in imposing the *règlement* on the Assembly. For having been called upon to reconcile their religion with the demands of active citizenship, the deputies found themselves renouncing certain religious dogmas as well as their equality before the civil law.

From the perspective of historical hindsight, the Sephardim, with their secular priorities and their anemic and static form of Judaism, prevailed. Most immediately, however, neither they nor the majority of the Ashkenazim were satisfied.[99] Furtado, apparently trusting the government's benevolence and convinced that the Jews of France needed regeneration through an enlightened and quasi-secular communal structure, stood isolated among the disgruntled and the dissatisfied. Yet even he would become disillusioned, as the Sanhedrin "sanctified" the responses of the Assembly and Napoleon rescinded even more of the civil rights of French Jewry.

5

Napoleon and the Sanhedrin

Napoleon had explained in his August 23 instructions sent to Champagny that the Sanhedrin was to translate the responses of the Assembly into articles of faith and principles of religious legislation. The recreation of a legislative body of a supposedly defunct nation may have appealed to Napoleon in yet another way. The Jews, dispersed throughout all of Europe, might find themselves sympathetic to such a beneficent ruler; this sympathy could then be used to Napoleon's advantage in his battles against both Germany and Poland.[1] That the Jews would be equally committed to the Sanhedrin of 1807 as to that of the past appears to be a naive hope on the part of Napoleon; nevertheless, the convening of the Sanhedrin after the Assembly of Notables had dutifully answered in their eighth response that the rabbis had no judicial powers and after the deputies had insisted that the Jews no longer formed a nation indicates the extent to which the Jews of France would comply with the contradictory demands of their Emperor.

Napoleon's ulterior political motives and inconsistent expectations notwithstanding, Furtado and his Commission of nine immediately began to direct their energies towards insuring the smooth adoption and sanction of the Assembly's decisions. On January 21, 1807, Furtado wrote a memorandum to the Imperial Commissioners in which he discussed the arrangements which remained to be made. A leader and two advisors have yet to be named, he wrote, and it would be more convenient if the government proposed these nominations in order to avoid the inevitable "intrigues and factions."[2] In essence, Furtado wished to avoid giving the Sanhedrin any chance for independent expression.[3]

Shortly after receiving Furtado's letter, the Commissioners recommended to Champagny, probably on the basis of Furtado's suggestions, that David Sinzheim be chosen "chef" of the Sanhedrin and the "assesseurs" be Sègre, Rabbi of Verceil, and Cologna, Rabbi of Mantua. It is necessary that we select a German as *chef*, they explained, since our principal goal is to influence the spirit and doctrines of those who have elicited so many complaints.[4] Two days later, Champagny informed Sinzheim, Sègre, and Cologna of their responsibilities.[5]

If Furtado and the Commissioners were sure of the position in which they wished to place the Sanhedrin, they were unsure of the way to present the decisions and the additional tasks, if any, that Napoleon had in mind for that body. Champagny decided, in the absence of any detailed instructions from the Emperor and with the hope that some such help would come soon, to begin the sessions and if necessary to prolong them indefinitely.

On February 4, the deputies convened to verify the powers of the members, confirm the selection of officers, and accept the manner in which all issues would be presented. Every matter would be presented to the Sanhedrin by two members of the Commission of nine, Cracovia and Furtado. During the week following the presentations, the members of the Sanhedrin would be able to present their observations in writing to the Commission of nine who would communicate them to the Imperial Commissioners before bringing them before the united Sanhedrin. Eight days after the presentation of a report, the members were to vote orally, yes or no. Absolute majority was necessary; there was to be no discussion.[6]

The first meeting of the Sanhedrin took place on February 9. The format followed was to be the same for all eight sessions; the deputies, arranged in the fashion of the original Sanhedrin, heard reports delivered primarily by Furtado and subsequently adopted each decision unanimously.[7] As decided in advance, discussions and debates, so common in the Assembly, were nonexistent.[8]

At the February 8 meeting, Furtado delivered a report introducing the first three decisions (polygamy, divorce, and marriage).[9] Rather than discuss the details of these decisions, Furtado chose instead to emphasize the "liaison intime" between the duties prescribed by religion and the dictates established by society. After proclaiming that man's wisdom came from God, whose law was the fundamental principle of all order and morality, Furtado then indicated the dangers inherent in an excess and distortion of religiosity. Although less rigid than the young man who advocated abolishing all religious institutions, Furtado appears no more sympathetic to the cultural and moral atmosphere of the Jewish communities. Persecution may revive religious sentiments, he admitted; more often, however, it leads to fanaticism, in the same way that continual and daily contempt leads to superstition. Napoleon, in finally freeing the Jews from persecution and contempt, had made possible the emergence of productive and respected citizens. The Sanhedrin, by its sanction of the doctrinal decisions, would confirm that Judaism, rather than impeding this emergence, demanded it.[10]

Since a week was to elapse between the presentation of the decisions and their adoption, the first session adjourned immediately after Furtado's introductory remarks.

In his second report of February 12, which introduced the fourth doctrinal point (fraternity), Furtado made specific what he had only implied in the previous session. When the people of Israel formed a nation, he recalled, there was a religious obligation to follow all the laws (whether political and civil or religious) of the "divine legislator." Israel ceased to be a nation, however, and from that moment on the Jews were obliged "par la nécessité des choses" to follow the political and civil laws of the States in which they lived. They were to retain "dans toute leur vigeur" only those laws which pertained to their religious society.

When this distinction is understood, Furtado continued, and when it is equally understood that there is perfect conformity between our religious laws and the civil code, then we can no longer be accused of living differently from those around us. The Sanhedrin, by adopting these first four decisions, will be declaring publicly and unequivocally that the Jews, in fulfilling their duties as citizens and in expressing their sentiments of fraternity towards their fellow countrymen, are simultaneously fulfilling their duties as Jews.[11]

The Sanhedrin adopted the first decision on February 16, the second and third on February 19 and the fourth on February 23, all of them unanimously.[12]

Furtado addressed the deputies again on February 23 when he introduced the eighth and ninth decisions (usury). Two advantages, he explained, will result from an exposition of the true doctrine of Moses: the first will show that this doctrine accords with the most severe principles of justice; the second will establish that the habit of lending on interest, a reproach directed at the Israelites of some parts of France and unhappily with too much reason, is not at all the effect of their religious dogmas but rather an abuse resulting from their civil and political situation.[13] After reminding the deputies of the translation which the Assembly had given both to the Hebrew word *neshekh* and the often quoted passage from Deuteronomy, and describing in familiar terms the idyllic nature of pastoral life in Palestine, Furtado concluded with an admonition to the rabbis. Do not confuse appearance with reality, he warned them, or false zeal with true piety; know that all too often the man who wishes to appear the most religious is not always the most honest.

With these words as well as with his previous descriptions of the degenerative expressions of religion, Furtado revealed his deep criticism of and estrangement from traditional Jewish life. His unveiled disdain, however, did not prevent the Sanhedrin from adopting unanimously the fifth, sixth, and seventh decisions (morality, civil and political relations and useful professions).[14]

The deputies, well on their way to completing the adoption of the Assembly's decisions, were finally informed of their tasks in a letter written by Napoleon sometime in January and received by the impatient Champagny around February 16.[15] In order to proceed in an orderly fashion, Napoleon wrote, "it is necessary to begin by declaring that there are in the laws of Moses both religious and political dispositions."[16] While the former are immutable, the latter are susceptible to modification, and it is only the Sanhedrin which can establish this distinction. Once this principle is declared, the Sanhedrin must apply it to prohibiting polygamy in the West, extending fraternity to all men without exception (provided the Jews enjoy the same rights as they), defending the country, requiring mixed marriages and, finally, obeying the laws pertaining to lending on interest. In addition, the Sanhedrin must proclaim that divorce and marriage are to be subject to the observance of the formalities prescribed by the civil code.[17]

On February 25, the Imperial Commissioners informed Champagny that the decisions of the Sanhedrin would receive the modifications contained in the last instructions, after which its mission would be terminated.[18] Either Furtado had already anticipated these instructions in his speech of February 12, or he revised the speech before publishing it. In either event, except for the obligation of mixed marriages, he assured their inclusion in the preamble and doctrinal decisions.

On March 2, the Sanhedrin completed its task by adopting the eighth and ninth decisions as well as a preamble to all the preceding decisions. The Imperial Commissioners had not been mistaken when they promised Champagny compliance with Napoleon's instructions. The preamble, which was probably written by Furtado, was virtually a repetition of Napoleon's distinction between religious and political dispositions.[19]

The deputies were not to be left with any doubts concerning the conformity of the decisions and preamble to Jewish law. "Doctors and Notables," Rabbi David Sinzheim proclaimed, "your religious, civil and political principles are known to me; I am pleased to find that they conform to the spirit of the law and I thank God."[20] Furtado also assured the deputies of the wisdom of their decisions. He was less concerned, however, with theological justifications. On the contrary, his satisfaction was derived primarily from the Sanhedrin's acceptance of a universal basis for the union of mankind and a secular standard for the evaluation of contemporary Jewish practices.[21]

On March 9, Rabbi Sinzheim delivered the final address to the Sanhedrin. He reminded the deputies of the distinctions they had made between civil and religious acts and their condemnation of antisocial opinions. On behalf of all Jews, he then addressed a prayer to the God of Jacob. We shall no longer offer You sacrifices, nor sanctify You with imposing ceremonies, he declared, but at least our hearts will be free from fear and our voices will be raised to proclaim the glory of Your name.[22] With the conclusion of this apologetic prayer and the recognition of gratitude to the Emperor and "chef," the Sanhedrin was terminated.

The responses which the Sanhedrin had sanctioned differed from those provided by the Assembly both in their form and emphasis. While the Assembly had answered specific questions, the Sanhedrin provided what were to be considered definitive statements on all issues which concerned Jew and non-Jew. These statements, moreover, were not at all explanatory, as were those of the Assembly, but rather declared, often very concisely, the official Jewish position. Despite its more emphatic and conciliatory resolutions, however, the Sanhedrin did not comply with Napoleon's views on intermarriage. The Grand Sanhedrin declares, Article III stated, "that marriages between Israelites and Christians, contracted in conformity with the laws of the civil code, are binding and civilly valid, and although not to be invested with religious forms will entail no anathemas."[23]

The Sanhedrin did declare, nevertheless, that all Jews called to military service were freed during the duration of their service from any observances which conflicted with military life. Every Jew, moreover, born and raised in France and Italy, was religiously obligated to view that country as his own, to serve and defend it, obey all laws, and conform in every transaction to the dispositions of the civil code.[24] In essence, as the preamble had stated, the Jews were to cease to regulate their civil and political lives in accordance with Jewish law or tradition.

There is no doubt that Napoleon's instructions provided the stimulus for this clearcut distinction between purely religious obligations and social and political duties. Nevertheless, this did not represent a significant departure either from principles debated by the revolutionaries or those acknowledged by the Sephardim. In setting forth the separation of belief and ritual from daily life, the dissolution of nationhood and the reinterpretation of the messianic dream, however, the doctrinal decisions provided a definitive formula and an enduring rationale for a profound break with Jewish tradition. Herein lies the real significance of the Sanhedrin.

In addition to his notes on the Sanhedrin, Napoleon had included in his February instructions the tasks remaining to be accomplished by the Assembly and sanctioned by the Council of State. Essentially the Assembly was to determine the organization of the synagogues and rabbis (which they had done on December 9), establish the requirement that every Jewish conscript serve in the army or find an "Israelite" replacement, recommend mixed marriages, and allow only two out of every three marriages in a district to be between Jews and Jewesses. Finally, the Assembly was to decide upon the disciplinary measures necessary to regulate the economic practices of the Jews.[25]

The objectives to be achieved by the adoption of these proposals were also clearly outlined by Napoleon. When a proportion of the youth are required to enter the army, he declared, they will stop having specifically Jewish interests and feelings; they will assume French interests and feelings.[26] Mixed marriages would successfully dilute the "blood" of the Jews until it no longer had any unique characteristics, while economic restrictions, in preventing the Jews from devoting themselves exclusively to usury and brokerage, would direct their energies towards other occupations and professions. Specifically, Napoleon wished to have those Jews who chose to engage in business authorized to do so by the local authority, and to prevent for ten years any nonpropertied Jews from lending money in exchange for mortgages.[27]

It is necessary to put an end to the evil, Napoleon concluded, by preventing it; it is necessary to prevent it by changing the Jews. Thus economic restrictions would achieve the former and intermarriage the latter. Convinced that these measures would be beneficial both to the Jews and the rest of the French, Napoleon demanded that the Assembly, in agreement with the administration, ordain their enactment. Aware that he would be absent from Paris and involved almost exclusively with his military pursuits, Napoleon left the accomplishing of this last part of his plan to his commissioners and ministers.

The Imperial Commissioners, however, had already prepared extensive reports on the means to settle the economic crisis among the Northeastern Jews and their debtors. Shortly after the May 30 decree, both Portalis, Minister of Cults, and Champagny, Minister of the Interior, had sent Napoleon their plans. "The question of the civil status of the Jews of France is not solely one of religious tolerance,"

Portalis wrote on July 8, 1806, "but also one of politics."[28] The Jews, the Minister reasoned, whose religion is all embracing, formed a nation within a nation and were neither French, German, English, nor Prussian; they were Jews. Portalis' plan included verifying the credits of all Jews engaged in commerce, preventing the Jews from using "lettres de change" with those citizens who were not engaged in commerce, limiting the taking of mortgages to property owners, and restricting the number of Jews entitled to dwell in France.

On August 20, 1806, Champagny submitted his plan to Napoleon. Differing substantially from the views of the Minister of Cults, Champagny was unwilling to support any measures against the Jews which were either "beyond those which their duties as subjects and citizens required" or would cause them "to renounce some part of their belief or practices."[29] He advocated, therefore, establishing a legal rate of interest to which all Frenchmen, including Jews, would be bound.[30]

Napoleon had clearly indicated, however, that he contemplated specific measures against the Jews which were comparable to those suggested by Portalis. Thus Champagny had no alternative but to see that Napoleon's proposals were adopted in the manner suggested. This required that the Assembly consent to the specifics of the measures which would then be legislated by a simple decree of the Council of State. The Jews, Champagny wrote to the Imperial Commissioners, permitted to enjoy from now on a beneficial legislation and the protection of the government, will offer themselves the just and reasonable conditions which will allow them to merit this kindness.[31] The fact that the initiative for these measures was to come from the Jews, he reasoned in an attempt to assuage his own misgivings, would make them honorable and acceptable to the Jewish nation, while their imposition would imply public censure.[32]

Molé, Portalis, and Pasquier, neither as optimistic nor as unrealistic as Champagny, assured the Minister that the Assembly would never agree to the proposed measures. It would be impossible, they concluded, to obtain more than that the Assembly entreat the Emperor to take those measures necessary to curb the disorders one accuses the Jews of creating; the Council of State would be required to legislate the specific measures.[33] Nevertheless, as late as February 26, Champagny remained convinced that the Assembly could and would solicit the government to help achieve "the *mélange* of the Jewish race with that of the French, the repression of usury, and the exercise of industry, particularly that of agriculture."[34]

The Commissioners were correct in their assessment of the point beyond which the Assembly would not go. Even they, however, did not anticipate the reactions of the deputies to the general and vague *arrêté* finally agreed upon and proposed by the Commission of nine to the Assembly.

On March 25, Furtado announced to the assembled deputies that he, as spokesman for the Commission of nine, would report on the work of the Sanhedrin, a proposed address of gratitude to Napoleon, and a project for an *arrêté* to implore the government to take those measures which would avoid a repetition of the abuses necessitating the May 30 decree.

In effect, Furtado communicated to the Assembly the essence of Napoleon's directives but in a manner which he undoubtedly felt would assure their acceptability and therefore their acceptance. The Sanhedrin, he began, has consecrated what this Assembly, composed almost entirely of laymen, had deliberated in advance. The essence is the same, the form alone is different.[35] Continuing to review the accomplishments of the Sanhedrin while praising those of the Assembly, Furtado arrived at the issue of the May 30 decree. After he reminded the deputies, who needed no such reminder, that the Assembly had been convened because of the abusive actions of certain individuals residing in the Northeastern departments, Furtado expressed the hope that the deputies could settle this matter and thus conclude their work.[36]

The address to Napoleon, which Furtado and his Commission had prepared, included, among praises for the Emperor and hopes that the May 30 decree would be permitted to expire, the invitation to the government to take the measures it deemed necessary to prevent any future disorders.

Decided that the Commissioners will be asked to transmit to his Majesty the wish which has been humbly formed by the Assembly, that his Majesty will make those arrangements which he believes proper, so that in the future some Israelites, either by second hand dealing, or by taking mortgages, will be unable to cause the disorders in trade and fortunes which have elicited complaints and which too often have brought shame and punishment on all their coreligionists.[37]

Furtado had attempted to introduce the *arrêté* in a manner which was flattering to the deputies and solicitous of the government's positive intentions. The Assembly, however, obviously aware in advance of the contents and significance of the *arrêté* (some of the reports opposing its adoption had been written prior to the discussion), showed itself unwilling to be influenced either by the government or the Commission. In fact, Furtado had hardly finished his report when the deputies rose to express their dissatisfaction. The *arrêté* was unnecessary, one member concluded, since the Sanhedrin had sanctioned the decisions of the Assembly and fixed the points of Jewish doctrine. Another member, with a prepared opinion in hand, read his objections which were based on the potential harm which could be done to the Jews. The *arrêté*, he declared, in focusing on the Jews, is in effect asking Napoleon to treat the Jews differently from other citizens. Neither the Jews nor special legislation against the Jews ought to deal with those who are guilty of usury in the future. "Thank goodness," the deputy concluded, "that the time when one only saw in a guilty party a member of some sect or cult is already behind us: let us enjoy in peace the favors of the government; let us hope that all our coreligionists will render themselves worthy and let us abandon those who do not to those laws common to all Frenchmen. I demand that the *arrêté* that your Commission proposes to you be suppressed as useless and injurious to our rights."[38]

Aware that the *arrêté* would not be adopted without additional debate, Furtado adjourned the Assembly, not before, however, the report of the Commission and the project of the first part of the address to Napoleon were accepted.

The deputies gave no indication at their next meeting, held on March 27, that they were any more sympathetic to the *arrêté*. The only proposal which was acceptable to all was the creation of a deputation of eight members who would inform the Imperial Commissioners of the Assembly's opinions. The deputation, composed of MM. Rodrigues frères, Formiggini, Lipman Cerf-Berr, May (of Neufchâteau), Wittersheim l'aîné, Abraham Cahen and Goudchaux, would report to their colleagues as soon as they had met with Molé, Portalis, and Pasquier. Until that time, there was nothing more to be accomplished by the Assembly.

On March 30, the deputation reported to the assembled deputies. There is reason to believe, however, that this report was edited by Furtado possibly before being presented. We have located a manuscript written by one of the members of the deputation, which, when compared to what was recorded in the minutes, reveals changes consistent not only with Furtado's style, but also with his attempts to insure the adoption of the *arrêté*.[39]

The account presented in the *procès-verbaux*, in addition to including descriptions typical of Furtado such as "chimériques," is stronger in its affirmation both of the justifiability of the *arrêté* and the unjustifiable fears of the deputies. We need only to juxtapose the significant paragraphs of each version to illustrate these differences in emphasis. The Commissioners, the draft reports,

made us feel that we could not penetrate the great and profound views of the genius who governs us and that in putting into his hands the task of taking those measures which he judged to be proper, we must be assured in advance that our coreligionists would have nothing to fear; on our part, we have observed to the Commissioners that neither we nor our colleagues have ever had the slightest doubt in this respect, but that all our fears concern the interpretation that malevolence or prejudice could give to this decision.[40]

The same paragraph, however, when presented to the deputies became:

The Commissioners, after having reviewed all that had happened, added that they could not penetrate, any more than we, the great and profound insights of the Prince who governs us; that, since they were unable to propose the means to prevent those disorders which necessitated the decree of May 30, their opinion was that we must restrict ourselves to putting in this decision the wish that the means will be taken; that our well known loyalty required this disposition; that the fears that several members of the Assembly showed with regard to the interpretations that malevolence might attempt to give to the decision proposed by the Commission of nine were entirely unfounded; that after all we could assure you, Gentlemen, that it was far from the thoughts of his Imperial and Royal Majesty to establish a special legislation with regard to your coreligionists in the Empire and the Kingdom of Italy.[41]

Although the manuscript merely indicates that the observations presented to the Commissioners would be reported, the minutes provide us with the details. Essentially the deputation repeated to Molé, Portalis, and Pasquier the unwillingness of the Assembly to accept the *arrêté* both because it humiliated the Jews by establishing a line of demarcation, and because its adoption would undoubtedly fortify the fears on the part of the wealthy who wished to invest and lend their money as well as exacerbate the existing prejudices against all Jews.[42]

In spite of the assurances provided by the deputation, there were many deputies who remained unconvinced, and the discussions in the Assembly continued to be emotionally charged.[43] Fortunately, although the minutes reveal little of the subsequent debates which took place, we can approximate their intensity and substance by examining an additional manuscript prepared by a number of the deputies.[44]

The arguments already expressed in the meetings of the Assembly and the report of the deputation are presented again, more forcefully and in greater detail. In addition, however, the opposition added a new criticism which reveals the painful and contradictory position of those fighting against the adoption of the *arrêté*. The *arrêté*, these deputies maintained, is humiliating for all "Israelities," is perhaps imprudent in its consequences and, worst of all, evidences a distrust of the good intentions of the government which cannot enter into the heart of any Israelite.[45] The deputies were expressing simultaneously both an avowed faith in Napoleon, which was probably only partly real, and a distrust of the French, which was unquestionably real.[46] The provisions of the *arrêté* might be misused in the future, they argued, and furthermore we do not show faith in that future by adopting those provisions. Committed to the final abolition of differences based on sect, as were those who spoke in the May 25 and 27 meetings, the deputies concluded that Jews must be punished not as Jews but as Frenchmen.

If we assume that the Assembly, or at least a number of its deputies, was aware of Napoleon's February instructions, which appears to be a justifiable assumption, it becomes surprising that no mention was made of the issues of mixed marriage and enforced conscription. One wonders, moreover, how any faith in Napoleon's intentions (especially among the Ashkenazim) was compatible with the knowledge that the Emperor planned a slow and sophisticated destruction of Jewish existence. Except for Furtado as the chief defender of the government's position, the protagonists in the struggle against the *arrêté* are unknown. Although only able to surmise the identity of the opposition, we are led to assume that for one of the few times both the Sephardim and Ashkenazim united (probably under the leadership of the former) to prevent any further discrimination.[47]

An increasingly angry Furtado finally put an end to the discussions. The President rose to the platform, the minutes tell us, and in a vehement discourse developed the powerful reasons which militated the adoption of the project.[48] Furtado's speech, quoted only in small part in the *procès-verbaux*, exists in manuscript form.[49] Obviously weary of the debates and unsympathetic to those who sought to dismiss the *arrêté*, he used all his eloquence to persuade and to chastise the deputies. The fears of those opposing the *arrêté* are mere phantoms and their assumptions erroneous and gratuitous. According to these assumptions, Furtado declared, since the Catholics and Protestants have never had anything comparable, we ought not to have been convened, we ought not to have had a Grand Sanhedrin and it ought not to have presented its decisions. "Why have those opposed to the *arrêté* accepted their mission? Why have they come? Why have they participated in the meetings? What a singular contradiction between their conduct and their beliefs!"[50]

More sensitive to the demands and expectations of the French political leaders than to those of the deputies, Furtado accepted the *arrêté* as logically consistent with the ideological and pragmatic premises of the Assembly and Sanhedrin. He continued to remain committed, moreover, to the justification of paternal surveillance and the need for additional legislation both to maintain a peaceful situation and to prevent a reccurrence of the past disorders. In addition (and perhaps this is why he could be so sanguine about the future), he had in mind the specific measures which he hoped to see the government adopt.

As President of the Assembly, Furtado had submitted a *mémoire* to the Minister of Interior in which he outlined the means of avoiding both the prolongation of the decree and the inconveniences associated with its expiration.[51] Although the draft of the *mémoire* as well as the finished copy are undated, we can assume by Furtado's references to the consistory (accepted by the Assembly on December 9, 1806) and the Sanhedrin (whose eight meetings extended from February 9–March 9, 1807) that he sent his proposal to the Minister of Interior sometime during the late winter of 1807.[52]

As in his earlier *mémoire*,[53] Furtado pointed to the existence of unjust laws as the reason for the Jews' lack of participation in the arts and professions and to a justifiable fear of ill-treatment on the part of the Jewish community for its estrangement from agricultural pursuits. In spite of these obstacles, Furtado continued, of the 45,000 Jews included in the departments subject to the decree, only 600, all of whom cannot be considered usurers, occupy themselves exclusively with lending on interest.[54]

Although Furtado sought to emphasize the external causes for the Jews' estrangement from useful occupations, he showed himself to be less sympathetic to the oppressed communities than previously, and more concerned with finding an acceptable solution to the problem. To this end, Furtado proposed, perhaps hoping that the Ministers would be more amenable to his other suggestions, that those Jews who practiced usury be reported to the police and expelled from France if they repeated the offense. In addition he specified twenty-seven Jews from the Bas-Rhin who were known to be usurers.[55]

After indicating the role which the consistories could play in influencing the young to direct their energies and talents towards useful professions, Furtado then offered his alternative to the present decree. Aware of the fears of the government, he agreed that an abrupt end to the moratorium could cause undesired repercussions, but this fact did not justify the government's continuation of a general measure which confused the innocent with the guilty. Furtado proposed to discontinue the enforcement of the decree in the Sahr, Ruhr, Vosges and Metz, in any transaction unrelated to lending money on interest, and for all loans whose principal did not exceed three-hundred *livres*. As for the other loans, Furtado suggested an extension of five years during which the debtors would pay off one-fifth of their loans at a 5% or 6% interest each year.[56]

Thus, aware of the "nefarious" economic practices among *some* Jews of the Northeast and convinced that the rest of the French Jews would not be included in any new measures, Furtado viewed the passage of the *arrêté* not in terms of discrimination against the Jews, but rather in terms of soliciting a necessary intervention on the part of the government.

In a final demonstration of their willingness to accept the leadership of their President, forty-five out of fifty-four of the deputies finally adopted the *arrêté*. Furtado would have cause later, however, to regret this success.

Champagny, aware that the *arrêté* was not at all what Napoleon had anticipated, assured the Emperor in a letter dated April 2, that nothing more specific would have been accepted. The vote, the Minister explained, was difficult enough to obtain; it would have been easier to ask the deputies to depart from a religious practice than to accept measures which could appear to separate them from the rest of the French.[57]

On April 3, Molé, Portalis, and Pasquier wrote to Furtado that Napoleon had been informed of the *arrêté* and that the Assembly, after having so honorably terminated its work, could now separate. As for us, they wrote, "we shall never forget the zeal with which we have seen all the members animated and the assistance which we have derived from their enlightenment."[58]

Three days later, Furtado presided over the last meeting of the Assembly. After reading the letter he had received from the Imperial Commissioners, he explained to the deputies that their task was hardly completed; a perfect "incorporation" with their fellow citizens would require additional efforts.[59]

Acknowledging the wisdom of their President's words, the deputies adopted an *Exhortation* written primarily by Furtado and to be communicated to all the Jews of France and Italy.[60] These Jews, no longer forming a nation within a nation, were urged henceforth to devote themselves to their country and its defense, to agriculture, and to a conduct which would prove their detractors of eighteen centuries wrong. "Europe will decide your future," the *Exhortation* concluded, "but your conduct will dictate it. . . . Let us swear together an inviolable loyalty to the God of Israel, an inviolable loyalty to Napoleon the Great."[61]

Furtado thanked Napoleon privately in a letter written on the eve of the dissolution of the Assembly. The Jews, he wrote, are once again citizens of a country which has become their country. "Paris will become for us what Jerusalem was for our ancestors in the beautiful days of its glory. . . . Israelites in our Temples, French among our fellow citizens, this is who we are."[62]

With the *arrêté* finally adopted, Champagny could carry out Napoleon's instructions. On April 9, 1807, the Minister sent two projects to the Emperor, one pertaining to Jewish conscription and the other detailing the measures to be taken concerning the commercial transactions of the Jews. No Jew could fill a public office, Champagny wrote in terms less harsh than Napoleon's, unless two-thirds of the Jewish conscripts in his department served personally or obtained Jewish replacements. Although he was still opposed to a law which would afflict all the Jews, Champagny was now willing to impose restrictions on those Jews who were most often accused of usury. Thus he proposed requiring certain Jews, who were not among the bankers, manufacturers, and property owners, to obtain special permission by the prefect to engage in commerce. In addition, he advocated restricting the immigration of Jews who had no means of support and specifying to whom, among the non-Jews, the Jews could lend.[63]

On April 25, Champagny's projects, along with the *Règlement* passed by the Assembly on December 9, were sent to the Council of State. Around the same time, the Council also received a report, similar to Champagny's although more rigorous in detail, prepared by the Imperial Commissioners.[64]

The moratorium which had been granted to the debtors by the May 30 decree was to be enforced for only one year. There was no indication, however, even by the end of April that the government had any concrete alternative measures. Thus on May 27, 1807, in the absence of Napoleon who was in Poland, Régnier, the Minister of Justice, and Champagny met with the archchancellor and together they agreed to maintain the decree until Napoleon ordered otherwise.[65]

On June 13, after considerable debate resulting in numerous revisions, the Council of State adopted five projects. The first stated simply that the *Règlement* deliberated in the General Assembly of the Jews on the 10 (sic) of December 1806 would be executed and annexed to the present decree.[66] The second project contained the measures necessary for the application of the *Règlement*. The remaining three projects concerned the police functions to be exercised by the consistories, the means to end the May 30 decree and, last, the extraordinary measures to be taken in certain cases by special decree.

The Council did not go so far as to accept the prolongation of six years for all debts, which had been proposed by Champagny, but rather suggested a delay of six months or one year for certain debts with a payment of the whole sum and a delay of two, three, four, or six years for others with payments each year of one-half, one-third, one-fourth, or one-sixth of the total sums. The first of the extraordinary measures was the requirement that foreign Jews could establish themselves in France only by permission from the authorities based on a declaration from the consistory. In addition, certain Jews were required to obtain a special license in order to engage in commerce. Although the Council suggested even more severe restrictions, they were reserved for exceptional situations when "grave complaints" against the Jews made them necessary and when the Council of State and Minister of Interior, at the suggestion of the prefect, central consistory, and local consistory, agreed to them.[67]

Despite the fact that the Council had agreed to certain specific measures against the Jews, all of their projects consistently reflected their antipathy to special legislation and their support of civil equality. Indicative of their position were two opinions attached to the projects which rejected Champagny's restrictions on taking mortgages and his regulations concerning conscription.

For reasons unknown to us, the Council did not submit the projects to Napoleon until February 29, 1808. Perhaps other involvements dictated this delay, or perhaps the Council hoped to prevent even these relatively mild projects from becoming law. Whatever the reasons, the Jews, aware of the proposals of Champagny and the Commissioners, became more and more apprehensive of the government's intentions.

Furtado had never anticipated that the *arrêté*, which essentially he alone had forced upon the recalcitrant deputies, would be used to sanction measures such as those advocated by Champagny and the Council of State. In fact neither in his *mémoire* nor in his speeches had he even intimated the possibility of additional economic restrictions. Furtado had assumed, quite inaccurately, that the May 30 decree would be allowed to end and that only those measures which were necessary to insure a peaceful return to equality would be promulgated. As with the terrorist events during the Revolution, Furtado was angered and disillusioned with what he quickly understood to be a recision of the citizenship he valued so highly. Aware of his responsibility towards the Jews of France, he undertook, almost singlehandedly, the struggle to prevent any future discriminatory legislation.

The first step was a letter to Napoleon written by Furtado and signed by a number of influential Sephardic and Ashkenazic Jews "Sire," these men wrote, "rumors have brought terror to the souls of the Jews; . . . How can they conciliate the paternal views of your

Majesty, so solemnly proclaimed during the sessions of the Assemblies, with a system whose inevitable result would be to isolate them from the great family of the state, to perpetuate their humiliation and to make of them a nation within a nation?"[68] Informing Napoleon that they were aware of the situation in the Northeast, these deputies assured their Emperor that soon all the Jews would show their civil virtues. "The seed is in their heart," they pleaded, "one need only leave it there without interfering."[69]

Furtado wrote a second letter to Napoleon after he had learned that the Council of State had rejected Champagny's projects but had proposed its own instead. This letter, although unsigned but unquestionably by Furtado, was also written on behalf of a number of representative Jews.[70] Usury is an annoying abuse to society, Furtado repeated, but since it is a general abuse, the remedy must likewise be general. If the remedies proposed cannot be applied to the Empire, they should not be applied against the Jews. There is only one point, Furtado admitted, when specific measures might be necessary, but this can occur only after there has been time to judge whether the accomplishments of the Assembly and Sanhedrin have been sufficient. Even then, however, these measures should be directed against individuals rather than against Jews of a certain district.[71]

Furtado must have had more than just hearsay with which to combat the Council's projects, for he continued his letter with a refutation of the argument that the Jewish population was expanding and therefore needed regulation. It is true, he explained, that the population of the North and East has augmented, but this is because the Jews there helped all the poor who came to them. The Revolution, however, has destroyed the communities, and in addition the Jews are no longer wealthy enough to help others. Thus the project offers a remedy for something which no longer exists, and furthermore, if it were to exist in the future, there is no justification for such a "violent" solution. In every respect, Furtado continued, the decree of May 30 and the projects proposed to replace it are a sword of Damocles hanging over the Jews. With them one erects an invincible obstacle to any social incorporation between Israelite and Christian. "We were Frenchmen and citizens," he concluded, "we shall not become Jews."[72]

There is no record that either of these letters was ever presented to Napoleon. It is unlikely, however, at such a critical time, when even the Sephardic Jews were threatened with discriminatory legislation, that Furtado would have spent his energies composing letters which were never sent.

One letter, for which we do have an official record, was a *Réclamation* by the Portuguese, Spanish, and Avignonese Jews living in Paris,

Bordeaux, Bayonne, and the South of France.[73] For the last time the Sephardic Jews in alliance with their erstwhile enemies, the Avignonese, were to seek special consideration from the government. Deeply concerned, they decided that if they could not prevent the decrees, at least they could assure their exclusion from them. We have always been distinguished from others, they wrote. We have always enjoyed in France privileges refused to Israelites of other provinces. We have always been ruled by the same legislation as all other Frenchmen.[74] Once again, the traditional statements on the superiority of these Jews were brought forth to influence the government.

Despite the fact that Furtado joined the other Sephardic Jews in signing the *Réclamation,* he did not cease his efforts to prevent the passage of the decree. At the same time that the *Réclamation* was being presented to the government, Furtado and Maurice Lévy (from Nancy), were on their way to Prussia to see Napoleon in person. Arriving in Königsberg, the emissaries found that Napoleon had already left. Undaunted, they followed him to Dresden, where they asked Napoleon to grant them an audience.[75]

Historians have maintained that Furtado and Lévy ultimately saw Napoleon at Tilsit and that the Emperor received them graciously with a promise that the Jews would continue to enjoy the same rights as other citizens.[76] There is no acceptable evidence, however, that the representatives saw Napoleon personally or that they received the assurances which have been traditionally assumed. There can be no doubt that Furtado and Lévy actually made their trip. In addition to the letter from Dresden, we have a letter to Patto jeune from Furtado in which the latter writes that, with the exception of his trip to Poland, all his other activities were at his own expense.[77] If their trip is not to be disputed, however, whether they actually ever met with Napoleon and where, if so, is unfortunately left to conjecture. We find it most probable, considering the lack of more substantial evidence, that the two men, unable to see Napoleon, left Dresden and returned to Paris.[78]

The *mémoire* which Furtado is said to have presented to Napoleon in Poland, and which may never have been presented, was published in 1808.[79] In addition, we have located a manuscript which, while closely following the official document, offers a more accurate picture of Furtado's anger and frustration.[80] Although he wrote this *mémoire* to refute the specific projects proposed by Champagny to the Council of State, Furtado did not limit his observations to the particulars suggested by the Minister of Interior. Far removed from the underlying optimism with which he had advocated the adoption of the *arrêté,* he now found himself unable to accept any legislation which threatened to treat the Jews differently from other French citizens.

I shall concentrate on three issues, Furtado states in the opening paragraphs of the *mémoire*. "The first [payment of rabbis] contains an omission; the second [regulations for conscription] is useless; almost all the clauses of the third [economic restrictions] are dangerous."[81] The Protestants receive support for their religion, Furtado explains, and yet this support is denied the Jews, who have to pay the same taxes as others as well as their own private religious expenses. A requirement which demands that two-thirds of the Jews serve in person before any Jew may participate in public office is virtually impossible to put into practice, will inevitably lead to inaccuracies based on omissions, and will punish the innocent needlessly. Lastly, the economic restrictions proposed are in effect an abrogation of the civil status of the Jews, impede commerce and agriculture, and in no way confront the problem of usury. On the contrary, these restrictions will necessitate circumventions which may only result in an exacerbation of the very problem which they are to solve.

Furtado was not satisfied with restricting his comments to the general ramifications of the project; instead he continued by analyzing in detail all of the articles included in Champagny's proposals, and by illustrating point by point either their unanticipated negative repercussions or their infringement on the rights of the Jews.[82]

There are two alternatives, Furtado concluded in a phrase borrowed from Grégoire's speech to the National Assembly. "The existence of the Jews in France is either unacceptable and it is necessary to banish them, or their existence is not at all unacceptable and thus no longer is it the Jews we see but Frenchmen."[83]

Furtado's activities after publishing his *mémoire* remain unclear. We do know from a report of the Secretary of State that, together with "some members of the Assembly of the Jews," he attempted unsuccessfully to meet with Napoleon at Fontainebleau. At this time, he had hoped to present both his views on the proposed decrees, which he characterized as humiliating and discriminatory, and his demands for financial support for the rabbis and consistories.[84]

Since Napoleon was at Fontainebleau from September 22 to November 16, it has been assumed, despite the date given in the Secretary of State's report (March 1808), that this abortive attempt took place sometime in the fall of 1807, and that somehow subsequently Furtado had become convinced that he had successfully prevented any legislation against the Jews.[85]

In a letter written to Patto jeune on March 15, Furtado discussed a second trip he had made to Paris in which he had successfully prevented the promulgation of decrees which would have been the "eternal shame of Israel."[86] What had convinced Furtado that he had prevented the decrees? Had he met with Napoleon, Maret, or some other government representative after his return from Poland? In the same letter to Patto, Furtado complained about a group of Bordelais Jews who decided to send a special delegation to Paris. He revealed that he had advised them against this attempt because it reestablished the spirit of a corporation, because without a consistorial organization these Jews represented no one, and finally because it would be disadvantageous and humiliating to find themselves turned away. The Bordelais, however, had been unsympathetic to Furtado's reasoning; he now hoped that the Jews of Bayonne and in particular Patto would be wiser and would refrain from sending a delegation.[87]

Was Furtado speaking of a new attempt to see Napoleon which was never actually made, or was he reviewing what had in fact taken place at Fontainebleau in March as the Secretary had reported? Although one likes to recapture the exact chronology of events, there appears to be enough vagueness to prevent any definitive conclusions. We can state, nevertheless, that Furtado agreed to accompany the other Bordelais to Paris as late as March, 1808, that sometime before that he had been assured of the unlikelihood of the projects being translated into a decree, and that finally he was unaware of the fact that Napoleon was busy affixing his signature to measures far more restrictive than those proposed either by Champagny or the Council of State.[88]

On March 17, 1808, Napoleon approved a series of three decrees which were to serve as the foundation of French Jewry. The first two decrees, concerned with the organization of the Jewish communities, merely confirmed the organic ordinance adopted by the Assembly of Notables in December 1806 and clarified certain of its articles. The third decree included the altered projects of Champagny and the Council of State, against which the Jews of France had battled since the passage of the infamous *arrêté*; it successfully annulled or reduced all past loans made by the Jews and established new and repressive restrictions on commercial transactions, conscription, and residence.[89]

Although the moratorium was now officially terminated, all loans made by Jews to minors, women, unauthorized military, husbands or military and naval officers, were annulled.[90] In addition the decree permitted a reduction of those credits whose capital exceeded five percent by the accumulation of interests and annulled those debts whose capital exceeded ten percent.[91] Finally the courts could decide upon a delay for all legitimate and nonusurious credits.[92]

No less restrictive were those measures which regulated future commercial transactions. After July 1, every Jew wishing to engage in any form of commerce was required to obtain a special license issued annually and revocable when warranted. The prefect was to issue the licenses after he had received the necessary information provided by the municipal council and the consistory.[93] Thus the special licenses, reserved by Champagny and the Commissioners for certain restricted categories, had been made mandatory for all Jews engaged in commerce, without distinction or exception.

The articles concerning residence and conscription were equally rigorous. No Jew could henceforth establish residence in the departments of Haut- and Bas-Rhin and no Jew would be allowed to reside in the other departments unless he acquired a rural property and devoted himself to agriculture.[94] Last, no Jew could supply replacements for military duty; every Jewish conscript was to be subject to personal service.[95]

Only in the last two articles was there an attempt to soften these measures. The decree was to last for ten years with the hope that at its expiration there would be no difference between the Jews and the other citizens of France. If, however, this was not the case, the decree would then be extended.[96] Significantly, and perhaps herein lay Furtado's success (or that of the delegation of Sephardim), the Jews of Bordeaux and those of the departments of the Gironde and Landes, having given no cause for complaint and engaging in no illicit trade, were exempted from all the provisions of the third decree.[97]

If the exclusion of the Sephardic Jews was in fact a success for Furtado, this did not deter him from expressing himself once more. On April 17, 1808, he wrote a long letter to Maret, Minister and Secretary of State, in which he presented his observations on both the ideological and practical implications of the decree.[98] "If I had not been President of the Assembly in Paris," Furtado admitted, "I would not view this letter as a personal obligation. My goal is not to censor the decree but rather to examine it." His introductory promises to the contrary, Furtado begins by discrediting the need for such legislation. In words similar to those of the deputies who fought against the passage of the *arrêté*, Furtado reminds Maret that the decree was promulgated after the convocation of the Assembly and Sanhedrin and after the speeches delivered by the Imperial Commissioners. One should have done one of two things, either not convened the Assembly or renounced any particular legislation against the Jews.[99]

The practical consequences of the decree were no less distasteful. Significantly, Furtado concentrates on precisely those measures which actually resulted in divergencies of practice and interpretation as well as misapplication. The debtors will take advantage of the situation, Furtado writes. What kind of proof can the Jew offer that the amount had been furnished fully and without fraud? In essence, all debts contracted before the decree are retroactively annulled, for even the courts will interpret the cases recognized as legitimate in whatever way it chooses. How accurate was Furtado's prediction may be seen in a letter Champagny wrote to Napoleon on February 1, 1809. "The debtors of the Jews," the Minister stated, "have become masters of the fortunes of their creditors."[100]

Even those measures which pertain to future transactions, Furtado adds, will be resolved in ways prejudicial to the Jews. The necessary licenses, whose form is yet unknown, will inevitably lead many honest Jews to renounce commerce. For the rest of the Jews, how shall they receive their licenses? From recommendations by the municipal councils? That will condemn in advance a multitude of honest heads of family.[101] Eventually, Furtado concludes, the licenses will be sold out at a good price.[102]

In spite of all his criticisms, Furtado saw a means of mitigating the effects of the decree. The Jews from the departments of the Gironde and Landes have been exempted, he declares. Would it not be equally equitable to extend the exemptions to those Israelites residing in the departments of the South and West of France? In this way one would finally come to know who was actually guilty of usurious activities.[103]

Although Furtado had requested exemption for only a few, there is no doubt that he hoped to see all the Jews progressively freed from the yoke of the decree. In this instance, Furtado's suggestions were not in vain. On the basis of collective petitioning by the departments and favorable letters by the prefects, the government finally exempted almost 14,000 Jews.[104] With the suppression of Imperial conscription after 1814 and the relaxation of a strict application of the licenses, there was at least a partial escape for the majority of the Jews who continued to be subject to the decree until the beginning of April, 1818.

Furtado had written to his friend Pery during the fall of 1806 that the work of the Assembly might seem great from afar, but from a close perspective it was little. This might equally well be said of all the accomplishments of both the Assembly and Sanhedrin. For what was most obvious immediately following the convocation of these bodies was that the majority of the Jews of France had been reduced to second class citizens, emasculated economically, and discriminated against socially and politically.

Napoleon had reintroduced and cleverly reversed the whole process of emancipation. The accusations, such as those describing the Jews as a nation within a nation as well as the anti-Jewish intentions of many of the ministers, were a continuation of the debates held almost a decade earlier in the National Assembly. The Ashkenazim, who had been granted admission into the fraternity of France on the basis of a revolutionary logic and who declared in no uncertain terms their willingness to fulfill all the obligations of French citizens, were now denied their citizenship on the basis of practical considerations and a deep rooted hostility. Only the Sephardim, whose enfranchisement was a result not of ideology but of assimilation, were left to enjoy their equality. Ironically, they were again the privileged among the Jews. Yet even they were required to accept the re-creation of communal responsibility in the consistorial organization of all French Jewry; their privileged status was thus tempered by a required union with those Jews from whom they had dissociated themselves for more than two centuries. Their consolation lay, perhaps, in the realization that French Jewry would henceforth be required to fashion itself in the Sephardic image.

Despite his personal antipathies, Napoleon had not really intended to restrict the Jews indefinitely to an inferior status. He sought, as did many Jewish sympathizers during the Revolution, to destroy the traditional community and to eradicate what he considered to be the evils inherent in Jewish attitudes and habits. Where he differed from the revolutionaries, however, was in his determination to achieve this assimilation by force and with the promulgation of a particular and discriminatory legislation. The Jews, perhaps more conspicuously than other Frenchmen, felt the thrust of Napoleon's success in consolidating and institutionalizing the revolutionary heritage while simultaneously laying the foundation for a state whose powers and institutions were in some ways comparable to but always more absolute than the monarchy of the *ancien régime.*

Furtado differed from Napoleon neither in the standards which he erected as models for the Jews, nor in his evaluation of the traditional Jewish communities. Having become disillusioned with the excesses of popular democracy, moreover, he was willing to see a strong government guide the Jews to a full economic, political, and social assimilation. He was unwilling, however, to abide by Napoleon's paradoxical means and to accede to the treatment of the Israelites of France as Jews. [105]

Despite the decrees and despite the official sanction of discrimination against them, the Jews of France did not retreat from their struggle to justify the expectations of the revolutionaries. The consistories, assuming their responsibilities in 1809, undertook to implement what the Bordelais *nation* had long ago realized. Israelites in their temples, the Ashkenazim would henceforth be French among their fellow citizens.

Conclusion

After having lived publicly as Catholics for almost two centuries, the *nouveaux Chrétiens* emerged as Jews. They established a *nation*, organized oligarchically and exercising both civil and religious functions, and successfully developed an economic presence necessary to the commercial development of Bordeaux and reflective of the mercantile interests of the leading French statesmen. By the end of the 18th century, they were ideologically prepared to abandon the Ashkenazim, successful enough economically to elicit protection from the emerging bourgeois leadership, and sufficiently sophisticated to participate in the events which led to the destruction of the *ancien régime*.

The revolutionaries of 1789, who waged a deliberate and self-conscious campaign against both the Church and the monarchical state, acknowledged the privileged status of the *nation* and vindicated its unceasing efforts to dissociate from the Jews of the Northeast. On January 28, 1790, the Sephardim were recognized as Frenchmen and entitled to enjoy the rights of full and active citizens. In their turn, the Jews of Bordeaux abandoned their corporate status; their Judaism, already of limited spiritual significance and having lost its pragmatic function, became for many what the Church was to the revolutionaries—an impediment to the future progress and happiness of mankind.

The Ashkenazim had to await the passage of more than a year and a half before they too were admitted as citizens into the French state. Only when the revolutionaries could no longer ignore the logical implications of the Declaration of the Rights of Man were the Jews of the Northeast emancipated. Unable to prove that they were Frenchmen, the Ashkenazim were now required to prove that they, like the Sephardim, could become Frenchmen.

Emancipation had been granted to the Ashkenazim primarily as a result of the "enlightened" principles of the revolutionaries; it was partially rescinded as a result of the pragmatic concerns and emotional biases of the Emperor. The Sephardim had needed no logical justifications for their enfranchisement. They had been protected from the accusations levelled at the Jews of the Northeast and the discriminatory legislation promulgated as a result of those accusations. Nevertheless, they too were to be included in Napoleon's plan to unite all French Jewry.

Napoleon embodied both the dreams and the disillusions of the revolutionary years. Unable and unwilling to disavow completely the revolutionary heritage, yet determined to forge a powerful and centralized state to which all citizens owed allegiance, he undertook to redefine traditional Judaism and to establish an institutional body to represent and to control the Jews of France. He called forth an Assembly of Jewish Notables and with the romantic gestures of a younger Napoleon convened the *de facto* legislative body of ancient Israel. The result was a unified French Jewry publicly committed to a Judaism similar in content and intent to that of the Sephardim.

The responsibilities Napoleon assigned to the consistories he succeeded in establishing in 1808 were the economic, social, and political assimilation of French Jewry. These, along with the protection of the interests of the Jewish community which the consistories later assumed, bear a striking similarity to the self-defined responsibilities of the *nation*. As the Sephardim had sought to prove their *utilité*, so now all French Jews were to justify their admission into the French state by becoming useful and productive citizens. In the manner that the Sephardim had divested Judaism of its rabbinic heritage, so now all French Jewry was to acknowledge a Judaism shorn of its nationhood, deprived of its messianic dreams, and rendered subservient to French secular law and French political life. Yet the consistories, differing so little both ideologically and institutionally from the *nation* of the past, were unacceptable to some Sephardim, who saw in them the recreation of a particular status, the reestablishment of religious distinctions, and the abrogation of a full and equal citizenship. Their response was conversion, the solution of their ancestors in Spain and Portugal.

The rest of the Jews of Bordeaux joined with the Ashkenazim; together for the first time, they undertook to complete the transformation of French Jewry. Despite the compromises they made with Judaism and their commitment to embrace France as their country and the French as their fellow citizens, the Jews of France continued to remain marginal men. Ironically they became modern Marranos whose assimilation to their place of residence rested on a foundation of Jewish separateness. To be sure, the legal coercion and the fear experienced in past centuries had disappeared. In their place, however, were a no less keenly felt social pressure and shame. The Sephardim of Bordeaux had successfully bequeathed their entire heritage to French Jewry.

Glossary

Ahikha. (Hebrew, "thy brother").

Ancien régime. Old regime.

Anciens. Those taxpayers who had once been or were presently on the council of the *Sedaca*.

Arrêt. Judgment.

Arrêté. Ordinance; decision.

Ashkenazim. In its broadest sense denotes German Jews as well as their descendants throughout the world.

Assignats. Bonds issued by the National Assembly (1789-91) against confiscated Church property. Later regarded as currency and issued in small bills.

Aubain. Foreigner. Alien.

Bet-Din. (Hebrew, "house of judgment"). The Jewish courts of law whose authority, sometimes extending to all spheres of Jewish life, was greatest during the Talmudic and medieval period.

Biens nationaux. Property nationalized during the Revolution.

Cahiers de doléances. Grievance lists prepared at the time of the elections to the Estates-General in 1789.

Capitation. Literally, "poll-tax." Initiated by Louis XIV, it was levied in correspondence to income.

Commission Populaire de Salut Public. Popular Committee of Public Safety. Established on June 9, 1793 by those Bordelais who sought to challenge the Jacobin control of the National Convention. Unsuccessful in their efforts, the Bordelais were subsequently proscribed by the Convention.

Droit d'aubaine. According to French law, the estate of a deceased foreigner belonged to France.

Etat-civil. Civil status.

Etranger. Foreigner. Alien.

Imperium. Nation. State.

Intendants. Representatives of the King sent to the Provinces to supervize the local administrators.

Jurat. Municipal magistrate.

Kashrut. (Hebrew from Kasher "fit"). Regulations determining the Jewish dietary laws.

Lettres de change. Bills of exchange.

Lettres Patentes. Royal decrees.

Livre. French currency. Received the name *franc* during the Revolution.

Marchands Portugais. Literally, "Portuguese merchants." Often used in France for those of Spanish and Portuguese descent who, although suspected of being crypto Jews, were nevertheless publicly committed to Catholicism. Most of these emigrants from the Iberian Peninsula were assumed to be merchants.

Marrano. In Spanish, "swine." Used disparagingly by both Spanish and Portuguese to designate those Jews who had converted to Christianity but who were suspected of remaining faithful to Judaism.

Maskilim. Those engaged in spreading European culture among Jews in the 18th and 19th centuries.

Mémoire. Memorandum.

Musée. Formed in Bordeaux(1783) under the patronage of the *Intendant* St. Maur. Pledged itself to pursue social and political questions as well as philanthropy.

Nation. The official designation for the community of Bordelais Jews of Spanish and Portuguese origin.

Négociant. Merchant; trader.

Neshekh. (Hebrew). Usury; interest.

Nouveaux Chrétiens. Literally, "new Christians." The converted Jews of Spain and Portugal were referred to as new Christians not only in France but also in Spain (cristianos nuevos) and Portugal (cristãos novos).

Nouveaux convertis. Literally, "new converts." Those Protestants who converted to Catholicism after Louis XIV revoked the Edict of Nantes (1685).

Parlements. The principal bodies of justice in France under the *ancien régime*.

Philosophes. French "men of letters." It was generally through these popularizers and publicists that the ideas of the Enlightenment were spread.

Procès-verbal. Official report; proceedings.

Réclamation. Demand; protest.

Règlement. Regulation; ordinance.

Régnicole. Native.

Sedaca. (Hebrew, "justice; charity"). The charitable organization established by the Sephardim of Bordeaux. Later became synonymous with the Portuguese *nation*.

Sénéchal. Provincial feudal officer who was chief of Justice.

Sénéchaussée. Jurisdiction of the *Sénéchal*.

Sephardim. Descendants of Jews from the Iberian Peninsula.

Sheluhim. (Hebrew, "emissaries"). Messengers from Palestine sent abroad to raise funds.

Société des Amis de la Constitution. Society of Friends of the Constitution. Established in Bordeaux during the early years of the Revolution. One of the most popular of the Bordelais clubs, the *société* counted many wealthy Sephardim among its members.

Société de Bienfaisance. Charitable Association.

Talmud Torah. An elementary Jewish school maintained primarily for the poor.

Vingtième. Literally "twentieth." Originally designed as a five per cent tax on income. Successfully watered down by privileged influential groups.

Notes

Chapter 1

[1]"Sçavoir Faisons, que Nous inclinans liberallement à la supplication et requeste desdits portugais, comme gens desquels Nous voyons le bon zele et affection qu'ils ont de vivre sous Nôtre obéïssance, ainsi que Nos autres sujets en bonne dévotion, de s'employer pour Nôtre Service, et de la Republique de Nôtre Royaume, la commodité de laquelle ils veulent ayder de leurs biens Manufactures et industries: De sorte que cela Nous merît à les bien et gracieusement traiter: Pour ces causes . . . qu'ils puissent à leur loisir, toutesfois et quantes que bon leur semblera eux retirer et habiter, et ceux qui jà y sont venus ayent peu et puissent demeurer et resider en Nôtredit Royaume, Païs, Terres et Seigneuries de Nôtre obéïssance, et en telles Villes et lieux d'iceluy Royaume que bon leur semblera, . . . et avec eux amener les Femmes, Enfans . . . ; entrer en ce Royaume et en sortir, aller et venir sans aucun trouble et empêchement, et en icelui Nôtredit Royaume, trafiquer et exercer train de marchandise: Ensemble y acquerir tous et chaucuns, les biens tant meubles qu'immeubles, qu'ils y pourront licitement acquerir; . . ."— Archives départementales de la Gironde, C1089.

[2]*Ibid.*

[3]Camille Jullian, *Histoire de Bordeaux depuis les origines jusqu'en 1895* (Bordeaux: Feret et Fils, 1895), p. 428.

[4]Archives départementales de la Gironde, C1089.

[5]*Ibid.*

[6]Historians such as Cardozo de Bethencourt, Ad. Detcheverry, and Francisque-Michel give the twelfth. This is inaccurate.

[7]Archives départementales de la Gironde, C1089.

[8]*Inventaire sommaire des archives départementales antérieures à 1790* (Bordeaux: 1928), registres d'enregistrement du parlement, IBI à 58.

[9]Théophile Malvezin, *Histoire des Juifs à Bordeaux* (Bordeaux: Charles Lefebvre, 1875), pp. 113–114.

[10]*Ibid.*

[11]Henry Léon, *Histoire des Juifs de Bayonne* (Paris: Armand Durlacher, 1893), p. 19. Louis Francia de Beaufleury, *Histoire de l'établissement des Juifs à Bordeaux et à Bayonne depuis 1550* (Paris: 1799), p. 17.

[12]"Mémoire présenté par MM Lopes Dubec père et Furtado aîné, députés des Juifs de Bordeaux, à M. de Malesherbes ministre d'Etat, en Juin 1788,"

Archives départementales de la Gironde, Série I, pp. 80–81.

[13]Malvezin, pp. 113–14.

[14]France, *Recueil général des anciennes lois françaises depuis l' an 420 jusqu'à la révolution de 1789* (Paris: Librairie de Plon Frères), Tome XVI, 1610–1643.

[15]Malvezin, pp. 121–2; p. 129.

[16]*Ibid.*, p. 128. France was again at war with Spain.

[17]*Ibid.*, p. 123.

[18]*Ibid.*, p. 129. The census was taken by Sebastian Diaz, "docteur regent," and Antoine de Mora, "marchand."

[19]Archives départementales de la Gironde, C1089.

[20]This geographic restriction often has been overlooked by historians.

[21]L. Cardozo de Bethencourt, "Le trésor des Juifs sephardim," *Revue des études juives*, XXV (1892), p. 240.

[22]Théophile Malvezin, *Histoire du commerce de Bordeaux depuis lés origines jusqu'à nos jours* (4 vols., Bordeaux: Imp. Nouvelle A. Bellier et Cie., 1892), II, pp. 308–9.

[23]The Calvinists, or Huguenots as they were called in France, had at one time enjoyed the same civil rights as Catholics. In 1598, Henry IV, himself once a Huguenot, issued the famous Edict of Nantes which permitted Protestants to participate in public offices, attend Catholic universities and establish their own means of defense. Although the Edict was amended in 1629 by Cardinal Richelieu (there were no longer to be fortified cities, armies or military and territorial rights), the Huguenots were still free to enjoy their religious and civil rights.

[24]Warren C. Scoville has recently presented the hypothesis that other factors—war, famine and the government's desperate fiscal situation—were more significant than the revocation in retarding France's economic development. Warren C. Scoville, *The Persecution of Huguenots and French Economic Development 1680–1720* (California: University of California Press, 1960).

[25]*Ibid.*, pp. 255–6.

[26]Archives départementales de la Gironde, C1089.

The Ashkenazic Jews became a part of France at different periods throughout the sixteenth, seventeenth, and eighteenth centuries, when the German territories in which they were residing were annexed by France. In 1559, France was permitted to occupy Metz, Toul and Verdun, by the treaty of Cateau-Cambrésis, and in 1648, her jurisdiction over these areas as well as over Alsace was confirmed. It was not until 1697, however, with the treaty of Ryswick, that she acquired the city of Strasbourg. France annexed Lorraine last in 1766 upon the death of Stanislas Leszynyski. In each case, France affirmed the rights of all the inhabitants and attempted, not always successfully, to assert her sovereignty over these territories. The Ashkenazic Jews, receiving from the French monarchs special renewals of all rights and liberties which they had enjoyed under former rulers, found themselves often dependent upon the protection of the French monarchs against the local ruling groups. This protection was forthcoming when it coincided with the monarchs' need to assert their authority over the former German territories.

The most significant Jewish right which the French government affirmed was that which permitted the Jews to continue to live as separate communities governed by their own civil and religious laws. The typical Jewish community structure was retained, serving both to protect the Jews as a group and to provide the government, as well as other groups, with a well organized means of collecting money.

While the Jews were not treated identically in Alsace, Metz, and Lorraine, and while they fared better in Metz and Lorraine than in Alsace, there was no significant difference in their general economic and social position. Although each community had within it some wealthy men, the communities as a whole were poor and more often than not indebted to Jewish as well as Christian creditors. Simultaneously with the right to live as a separate community existed economic and social prohibitions which perpetuated the Jews' precarious financial situation. Thus the majority of the Jews were confined to lending money, petty trading, and at times dealing in used clothing. Socially, they were no less segregated. Social intercourse between them and their neighbors was restricted by those laws, likewise affirmed by the French monarchs, which had successfully maintained the social cleavages known throughout the Middle Ages.

[27]Malvezin, *Histoire des Juifs*, p. 175.

[28]Archives départementales de la Gironde, C1089.

[29]In 1651 Bordelais shipping accounted for only 2.5% of the movement of the port, in 1672, 11.5% and in 1683, 5%. Quoted in Giteau, "Vie économique et classes sociales dans le monde laïque," in Charles Higounet, ed., *Histoire de Bordeaux* (6 vols.; Bordeaux: Fédération Historique du Sud Ouest, 1962), IV, pp. 472–73.

[30]*Livre des Bourgeois de Bordeaux, XVIIe et XVIIIe siècles* (Bordeaux: MDCCCXCVIII). For the trade with Spain see Zosa Szajkowski, "Trade Relations of Marranos in France with the Iberian Peninsula in the 16th and 17th centuries," *Jewish Quarterly Review*, (July, 1959), pp. 69–78.

[31]Malvezin, *Histoire du commerce*, Vol. II, pp. 287–89.

[32]*Ibid.*, p. 295.

[33]Malvezin, *Histoire des Juifs*, p. 129.

[34]Archives municipales de Bordeaux, *Inventaire sommaire des registres de la Jurade: 1520–1783* (8 vols., incomplete; Bordeaux: 1896–   ), VI, pp. 668, 679-680. Malvezin, *Histoire des Juifs*, pp. 174–5.

[35]Georges Cirot, *Recherches sur les Juifs espagnols et portugais à Bordeaux* (Bordeaux: 1920), p. 172.

[36]*Ibid.*, pp. 159–60. Beaufleury, p. 33 and Malvezin, *Histoire des Juifs*, pp. 223–4 give the date 1705. Cirot, the most recent historian of the three, appears to be the most reliable in this matter.

[37]Not until 1728, in an ordinance confirming the privileges of the Jews of Bordeaux, did the king prohibit receiving Jews under twelve years of age. Archives départementales de la Gironde, C1089.

[38]"On ne peut être agrégé à la faculté de médecine sans être catholique. Les déclarations du Roy sont expresses sur ce point, . . ." Quoted in a letter written by the *nation* to the widow of the doctor Cardoze, Archives départementales de la Gironde, C1090. As an example of this, Jean Baptiste Silva,

son of the famous doctor of Bordeaux, converted to Catholicism before pursuing his medical studies. His father had been dismissed as doctor of the *Hôtel de Ville* of Bordeaux because he was an "étranger." The son became consulting doctor of the king and received letters of nobility. Cirot, p. 237.

Another example is Cardoze, who also converted to Catholicism. At his death, his widow claimed that her conversion was merely to aid her husband and that she was born and would die a Jew. The *nation* wished her to pay taxes as a Jew and a long dispute ensued concerning the accumulated taxes the widow owed. Archives départementales de la Gironde, C1090.

[39]Daniel and Joseph Fernandes had both converted to Catholicism and subsequently brought their complaints before the *jurats* of Bordeaux (1705–1707). Both men complained of having suffered physical attacks at the hands of the Jews. "Le nommé *Mendes* s'est présenté à luy [Daniel Fernandes], lequel a traité le pleignant de renié, qu'il voulloit quitter la loy mosaique et embrasser une qui ne le souveroit pas, à quoy le pleignant a respondu que ce n'estoit pas à luy à le reprendre; tout à l'instant ledit *Mendes*, d'une cane qu'il avoit à la main en a frappé icelluy pleignant de divers coups quy n'avoit rien aux mains pour se deffendre; sur ce temps est survenu le nommé *Peyreyre* fils, lequel, prenant le party dud. *Mendes*, d'une cane qu'il avoit aussie à la main, en a frappé de plus de vingt coups led. pleignant, sur les épaules et sur les bras. . . ." Archives départementales de la Gironde, 12B204.

[40]Malvezin, *Histoire des Juifs*, pp. 133–34.

[41]The first syndic was Leon Peixotto.

[42]Cirot, pp. 85–99.

[43]*Ibid.*, pp. 80–81.

[44]*Ibid.*, p. 75.

[45]*Ibid.*, p. 50.

[46]Arthur Hertzberg, *The French Enlightenment and the Jews* (New York: Columbia University Press, 1968), p. 25. According to this author, the decrees of 1686–87 by Colbert de Croissy, which permitted foreigners to enter and leave France whenever they chose, were the signal for the Jews of Bordeaux and Bayonne to drop their Christian practices.

[47]Zosa Szajkowski has stated that the majority of the Marranos who came to France from the 15th-17th centuries remained Christian and that few returned to Judaism. Zosa Szajkowski, "Notes on the Language of the Marranos and Sephardim in France," *For Max Weinreich* (1964), p. 239. Zosa Szajkowski, "The Marranos and Sephardim of France," *The Abraham Weiss Jubilee Volume* (1964), p. 107. This assertion, based primarily on a list of lost names and lost Sephardic communities such as Nantes, Rouen, and Montpelier, is challenged by I. S. Révah, who states that the majority, rather than remaining Christian, emigrated from France or died as judaizers. I. S. Révah, "Les Marranes," *Revue des études juives*, CVIII (1959–60), pp. 65–67.

[48]For example, in Bordeaux 20% of the marriage contracts of the *négociants* exceeded 100,000 *livres* while in Toulouse the largest contract was 100,000. François Georges Parisit, ed., *Bordeaux au XVIII siècle* (Bordeaux: 1968), p. 351.

[49]Malvezin, *Histoire du commerce*, vol. III, pp. 34–60.

[50]M. de Peña, "Contribution à l'étude du commerce de Bordeaux avec

l'Espagne au XVIIIe siècle," *Revue historique de Bordeaux* (1958), pp. 177–97.

[51]Jean de Maupassant, *Abraham Gradis (1699?–1780): Un grand armateur de Bordeaux* (Bordeaux: Feret et Fils, 1917).

[52]Archives départementales de la Gironde, Répertoire Numérique du Fonds des Négociants, 7B2147; 7B1590–1612; 7B2563–2565; 7B2021–2127.

[53]In a list of 806 *négociants,* 26 were Jewish. The population of Bordeaux at the time was approximately 100,000, that of the Jews approximately 1,500. *Almanach de Commerce d'Arts et Métiers pour la ville de Bordeaux; Pour l'Année Commune Mil Sept Cent Quatre-Vingt-Cinq,* Archives départementales de la Gironde, 3I/L4.

[54]*Livre des Bourgeois de Bordeaux, XVIIe et XVIIIe siècles* (Bordeaux: MDCCXCVIII). It is difficult to ascertain just how many Jewish families were titular members of the bourgeoisie. In the *Livre des Bourgeois,* there are those Sephardim listed for the 18th century whose letters dated back to the 17th century. Yet in this same *Livre,* these Sephardim are not listed for the 17th century. Thus although we found 18 families listed for the 18th and 7 families listed for the 17th centuries, the actual figures are undoubtedly much higher.

[55]Parisit, p. 358. 25,600 *livres* is equivalent to approximately twice as many modern *francs.*

[56]Archives départementales de la Gironde, 3E21722, 3E21731, 3E21733, 3E21721, 3E21728, 3E21720, 3E21727, 3E21726. It is informative to add to these statistics that an unskilled worker earned 200 *livres* a year.

[57]The statistics come from the years 1800–23. This accounts for the use of *francs* rather than *livres.* Unfortunately there are no statistics prior to the year 8 and thus we are unable to use this type of information for the early part of the 18th century. Because of the economic disasters of the revolutionary years, however, and their effect on the Bordelais community, we can safely assume that those Sephardim who died after the Revolution were less wealthy than before 1789.

[58]Archives départementales de la Gironde, $\frac{BX.}{t}$ 1, fol. 43v°, 62v°, 137v°, 158v°, 161v°; $\frac{BX.}{t}$ 2, fol. 1v°, 2v°, 4v°, 30v°, 35v°, 50v°, 53v°,59v°, 76v°, 77v°, 88v°, 89v°, 97v°, 108v°, 110v°, 121v°, 123v°, 144v°, 150v°, 153v°, 164v°, 167v°, 176v°; $\frac{BX.}{t}$ 3, fol. 4v°, 52v°, 56v°, 80v°, 88v°, 97v°, 112v°, 115v°, 120v°, 147v°, 157v°, 158v°, 160v°, 167v°, 168v°.

[59]*Ibid.,* C2915.

[60]Among the *marchands de planches* more than 10% paid more than 100 *livres.* Parisit, pp. 356–7.

[61]According to a census taken in 1751, there were 330 heads of families. Archives départementales de la Gironde, C1089.

[62]In 1790, 55,259,589 *livres* out of 56,996,077 were paid on the property tax; M. Marion, *Dictionnaire des institutions de la France aux XVII et XVIII siècles* (Paris: A. Picard, 1923), p. 556.

[63]Archives départementales de la Gironde, C2992. The statistics are for the *vingtième* of industry of 17⁻7. In addition, individual Sephardim paid additional taxes in the other categories. Archives départementales de la Gironde, C3002.

[64]Cirot, p. 50.

[65]The first mention of the *capitation* in the minutes of the *nation* is on September 7, 1738. "Registre des déliberations de la nation portugaise depuis Mai 1710, tiré des anciens livres pour servir au besoin, lequel registre servira pour y coucher toutes celles qui seront passées de l'avenir dans le corps, commencé du sindicat de sieur David Lameyra à Bordeaux le premier Juin 1753," Archives départementales de la Gironde, Série. I.

The *nation* paid the *capitation* in the same manner as other *corps,* that is it was taxed as a group and given the responsibility of dividing the amount among its members. In a *capitation* list of 1741, the Portuguese were included in the list of *métiers* while the Protestants were listed as individuals according to their professions. In 1744, we find the "Rôles de la nation Juive, corps portugais," in which the full tax and the amount paid by each member is recorded on the form used for all other *corps*. Archives départementales de la Gironde, C2716.

[66]Archives départementales de la Gironde, C1090.

[67]*Ibid.* Sometimes the *nation* would arrange to pay the expenses of those Jews it expelled. "Registre," N° 11D.

[68]Cirot, pp. 57–68.

[69]Archives départementales de la Gironde, C1089.

[70]"Registre," N° 215.

[71]In 1730, a number of members of the *nation* refused to pay their taxes. The *nation* asked the *intendant,* M. de Boucher, to intervene and on April 12, 1730, he issued an *ordonnance* requiring that all those included in the *rôle* of the *nation* pay their taxes. Archives départementales de la Gironde, C 1090.

In the 1750's, we find the *nation* having trouble filling the role of syndic and fines were instituted of 500 and ultimately 1000 *livres* for those who refused the position. Archives départementales de la Gironde, C1090. "Registre," N° 547.

[72]Archives départementales de la Gironde, C1089.

[73]Malvezin, *Histoire des Juifs,* p. 212. The non-Sephardic Jews of Bordeaux (the German, Avignonese, and Italian) had long been the target of both Bordelais and Sephardic competition.

"C'est avec bien du plaisir que nous [Chamber of Commerce of Bordeaux] avons apris par votre lettre du 16 de ce mois la décision quy fut donnée le 15 . . . que les Juifs avignonnais seroient expulsés hors du Royaume, . . ." If the Avignonese stayed any longer, these businessmen wrote, the merchants and *boutiquiers* would have been forced to abandon their commerce. "Copies des lettres missives de la Chambre de Commerce le février 1725 et finy le 27 avril 1744," January 23, 1734, Archives départementales de la Gironde, C4262.

On February 21, 1722, in an *arrêt* concerning the confiscation of property of the Sephardic Jews, the Avignonese Jews of Bordeaux were expelled (Malvezin, *Histoire des Juifs,* p. 173). On April 12, 1730, all vagabond Jews were ordered out of Bordeaux (Malvezin, *Histoire des Juifs,* p. 177). This expulsion was requested by the Sephardic Jews who feared, justifiably so, the threat to their position by poor, uncultured, but potentially competitive Jews. The *arrêt* of 1734 renewed the expulsion orders of 1722 and exempted only a few wealthy Avignonese (Malvezin, *Histoire des Juifs,* p. 185). This *arrêt* was followed in

1735 by a decision on the part of the *nation* to provide for only ninety families at one time and to limit those families to Sephardic Jews (Cirot, p. 30). Not until 1764 did the king permit the six Avignonese families previously protected from the expulsion decrees to organize themselves with their own syndic and to tax themselves. They were to be dependent, however, upon the bakeries and butcher shops of the *nation* and were to have no authority to expel unwanted Jews (Malvezin, *Histoire des Juifs*, pp. 208–16).

[74]Archives départementales de la Gironde, C1089.

[75]"En effect si ceux qui doivent représenter la nation sont toujours les mêmes, si'ils sont perpétuels, qui peut douter qu'ils ne se ménagent réciproquement dans la répartition des impositions, et par une conséquence inévitable, qu'ils ne surchargent le reste de la nation." Archives départementales de la Gironde, C1090. This accusation must be tempered by the fact that there were some Sephardim who refused the position of syndic. There is no doubt, however, that the wealthy controlled the community—a situation little different from other Jewish communities of the 18th century.

[76]Archives départementales de la Gironde, C1090.

[77]*Ibid.*

[78]The Sephardic Jews traced their descent to the tribe of Judah.

[79]For a detailed account of the Ashkenazic Jews of France, see Robert Anchel, *Les Juifs de France* (Paris: 1946) and Zosa Szajkowski, *The Economic Status of the Jews in Alsace, Metz and Lorraine (1648–1789)* (New York: 1954).

[80]Malvezin, *Histoire des Juifs*, pp. 177–79.

[81]*Ibid.*, pp. 178–79.

[82]Archives départementales de la Gironde, C1090. This letter was in answer to the request of M. le Chancelier for details on whether the "Israelites" of Bordeaux practiced their religion and if they had any synagogues. M. de Boucher's suggestions were supported by M. le Chancelier in a letter written on June 4, 1734.

[83]Archives départementales de la Gironde, C1090. M. de Tourny gave an interesting explanation for the *lettres patentes* of 1723, "Je sçay qu'il est echapé au conseil en 1723 une déclaration du Roy, où l'expression des Juifs était employée et quelques lettres de ministres dans le même cas en leur faveur, . . ." Apparently the "royal slip" of 1723 was to be disregarded.

[84]See pp. 34–35.

[85]The *jurats* now had less control over the *nation,* and in 1761 they freed the Jews from the patrol on the Sabbath. The *nation,* in gratitude for the privilege, gave a M. Douin a bill of 6000 *livres* owed the Jews. "Registre," N° 306.

[86]Neither the German nor the Flemish merchants were ever able to attain such a complex and complete organization.

[87]In this respect Abraham Furtado's personal letters and diaries, although written at the end of the 18th and beginning of the 19th centuries, will provide us with important sources of information.

[88]Archives départementales de la Gironde, C1090. *Tala* refers to the traditional prayer shawl, *cecis* to the fringes of the shawl and *sosopha* to the ram's horn.

[89]The oldest register of a circumcision is in 1706. Between March 27 and

August 10, 1718, we find 18 circumcisions, only one of whom was a child. Cirot, p. 174.

[90]The source for the interpretation of the Shofar blowing which M. de Puddefer gives is unclear. Perhaps, this represents the Sephardic interpretation of Genesis, chapter 21, v. 17 which was traditionally read on the New Year.

[91]"Registre," N[os] 58, 62, 66, 273, 274, 400, 422.

[92]*Ibid.*, N[os] 538, 249. Since most of the signatures of the *Sheluhim* are in Spanish, we can assume that the *nation* was supporting only the Sephardic Jews of these communities. Contact was also established with the German communities of Hamburg and Altona, since the *nation* was responsible for overseeing that the wine bought by these communities from the Christian merchants Hamensen & Sons and Schroder & Schyler was kosher (certificates to that effect were issued). The Jews of London and Amsterdam also bought their wine from Bordeaux, and in all these transactions the *nation* received 4 *livres* a ton which was applied to the poor fund. An interesting incident occurred when Jonathan Eibeschütz, Rabbi of Hamburg, questioned the legitimacy of the Sephardic certificates. After correspondence between the communities, the *intendant* intervened and the tax was allowed to remain.

[93]Apparently one way of rebelling against the omnipresence of the syndic was to follow the traditional methods of engagement (where a certain formula said between a man and woman in the presence of witnesses was sufficient) and marriage. The syndic and deputies were quick to bring these cases before the *Bet Din* where they were always pronounced illegal.

[94]"Registre," N°s 85, 104, 121, 433, 545.

[95]Archives départementales de la Gironde, C1090, n.s., n.d.

[96]"Registre," N°s 273, 274.

[97]*Ibid.*, N° 280.

[98]*Ibid.*, N°s 280, 422.

[99]In 1762, the *nation* gave 2,400 *livres* for a ship and in 1782, during the war with England, gave 60,140 *livres*, enough for approximately one-fifth of a ship. *Ibid.*, N°s 299, 505.

On December 12, 1754, Péreire suggested that the *nation* lend 6000 *livres* to an influential Parisian who would be able to benefit the Sephardim. Meanwhile Péreire received an annual pension of 400 *livres* a year which was soon raised to 800. *Ibid.*, N°s 228, A. F. 59, 301.

[100]"Lesdits Marchands Portugais nous ont très-humblement fait exposer, par le Sieur Rodrigues Péreire leur Agent, à Paris, Membre de la Société Royale de Londres, notre Pensionnaire et notre Ami, Sécrétaire-interprète pour les langues Espagnole et Portugaise, que leur admission en France, et la confirmation de leurs privilèges, qui depuis plus de deux siècles leur a été accordée de règne en règne, ont été justifiées, tant par leur attachement inviolable pour les Rois nos Prédécesseurs, et pour notre Personne Sacrée, que par leur application et leurs talents dans le commerce, à la prosperité et à l'étendue duquel ils ont contribué dans notre Royaume, par le moyen de leurs relations au dedans et au dehors, et qu'ils ont même étendu par les nouvelles branches qu'ils y ont ajoutées, le tout à l'avantage du Public et de nos revenus,

sans qu'il soit jamais résulté de leur séjour en France, et de leurs usages particuliers, aucun inconvénient pour nos autres sujets . . . . Maintenons lesd. Marchands Portugais, tant ceux qui sont déja établis et domiciliés dans notre Royaume, Pays, Terres et Seigneuries de notre obéissance, que ceux qui viendront y venir dans la suite, dans la pleine possession et paisible jouissance desdits privileges . . . leur permettons d'y demeurer et vivre suivant leurs usages, . . . voulons qu'ils soient traités et regardés ainsi que nos autres sujets, nés en notre Royaume, et qu'ils soient réputés tels, tant en jugement que dehors; faisant très-espresses inhibition et défenses de leur donner aucun trouble ni empêchement." France, *Lettres Patentes,* June, 1776. Copy in the private library of M. R. Weill, Talence, France.

Not only was Péreire paid a generous sum, but also an additional 3000 *livres*, at the suggestion of Péreire, was lent to an unnamed Parisian. "Registre," *op. cit.,* N⁰ 455.

¹⁰¹Solomon Lopes-Dubec, "Autobiographical account," Jewish Historical General Archives, Jerusalem, Zf5.

¹⁰²After the revocation of the Edict of Nantes in 1685, the Huguenots never regained their lost privileges. On the contrary, as the Sephardim developed their communal organization and received royal protection for the exercise of their religion, the Protestants retreated to a life of religious subterfuge. The *nouveaux Chrétiens* had emerged as Jews; many of the Protestants became *nouveaux convertis.*

One year after the *Lettres Patentes* of 1723, Louis issued a decree in which, according to Article 1, it was prohibited to practice any religion other than the Catholic or to assemble for any religious purpose. Punishment was the galleys for the men, shaving and life imprisonment for the women, and confiscation of property in both cases. Article 3 obliged all parents to baptize their infants during the first twenty-four hours following their birth, and Articles 4–7 demanded that they be raised according to the Catholic religion. The *Parlement* of Bordeaux registered the decree on June 16, 1724. Although some of the more wealthy and influential Protestants (especially those of Bordeaux) escaped the rigors of this "declaration du roi concernant les religionnaires," this was the exception. For most, the next sixty-four years were filled with maltreatment, discrimination, and persecution; as late as 1782, the Catholic curies were registering the children born of suspected practicing Protestants as bastards. J. Cavignac, "Les assemblées au désert dans la région de Sainte-Foy au milieu du XVIIIᵉ siècle," *Revue historique de Bordeaux,* XVI (July-December, 1967), pp. 97–119.

¹⁰³For a detailed account of Péreire and de Pinto, see Hertzberg, pp. 141–153.

Chapter 2

¹For a discussion of the situation of the Protestants in France, see Chapter I, notes 23, 24, and 102.

²"Notre justice et l'intérêt de notre royaume ne nous permettent pas d'exclure plus longtemps, des droits de l'état civil, ceux de nos sujets ou des

étrangers domicilés dans notre empire, qui ne professent point la religion catholique . . . . La religion catholique que nous avons le bonheur de professer, jouira seule, dans notre royaume, des droits et des honneurs du culte public, tandisque nos sujets non catholiques , . . . ne tiendront de la loi que ce que le droit naturel ne nous permet pas de leur refuser, de faire constater leurs naissances, leurs mariages et leur morts, afin de jouir, comme tous nos autres sujets, des effets civils qui en résultent." France, *Recueil général des anciennes lois* N° 245, "l'Edit concernant ceux qui ne font pas profession de la religion catholique," pp. 472–73.

[3]For example, article 2: "Pourront en conséquence ceux de nos sujets ou étrangers domicilés dans notre royaume, qui ne seroient pas de la religion catholique, . . ." *Ibid.*, p. 474.

[4]"N'entendons néanmoins que ceux qui professent une religion différente de la religion catholique, puissent se regarder comme formant dans notre royaume un corps, une communauté ou une société particulière, ni qu'ils puissent, à ce titre, former en nom collectif aucune demande, donner aucune procuration, prendre aucune délibération, faire aucune acquisition ni aucun autre acte quelconque." *Ibid.*

[5]Zosa Szajkowski, "Protestants and Jews of France in Fight for Emancipation," *Proceedings of the American Academy for Jewish Research,* XXV (1956), p. 123.

[6]Malvezin, *Histoire des Juifs,* p. 244.

[7]*Ibid.*, pp. 247–8.

[8]*Ibid.*, p. 247.

[9]See p. 28 for the details of Article 3.

[10]Malvezin, *Histoire des Juifs,* p. 247. Fonseca remained in Paris for only a short time. Having become ill, he left for home on May 4th, "Notes of Solomon Lopes-Dubec on the Bordeaux delegation to Paris, 1788," Jewish Historical General Archives, Jerusalem, Zf3.

[11]After the dissolution of the *nation,* however, Furtado would emerge as an influential spokesman for the Sephardic Jews. As we shall see, Furtado's personal convictions and influence would help to define the course of French Jewish history.

[12]"Journal of the Bordeaux Jewish Commission in Paris, 1788," Jewish Historical General Archives, Jerusalem, Zf1. This journal appears to have been written by Furtado.

[13]*Ibid.*

[14]"Et sans avouer ouvertement, dans les conversations que vous aurez avec lui la différence qui existe entre leurs moeurs et les nôtres, pour ne pas trop les déprécier, ni convenir qu'il y en ait aucun dans le dogme religieux, vous pouvez représenter qu'ils le surchargent de beaucoup de cérémonies ridicules, d'idées rabbiniques, et qu'ils sont en quelque manière tellement asservis à toutes sortes de superstitions ou de bigoterie, que cela les a encore rabaissés à nos yeux au point de ne nous être jamais permis avec eux d'alliances sous les liens du mariage." Malvezin, *Histoire des Juifs,* pp. 251–2.

[15]"Mémoire présenté par MM Lopes-Dubec père et Furtado aîné."

[16]*Ibid.*, pp. 17–18. How clearly this foreshadows statements made almost a

century later by Eastern European *maskilim*.

[17]*Ibid.*, p. 25. To Joseph II of Austria, the determination to centralize his realm transcended any concern he might have had for the retention of the privileges of either the nobles or the Church. He demanded rather that all his subjects be equally productive regardless of religious opinions or influential status. Thus monasteries and convents were destroyed, the Church was forced to renounce its connection with brethren in other countries, serfdom was abolished, property distinctions were removed, universal, gratuitous, and compulsory education was established, and conscription was made a universal liability. James F. Bright, *Joseph II* (London: Macmillan Company, 1897), Chapter VI.

The Jews were not to be excluded from this attempt to create a modern, secular nation-state. They were permitted to learn handicrafts, arts, and sciences and without restrictions to devote themselves to agriculture. The doors of the universities and academies were opened to them, Jewish primary and high schools were to be established, and adults were required to learn the language of the country. The body tax, *leibzoll*, was abolished as were special law taxes, passport duties, night duties, and other similar imposts. That Joseph did not intend to concede complete citizenship to the Jews, however, was clear. They were still forbidden to reside in those towns from which they had been banished previously, and they were allowed to dwell in Vienna only in a few exceptional cases, and with the payment of protection money.

[18]For example, concerning the *Lettres Patentes* of 1550, the authors stated that the king avoided designating the Portuguese and Spanish as Jews because of the feared repercussions on the part of the populace. In discussing the *Lettres Patentes* of 1723, Furtado and Lopes-Dubec omitted mentioning the money paid for these privileges and overlooked the fact that this was the first time the Portuguese were officially recognized as Jews. In addition, no mention was made of those times when the government leaned towards negating the privileges of the *nation*.

[19]"Mémoire présenté par MM Lopes-Dubec père et Furtado aîné," p. 113.

[20]*Ibid.*, p. 132.

[21]*Ibid.*, p. 134.

[22]*Ibid.*, p. 135.

[23]*Ibid.*

[24]*Ibid.*, p. 136.

[25]*Ibid.*, pp. 139–40.

[26]*Ibid.*, pp. 141–2.

[27]*Ibid.*, p. 142.

[28]*Ibid.*, p. 144.

[29]*Ibid.*, pp. 145–51.

[30]*Ibid.*, pp. 146–7.

[31]"Notes of Solomon Lopes-Dubec on the Bordeaux delegation to Paris, 1788."

[32]Szajkowski, "Protestants and Jews of France," pp. 120–21, footnote 5. This is taken from the "Second mémoire sur le mariage des Protestants," which Malesherbes wrote in 1787.

[33]*Ibid.*, p. 120. "Malesherbes' main reason for adopting a more favorable attitude towards the Jews was his conviction that such a change would contribute greatly toward the conversion of the Jews." Hertzberg, p. 323, has this to say: "His [Malesherbes] main reason for wanting some reform and kinder treatment of the Jews was that it would lead to their conversion; he was utterly opposed to the organized Jewish community."

Szajkowski and Hertzberg therefore limit Malesherbes' solution to one of anticipated Christianization. Although Hertzberg is correct in stating that Malesherbes was opposed to the organized Jewish community, this does not, as he implies, necessitate a conversionist policy.

Hopefully access will soon be gained to those papers of Malesherbes still withheld from the public. Then perhaps these questions can be answered more satisfactorily. For a somewhat general discussion of Malesherbes and his views on religious tolerance and religious separatism, see John M. J. Allison, *Malesherbes* (New Haven: Yale University Press, 1938).

[34]"L'édit concernant ceux qui ne font pas," pp. 472–73.

[35]"Journal of the Bordeaux Jewish Commisssion in Paris, 1788."

[36]Pierre Grosclaude, *Malesherbes, témoin et interprète de son temps* (Paris: Librairie Fischbacher, n.d.), pp. 642–43. Most of this comes from a letter written by Malesherbes to Mulinen, Councilor of State and Treasurer of Finances of the Republic of Berne.

[37]Jacob Katz has provided us with an excellent study of the terms 'nation-within-a-nation' and 'state-within-a-state' as they applied both to Jewish and non-Jewish groups. Although Katz did not mention Malesherbes or his use of the phrase *imperium in imperiis*, it is clear that Malesherbes belonged with those Frenchmen who at the end of the century began to question whether the Jews were really able to enter society. "In other words, were they prepared and fit to cast off their separate traditions and to merge with the surrounding society, or would they forever remain a religious, social, and ethnic entity, a state within a state, or, in the variation which began to appear at that time, a nation within a nation." Jacob Katz, "A State Within a State," *Proceedings of the Israel Academy of Sciences and Humanities,* vol. IV, N° 3, p. 44

[38]Dohm, a German, stood alone, except for Mirabeau, who merely translated Dohm's proposals into French, in advocating that Jewish communal organization be retained, that the rabbis continue to exercise the power of excommunication, and that the Jews be permitted to live and be judged according to their laws. For him, the Jews had already proven in the past that they were capable of being useful members of society. Their oppression by others was responsible for their present condition, and this condition could and must be altered. Dohm's plan was to permit and to convince the Jews, sometimes by discriminatory legislation in their favor, to participate freely in all areas of society, except that of public office. Christian Wilhelm Dohm, *Über die bürgerliche Verbesserung der Juden* (Berlin and Stettin: Friedrich Nicolai, 1781). Dohm's proposals concerning the retention of communal autonomy and the authority of the rabbis were contrary to what Mendelssohn proposed. This is perhaps because Dohm was responding to what the Jews of the Northeast most desired.

For Roederer, the chairman of a meeting of the Royal Society of Sciences and Arts of Metz which was considering whether or not there were means of making the Jews more useful and happy in France, the problem was more complex than others were willing to acknowledge. He asked questions which were basic to Jewish reform, namely, if the changes proposed were able to coexist with the religious and political laws of the Jews, and if a revolution in their political constitution would do away with what he considered to be praiseworthy in that constitution. Roederer did not subscribe to the theory that the culture of the Jews was necessarily inferior to that which they would be given by assimilation into the Gentile society—a theory which reflected the subtle influence of Deism and of *philosophes* such as Voltaire; he did accept, nevertheless, the dissolution of communal autonomy as necessary for the betterment of the Jews. Abraham Cahen, "L'émancipation des Juifs devant la société royale des sciences et des arts de Metz en 1787 et M. Roederer," *Revue des études juives*, I (1880), pp. 83–104.

A more fervent and inspired spokesman for the Jews was the Abbé Grégoire, one of the three to win the prize from the Metz society. Although it has previously been alleged that Grégoire was motivated in his work on behalf of the Jews by a missionary zeal, it has been suggested that in fact he was expressing an often overlooked neo-Jansenist belief in the ultimate triumph of the Catholic church. P. Grunebaum-Ballin, "Grégoire convertisseur? ou la croyance au 'retour d'Israël,' " *Revue des études juives*, CXXI (1962), pp. 383–98. Ruth F. Necheles, *The Abbé Grégoire 1787–1831* (Connecticut: Greenwood Publishing Corporation, 1971). In the realm of eschatology Grégoire might indeed have envisioned the conversion of all Jews to a purified and humanitarian Catholicism; in the realm of contemporary secular politics, however, he was working towards reforming the Jews, opening avenues of society to them, helping them to adjust to their new occupations, and generally attempting to make them productive and happy members of society. This activity did not change his opinion of the Jews of France whom he saw as ignorant, deprived, clannish, and committed to a Talmud which reinforced all these qualities. Henri-Baptiste Grégoire, *Essai sur la régénération physique, morale et politique des juifs* (Metz: Claude Lamort, 1789).

Chapter 3

[1]Suffrage was to be almost universal. For the third estate (peasants as well as bourgeois), those males who were French citizens, living in France, over twenty-five years of age, and paying a direct tax were entitled to vote. The country clergy were included among the ecclesiastics and the smaller nobility among the nobles. Finally, Protestants were also electors and eligible. For a detailed account of the early revolutionary period and the struggles among the three estates, consult Georges Lefebvre, *The Coming of the French Revolution* (New York: Random House, 1947).

[2]The most recent of the historians to concern himself with the revolutionary period is Arthur Hertzberg in *The French Enlightenment and the Jews.* In addition to his sections on the Enlightenment, Hertzberg includes a provoca-

tive chapter on the Revolution in which he attempts to demonstrate that in relation to the Jews revolutionary liberalism was in fact often totalitarian and revolutionary radicalism often anti-Semitic.

[3]David Feuerwerker, "L'émancipation des Juifs en France," unpublished Ph. D. dissertation (Sorbonne, 1961), Ephemerides.

[4]Ibid.

[5]Ibid.

[6]"Registre des délibérations."

[7]Michel Lheritier, Les débuts de la Révolution à Bordeaux (Bordeaux: 1919), pp. 55-6.

[8]Malvezin, Histoire des Juifs, p. 253. The Sephardic Jews used this fact to further support their position during the debates in the National Assembly.

[9]France, Archives parlementaires de 1787 à 1860 (Paris: 1868), première série (1787 à 1799), Tome II, pp. 392–414. I have also spoken to a well known Bordeaux historian, Pierre Bécamps, who states that he has found nothing concerning the Jews in the unprinted cahiers.

[10]Ibid., p. 393, number 24.

[11]Michel Lheritier, La Révolution à Bordeaux dans l'histoire de la Révolution française (Paris: Presses Universitaires de France, 1942), pp. 266-7.

[12]Maurice Liber, "Les Juifs et la convocation des Etats Généraux," Revue des études juives, LXIV (1912), pp. 255-61.

[13]Ibid., pp. 261-66.

[14]Ibid., LXV (1913), pp. 99-133.

[15]This was hardly coincidental since Dohm had written his pamphlet with the Ashkenazic Jews in mind. It is significant, however, that the Ashkenazim were asking to be taxed as part of the general population. Never having had to pay burdensome sums for protection, the Sephardim chose to retain their corporate status in areas of taxation.

[16]Zosa Szajkowski has written some important monographs on the pre-revolutionary situation of the Jews of Northeastern France. Consult: Autonomy and Jewish Communal Debts During the French Revolution of 1789 (New York: 1959). The Economic Status of the Jews in Alsace, Metz and Lorraine (New York: 1954). "Relations among Sephardim, Ashkenazim and Avignonese Jews in France from the 16th to the 20th Centuries," YIVO Annual, X (1955), 165–96.

[17]Archives départementales de la Gironde, Série I. Hourwitz, a Polish Jew, was a pariah within the Ashkenazic community. He fought frequently for the abrogation of communal control over the lives of the Jews and expressed a biting hatred for the pervasive influence of the rabbis. For a description of the taxpaying procedures of the nation, see Chapter I, note 65.

[18]The late Grand Rabbi of Bordeaux, Joseph Cohen, was kind enough to let the author have a copy of this letter.

[19]Malvezin, Histoire des Juifs, p. 254.

[20]It had been understood that when the Constitution was finished, the Declaration would be reviewed and completed. Lefebvre, p. 147.

[21]After August 1789 it was no longer a question of amelioration or reform. Instead we have the struggle for emancipation based on programmatic

ideological grounds and implying that natural rights had been withheld from the Jews.

[22]Bibliothèque Nationale, Ld[18]429. The address was signed by Furtado l'aîné, Azevedo, David Gradis électeur, Lopes-Dubec.

[23]Maurice Liber, "Les Juifs et la convocation," LXVI (1913), pp. 186–96.

[24]Hertzberg, p. 348, quotes a letter from Berr Isaac Berr written in the spring of 1790 in which he refuted the speech made by De la Fare, Bishop of Nancy. Berr made an offer in which the Assembly would give the Ashkenazim all rights with the exception of the right to hold public office and the Jews on their part would retain their full internal autonomy.

The issue of communal autonomy not only would become a major threat to Jewish emancipation, but also would succeed in dividing the Ashkenazic community. Many of the younger Jews began to regard Berr Isaac Berr's proposals with the same annoyance as did the Sephardim.

[25]Legally, the Parisian Jewish community did not exist, but in fact on the eve of the Revolution there was a significant number of Ashkenazic, Sephardic, Avignonese, and Comtadin Jews living in Paris. This mixed community differed from the other centers of French Jewish life both in its heterogeneous composition and in its lack of communal organization. These two major differences produced a more liberal community and made possible both an awareness of the social and political developments in France during the Revolution and a desire to participate in them.

[26]Liber, "Les Juifs et la convocation," LXVI (1913), p. 184.

[27]A description of the involvement of some Sephardic leaders in the municipal affairs of Bordeaux may be found in Zosa Szajkowski, "The Sephardic Jews of France During the Revolution of 1789," *Proceedings of the American Academy for Jewish Research*, XXIV (1955), pp. 137–64.

[28]Archives départementales de la Gironde, C4438.

[29]This aspect of similarity between the bourgeois values of the *nation* and those of the early revolutionaries should be taken into account, for emancipation was primarily a bourgeois phenomenon.

[30]Michel Lheritier, *Les débuts de la Révolution à Bordeaux*, (Bordeaux: 1919), p. 82.

[31]Here we see a further extension of Malesherbes' *Imperium in Imperiis*. The Jews are no longer one among many corporate groups; on the contrary, they have become the only subgroup whose corporateness creates an unbreachable barrier between them and the rest of the population of France.

[32]Malvezin, *Histoire des Juifs*, p. 258.

[33]Feuerwerker, volume III, p. 230.

[34]*Ibid.*, volume I, p. 157.

[35]"M. Furtado l'aîné qui avoit été aussi nommé Député n'a pas accepté." "Registre des délibérations." Contrary to what some historians have maintained (Hertzberg, p. 326), Furtado did not accompany the others.

By including Salom among the deputies, the *nation* was confirming that the Avignonese and Portuguese Jews were in fact united. This union was to endure and both groups worked together in the philanthropic society which replaced the dissolved *nation*.

[36]"Journal of the Bordeaux Jewish delegation to Paris, 1790," Jewish Historical General Archives, Jerusalem, Zf6.

[37]*Ibid.*

[38]*Ibid.*

[39]Although the petition is dated December 31, it appears that the deputies wrote it and sent it to Bordeaux for approval subsequent to their journey to Paris. "Quant à l'adresse à présenter, celle qui a été envoyée à Bordeaux, de l'avis de tous ceux à qui nous l'avons communiquée et de M. Garat lui même est parfaitement conforme aux circonstances, nous allons donc la faire imprimer." *Ibid.*

[40]*Adresse à l'Assemblée Nationale,* Archives municipales de Bordeaux, P 8.

[41]*Ibid.*

[42]*Ibid.*

[43]Bibliothèque Nationale, In 8° Ld[18]450.

[44]"Journal of the Bordeaux Jewish delegation to Paris, 1790."

[45]*Ibid.*

[46]Of course it was assumed that the Bordelais Jews would have to meet the conditions applicable to all the other citizens.

[47]Feuerwerker, volume III, pp. 287–8.

[48]Reprinted in *L'Assemblée Nationale Constituante,* (Paris: Editions d'Histoire Sociale, 1968), pp. 1–2. Many historians have mistakenly assumed that this included the Jews of Avignon and the rest of the papal provinces.

[49]*Gazette Nationale,* ou *Le Moniteur Universel* N° 42 (Jeudi, Février, 1790). Archives municipales de Bordeaux.

"M. Garat l'aîné. Un courrier extraordinaire, arrivé hier de Bordeaux, m'a apporté une lettre dont je demande la permission de vous faire lecture. Cette lettre porte que, 'le lundi, après l'arrivée du décret rendu par l'Assemblée nationale, quelques jeunes gens formèrent à la bourse de Bordeaux une cabale contre les Juifs; que cette cabale se manifesta aux spectacles le soir du même jour, mais que tous ces désagréments finirent là.' "

" 'Les Juifs eurent la satisfaction de recevoir le lendemain des excuses de quelques-uns de leurs ennemis, et l'expression de l'interêt que mille autres citoyens avaient pris à leur peine.' "

[50]On August 4, 1789, the clergy had renounced their tithes and dues. On November 2, 1789, the Assembly decreed that all Church property was at the disposal of the nation. Land and buildings were to be sold by auction, and liabilities were assumed to be taken over by the state. It was not until October, 1790, however, that the National Assembly dissolved the corporations, including religious communities. Their debts were assumed by the government by the decrees of June 14 and July 30, 1791 and by the law of August 15, 1793. Szajkowski, *Autonomy and Jewish Communal Debts.*

[51]Jacques Godard, *Discours prononcé le 28 Janvier 1790 par M. Godard, Avocat au Parlement,* p. 5, Bibliothèque de la ville de Bordeaux. The estimated Jewish population of France during the Revolution is about 40,000.

[52]*Petition des Juifs établis en France adressée à L'Assemblée Nationale le 28 janvier 1790 sur l'ajournement du 24 décembre.* Reprinted in full in Feuerwerker, volume III, pp. 292–351.

[53]*Ibid.*, p. 336.

[54]*Ibid.*, p. 304.

[55]Malvezin, *Histoire des Juifs*, pp. 263–4.

[56]Reprinted in *L'Assemblée Nationale Constituante*, (Paris: Editions d'Histoire Sociale, 1968), pp. 1–2.

[57]The law of September 27, 1791, also included the Jews living in Avignon and Comtat Venaissin, for these provinces had sought and attained incorporation into France on September 14, 1791. The Jews of these provinces, however, had been emancipated previously by the provinces themselves and thus were enjoying civil rights before they were recognized legally as French citizens. H. Chobaut, "Les Juifs d'Avignon et du Comtat et la Révolution française," *Revue des études juives*, 101 (1937), pp. 5–52; 102 (1937), pp. 3–39.

[58]Zosa Szajkowski, "French Jews in the Armed Forces During the Revolution of 1789," *Proceedings of the American Academy for Jewish Research*, XXVI (1957), pp. 139–60.

[59]Zosa Szajowski, "Jewish Emigrés During the French Revolution," *Jewish Social Studies*, XVI (1954), pp. 319–34.

[60]Laumond, the first prefect of the Bas-Rhin in the year X of the new regime, discussed the Jews in his "Statistique du département du Bas-Rhin." When asked if the hatred towards the Jews had abated, Laumond answered: "En considérant cette question en général, on pourrait dire *non*. Comme ils n'ont rien changé à leur genre de commerce . . . il n'y a pas de raison suffisante pour qu'ils soient plus aimés; mais il y a peut-être plus de justice distributive à leur égard qu'auparavant. On ne confond pas tous les Juifs dans la même catégorie, et *le respect public accompagne ceux en petit numbre, qui s'en rendent dignes*. . . . Les Juifs ne sont point aimés parce qu'ils ne sont point aimables; qu'ils le deviennent et les dispositions changeront." Rod. Reuss, "Quelques documents nouveaux sur l'antisémitisme dans le Bas-Rhin de 1794–1799," *Revue des études juives*, 59 (1910), pp. 275–6.

[61]Bordeaux, *Documents de la période révolutionnaire*, $\frac{8}{L19}$, $\frac{8}{L20}$, $\frac{8}{L21}$, $\frac{8}{L22}$, Archives municipales de Bordeaux.

[62]Many Jews of Bordeaux lived in the Rue Bouhaut and Rue du Coheran district.

[63]Marcel Marion, "Du rôle des Juifs dans la vente des biens nationaux dans la Gironde," *Actes de l'académie nationale des sciences, belles-lettres et arts de Bordeaux*, 3ᵉ série (1908), pp. 5–19.

[64]Bordeaux, *Documents de la période révolutionnaire*, $\frac{8}{L20}$, volume II, D 129, "Registre des arrêts du Bureau municipal, An II."

[65]"Les Juifs sont ceux que la Révolution a le plus favorisés. Cependant, cette nation, au lieu de contribuer au bonheur de la République et à la tranquillité de la citée, cherchent au contraire à mettre la désolation parmy les citoyens. . . . Ce même membre observe qu'il a vu des Juifs dans la Rouselle aller de magazin en magazin pour acheter d'huiles, c'est ce qui a fait hosser à prix exorbitant dans cy peu de jours toutes ces denrées." Bordeaux, *Documents de la période révolutionnaire*, $\frac{8}{L22}$, volume IV, 165, number 23, "Extrait des registres de Délibérations de la Section des Hommes Libres."

[66]Pierre Bécamps, "Les relations avec les neutres au temps de la Révolution:

l'agence commerciale de Bordeaux," *Revue historique de Bordeaux,* IV (1955), p. 314.

Despite the accomplishments of the commercial agency and the subsequent attempts by many Bordelais, including the Gradis family and Lopes-Dubec, to develop more sophisticated banking and credit institutions, the old commercial splendor of Bordeaux was never restored. Le Havre replaced Bordeaux as an important port, England assumed the role of supplying the Northern European countries, and the protectionist policies of post-Napoleonic France favored the development of industry at the expense of commerce.

[67]A peddler, Azevedo, played a prominent role in the departmental surveillance committee and in July, 1794, was named first deputy to the city council. Shortly thereafter Azevedo was among those chosen to form a military commission to judge Lacombe, President of the infamous Revolutionary Tribunal. "Arrêté du représentant du peuple, délegué par la Convention Nationale, dans les départements du Bec-d'Ambès et de Lot et Garonne, en séance à Bordeaux, du 26 Thermidor, an 2 de la République française une et indivisible," Jewish Theological Seminary, New York.

Markedly different from the atmosphere in Bordeaux and the Popular Commission was the *Société Montagnarde et Régénérée des Amis de la Constitution de 1793* of Saint-Esprit-de-Bayonne,one of the two Jacobin strongholds of the entire department of the Landes. This society, composed almost exclusively of Jews (Fonseca neveu was President, JDJ Pereire and Nunes Hananel were Secretaries) took the initiative in installing the cult of Reason in Jean Jacques Rousseau (St. Esprit). Leon, p. 164.

For the Jews of Saint-Esprit, there was far more to be gained by identifying themselves with the Jacobin cause, which might both alleviate their past difficulties and finally permit an acceptance comparable to that achieved by the Bordelais Jews.

[68]In a monograph on the Jews of Bordeaux, written for a series of studies on the Bordelais population, we find the following: "Mais comme le culte n'était pas encore officiellement organisé en harmonie avec la nouvelle situation faite à la communauté de Bordeaux, et qu'on ne pouvait pas la laisser absolument sans direction, il se forma une administration sous le nom de *Société de Bienfaisance,* qui s'occupa des affaires publiques jusqu'au 13 avril, 1809, époque à laquelle fut institué le *Consistoire israélite de Bordeaux." Monographie du culte israélite à Bordeaux* (Bordeaux: G. Gounouilhon Imprimeur, 1892), p. 10.

[69]See note 35.

[70]Michel Lheritier, *Liberté (1789–1790). Bordeaux et la Révolution française* (Paris: 1947), pp. 253–4.

[71]Lheritier, *La Révolution à Bordeaux dans l'histoire,* p. 43.

Little has been uncovered thus far concerning the connection between the Musée and the Masonic lodges of Bordeaux. "Nous ne pouvons également qu'évoquer ici la question des rapports entre le franc-maçonnerie et la Société du Musée, . . . Les francs-maçons y auraient été nombreux, et la devise maçonnique, 'Liberté-Egalité' devient celle du Musée." G. Hubrecht, "Notes pour servir à l'histoire de la franc-maçonnerie à Bordeaux," *Revue historique de*

Bordeaux (Janvier-Mars, 1954), p. 150, footnote 33.

Freemasonry flourished in Bordeaux during the last twenty years of the *ancien régime* and again during the First Empire. The masons devoted themselves to banquets and philanthropy, but political concerns were not totally lacking, and the lodges took the initiative in public festivities. Although the Freemasons were not revolutionary before 1788, they were influential in popularizing the ideals of Liberty, Equality, and Fraternity and the practices of meeting in assemblies, balloting, and organizing orders of the day. In addition, many masons were involved in editing the *cahiers de doléance* and some were chosen as deputies to the Estates General. The lodges, some of which refused to admit Jews and actors, did not lose their Christian character until after the Revolution. "Par ailleurs, tout en cultivant la tolérance, les loges demeuraient sur le plan chrétien; elles célébraient la Saint-Jean, se plaçaient parfois sous le patronage de saints, se rendaient en corps à messes telles que celle célébrée à l'occasion du retour du Parlement." *Ibid.*, p. 149

[72]*Le Musée aux citoyens de Bordeaux*, 1791, p. 14, Archives municipales de Bordeaux, R 6.

[73]"Registre des délibérations du Bureau municipal," *Documents de la période révolutionnaire*, $\frac{8}{L20}$, D 102.

[74]"Registre des délibérations du Bureau municipal," *Documents de la période révolutionnaire*, $\frac{8}{L19}$, number 97; $\frac{8}{L20}$, D 123; $\frac{8}{L20}$, D 102.

Among Furtado's activities were the overseeing and verifying of pharmaceutical patents.

[75]*Documents de la période révolutionnaire*, $\frac{8}{L22}$, 165. This is a report in Furtado's own handwriting of the details of the search.

[76]Abraham Furtado, "Folie de jeunesse." This manuscript, which is incomplete (one-hundred and twenty pages), is in the private possession of Pascal Thémanlys. The title which Furtado has given this manuscript is interesting. Perhaps he decided to call it *Folie de jeunesse* only after rereading it a few years later and realizing the inadequacy of his thinking. Another possibility, however, is that the *Folie* is not the author's but rather that of society, for according to Furtado, religion had prolonged "l'enfance du genre humain." Although the *Folie* is undated, Furtado's mood, assumptions, intellectual companions, and direct references indicate that it was written sometime during 1791.

[77]*Ibid.*, p. 90.

[78]"Ces idées de réprobation, de damnation éternelle que l'on attache à toute autre croyance que la sienne rendent, si l'on peut s'exprimer ainsi, le genre humain étranger à lui-même . . . . La morale prescrit la justice, l'indulgence, l'égalité, l'exercice ou la pratique de tous les devoirs sociaux envers tous les hommes indistinctement, et sur tous ces objets, les religions ont consacré les plus monstrueuses différences." *Ibid.*, pp. 24–6.

[79]*Ibid.*, p. 57.

[80]On June 9, 1793, seven days after the proscription of 29 deputies from the National Convention, Furtado, as one of 9 "commissaires du conseil général de la commune de Bordeaux" and Lopes-Dubec, one of two "membres du tribunal de commerce de Bordeaux" were among those Bordelais who joined

together to form the *commission populaire de salut public*. *Commission Populaire de Salut Public* (Bordeaux: A. Levieux), Jewish Theological Seminary, New York.

On June 10, the *commission* decided on the actions which it would take. A departmental army of about 1200 men would be equipped and kept in reserve to obey orders. Emissaries would be sent to other departments to propose that they take similar measures, and finally the various detachments would march on Paris where they would protect the liberty of discussion of the Convention and the persons of its members.

[81]For a detailed account of Furtado during the Revolution, see Frances Malino, " 'Mémoires d'un Patriote Proscrit' by Abraham Furtado," in *Michael, IV* (Tel Aviv: Diaspora Research Institute, 1976).

[82]Szajkowski, *Autonomy and Jewish Communal Debts*, p. 46, note 119.

[83]*Ibid.*, pp. 73–4, 127–30.

[84]*Mémoire à consulter et consultation*, reprinted in full in Beaufleury, pp. 161–195. *Mémoire pour les citoyens Despiau et Pujos, de Bordeaux*, Archives municipales de Bordeaux, p. 8.

[85]A corporation, the two men wrote, "étoit une assemblée de plusieurs personnes unies en corps, établie et formée par l'ordre ou par la permission du prince. Ceux qui ont permission de former un corps ou communauté, ont aussi leurs droits, leurs affaires, auxquelles ne pouvant vaquer tous ensemble, ils peuvent y préposer des personnes qui en prennent soin, sous la dénomination de syndics, . . ." *Mémoire pour les citoyens*, p. 21.

[86]Markedly different from the definition offered by Despiau and Pujos was the declaration by the Bordelais Jews that a corporation was "une réunion d'hommes exerçant un même art ou une même profession; que pour y aspirer il fallait passer par les épreuves de l'apprentissage, et que pour y être reçu il falloit subir un examen, pour exercer une profession, et faire ce qu'on nommoit le chef-d'oeuvre pour exercer un art ou métier; . . ." *Mémoire à consulter*, p. 183.

One cannot help but feel that despite some real confusion in accurately defining the status of the *nation*, the Sephardim could and would have defended their existence as a corporation had it been advantageous to do so.

Chapter 4

[1]Louis Madelin, "Napoleon," in *The European Past*, vol. I (New York: Macmillan, 1970), p. 432.

[2]Malvezin, *Histoire des Juifs*, p. 276.

[3]*Ibid.*, pp. 274–81. Although the Sephardim had long since ceased to practice polygamy, they did differ from the French both in the form and justification for divorce as well as the conditions required for validating marriage. As in the past, they followed French law in all matters of inheritance.

[4]Berr Isaac Berr, *Lettre . . . à M. Grégoire*, p. 22.

[5]On September 4, 1802, a prefect described to Portalis the situation among the Jews of Meurthe: "Les uns cherchent à maintenir les règlements de discipline tant religieuse que civile qui existaient entre eux et que l'ancien

gouvernement avait même consacrés. Les autres ne voyant dans une partie des mêmes règlements qu'un joug insupportable appesanti arbitrairement sur eux par quelques familles ou par quelques individus ont fait constamment leurs efforts pour s'y soustraire." Robert Anchel, *Napoléon et les Juifs* (Paris: Presses Universitaires de France, 1928), pp. 45–6.

[6]*Ibid.*, p. 42.

[7]*Ibid.*, pp. 66–7.

[8]*Ibid.*, p. 76. The civil code had not established any legal rate of interest, but rather relied on the acceptable and going rate. Not until September 3, 1807 (fifteen months after the May 30th decree) was the legal rate of interest set at no more than 5% in private credit and 6% in commercial credit. Penalties were provided for not observing the legal rate.

[9]In a manuscript entitled "Petition à Sa Majesté l'Empereur et Roi" written by the Ashkenazic Jews in response to the May 30th decree, we find the following: "Lorsque votre Majesté elle-même est venue dans le Bas-Rhin, et que dans le peu de journées qu'elle y a passé, . . ." Archives départementales de la Gironde, Série I.

[10]Robert Anchel, *Les Juifs de France* (Paris: 1946), p. 240.

[11]Louis Gabriel Bonald, "Sur les Juifs," *Mercure de France*, February 8, 1806, pp. 249–67. "Les Juifs ne peuvent pas être et même quoi qu'on fasse, ne seront jamais citoyens sous le Christianisme sans devenir Chrétiens."

[12]Henri Grégoire, *Observations nouvelles sur les Juifs et spécialement sur ceux d'Allemagne*, Bibliothèque Nationale, Ld[18]465.

Moyse P[xxxxx], *Réponse à un article sur les Juifs de M. de Bonald* (Bordeaux, 1806). In this pamphlet, published throughout France, Moyse Peixotto? refers to Mendelssohn to combat the injustices of Bonald's thesis.

In the Fonds de Cardozo de Bethencourt, p. 1491, Cardozo states that "Furtado a fait une réponse en 1806 à un article sur les Juifs par M. Bonald qui fut inséré dans le Mercure du 8 février 1806. Sa réponse à M. Bonald ne fut point imprimée ayant été trouvée trop hardie." We were unable to locate this unpublished pamphlet.

[13]Israel Lévi, "Napoléon 1er et la réunion du Grand Sanhedrin," *Revue des études juives*, XXVIII (1894), p. 270, note 2 ("Mémoires of the Baron de Barante," member of the Council of State).

Throughout all the discussions concerning the decree of 1806 and that of 1808, the Council of State tended to liberalize the proposals of Napoleon and his sympathetic auditor, Molé.

[14]Maurice Liber, "Napoléon et les Juifs," *Revue des études juives*, 72 (1921), pp. 7–10; 14–15.

[15]M. Beugnot described the measures to be taken against the Jews as "une bataille perdue dans les champs de la justice." Lévi, "Napoléon 1er", p. 270, note 2.

[16]Liber, "Napoléon," p. 18.

[17]*Ibid.*, pp. 21–23.

[18]Anchel, *Napoléon*, pp. 96–97. Ellis Rivkin (ed.), *Readings in Modern Jewish History* (Cincinnati: Hebrew Union College — Jewish Institute of Religion, 1957), Document I–A.

[19]*Ibid.*

[20]Archives Nationales, AF^{IV}pl, 1403, n° 6.

[21]Lévi, "Napoléon 1er," p. 273 (extrait des mémoires du Chancelier Pasquier).

[22]It would be Molé, often in conflict with the other two commissioners, who communicated to the Assembly both the wishes and biases of Napoleon. "Les rôles entre les Commissaires restèrent distribués comme ils l'avaient été précédemnent: M. Molé, toujours menaçant; M. Portalis et moi, nous efforçant de ramener, par des formes plus conciliantes, les esprits que notre impétueux collègue ne cessait de cablcr." *Ibid.*, p. 275 (extrait des mémoires du Chancelier Pasquier).

[23]Anchel, *Les Juifs de France*, p. 244.

[24]Anchel, *Napoléon*, p. 130. Surprisingly, M. Fauchet, prefect of the Gironde, subsequently attempted in vain to increase from two to four the number of deputies he was to select. Malvezin, *Histoire des Juifs*, p. 284.

[25]Malvezin, p. 285.

[26]*Ibid.*, pp. 285–6.

[27]*Ibid.*, p. 286.

[28]*Ibid.*, p. 288.

[29]Abraham Furtado, "Mémoire d'Abraham Furtado sur l'état des Juifs en France jusqu'à la Révolution," Pascal Thémanlys, Jerusalem. A printed edition, edited by Gabrielle Moyse (Paris: Librairie Durlacher), can be found in the Brandeis Library. The page numbers quoted will be those of the printed edition.

Arthur Hertzberg, p. 327, note 17, mistakenly equated this *mémoire* with the one prepared for the Malesherbes Commission. In addition to the omissions from and additions to the Malesherbes *mémoire* is the following statement, which leaves no doubt that Furtado wrote this second mémoire after the Revolution. "L'ancien gouvernement éclairé sur tout ce que tenoit aux habitudes aux opinions, aux moeurs, aux occupations, à la croyance des Juifs, allait rendre un édit en leur faveur. Si l'ouragan révolutionnaire n'eut pas éclaté, on aurait vu Louis XVI et son conseil faire pour les Juifs français autant et peut-être mieux que n'a fait l'Assemblée Constituante." Furtado, *Mémoire*, p. 40.

Gabrielle Moyse has suggested that Furtado prepared his report to present to the Imperial Commissioners who were communicating with the Assembly of Notables; "Ce rapport a peut-être été présenté aux délégués de l'Empereur communicant avec l'Assemblée des Notables israélites que Furtado présidait." Mrs. Moyse did not indicate her reasons for this conclusion.

Although the *mémoire* may have been written during the sessions of the Assembly of Notables, we cannot overlook the fact that it was almost a *verbatim* repetition of the 1788 *mémoire*, that it was written not only with an intention to defend the perfectibility of the Jews but also with a desire to instruct those who were ignorant of French Jewish history, and finally that, after July 15, Furtado himself was in daily contact with the representatives of the Emperor and therefore less likely to have occupied himself with a work of this type. Hence, the period during which the Ministers were obtaining information concerning the Jews and while Furtado was still in Bordeaux appears to be a more natural time for the *mémoire* to have been composed.

[30]Furtado, *Mémoire . . . sur l'état des Juifs,* p. 4.

[31]*Ibid.,* p. 40.

[32]*Ibid.,* p. 41.

[33]*Ibid.,* p. 45.

[34]*Ibid.,* p. 46.

[35]*Ibid.*

[36]*Ibid.,*p. 47.

[37]Lévi, "Napoléon 1er," p. 273 (extrait des mémoires du Chancelier Pasquier).

[38]Anchel, *Les Juifs,* p. 246.

[39]Pasquier wrote: "Il fut bientôt avéré les Juifs portugais étaient suspects à tous leurs coreligionnaires, qui les considéraient comme des apostats. Le président Furtado était plus qu'un autre en butte aux soupçons. On semblait croire qu'il ne tenait à sa religion que par ce sentiment de respect humain qui ne permet d'abandonner celle où l'on est né que dans le cas où l'on serait entraîné par la plus forte des convictions. Or, telle n'était pas la disposition d'esprit de M. Furtado, l'indifférence philosophique faisait le fondement de ses opinions. Les rabbins d'Alsace et ceux de l'ancien comtat d'Avignon, aux quels appartenait le premier rang pour la science, disaient de leur président qu'on voyait bien qu'il n'avait appris la Bible que dans Voltaire." Lévi, "Napoléon 1er," pp. 273–4 (Extrait des mémoires du Chancelier Pasquier).

[40]*Procès-Verbal des séances de l'Assemblée des Députés français professant la religion juive; imprimé d'après le manuscript communiqué par M. le Président* (Paris: Desenne, 1806). Curiously this volume, found in the private possession of Pascal Thémanlys, Jerusalem, includes the minutes of the Sanhedrin. Thus the publication date must be inaccurate. What is most probable is that the edition of 1806 was republished to include the decisions of the Sanhedrin.

Other editions include: Diogène Tama, *Collection des écrits et des actes relatifs au dernier état des individus professant la religion hébraique* (Paris: 1806); Id., *L'organisation civile et religieuse des Israélites* (Treultel et Wurtz, 1808); S. Romanelli, *Raccolta di inni ed ode de parechi Rabbini dell'Assemblea degli Ebrei e del Gran Sinedrio* (Mantua, 1807).

[41]Carmi, in his letters to his community concerning the progress of the Assembly, accused Furtado of modifying certain decisions (Anchel, *Napoléon,* p. 160, note 5). This accusation seems probable, since Furtado kept a close eye on the secretaries who were keeping the minutes and in addition reviewed them with the Imperial Commissioners before they were published. Most of the letters from the Commissioners to Furtado, of which there are about fifty extant, are brief and merely designate the time and place for their next meeting. One such letter, however, dated March 1, 1807 from Molé stated: "La rédaction dont vous me parlez Monsieur est celle qui a été approuvé par mes collègues et moi." Pascal Thémanlys, Jerusalem.

We have located two manuscripts, one a draft, in Furtado's hand, of the answers to the 11th and 12th questions (Thémanlys, Jerusalem), and the other the *Procès-Verbal* of the Assembly (Archives départementales de la Gironde,

3JI). We have found in the former a significant difference in both form and emphasis from the printed edition and in the latter only stylistic changes, also made by Furtado. An example of these changes may be seen in the copy of the August 12th meeting of the Assembly: "Un membre observe que le mot n'eut exclusivement applicable

pas ~~du-tout-exclusif~~ aux coreligionnaires. Il cite le chap: 29 v:4 de la est pris dans le sens plus général d'ami."

Genèse ou le mot ~~generique signifie~~ ami."

[42]Although the authorship of the questions is unknown, Napoleon probably gave this task to Molé.

[43]*Procès-Verbal.*   [44]*Ibid.*

[45]*Ibid.*   [46]*Ibid.*

[47]*Ibid.*   [48]*Ibid.*

[49]*Ibid.*   [50]*Ibid.*

[51]Also on August 12, some deputies expressed their opposition to including in the minutes the remarks made on the differences between German and Portuguese Jews (in the draft answer to the fourth question). Furtado declared that the minutes must take notice of whatever was said in the Assembly, and put the minutes to the vote. They were adopted by the majority.

[52]*Procès-Verbal.*

[53]*Ibid.*

[54]*Ibid.*

[55]Jacob Katz, *Exclusiveness and Tolerance* (New York: Schocken Books, 1962), p. 190, has made the following statements: "The rate of interest was legally fixed in France and this applied to moneylending between Jews as well as between Jews and Gentiles. The only difference was that, when both parties concerned were Jews, religious law demanded resort to the fiction of the *hetter 'isqua*. The Jewish notables could have simply stated that, with reference to lending money, there was no real difference in the Jewish law as between Jews and non-Jews." In fact the law establishing a legal rate of interest and the penalties for not observing that rate was promulgated on September 3, 1807, one year after the discussion in the Assembly. In addition, the Jews did make it quite clear that in the practical application of their law, which explicitly prohibited lending to one's "brother," there was no difference between Jews and non-Jews.

Katz continues by characterizing the Assembly's response as an *apologia,* "a presentation not previously used by the traditional authorities."

[56]Furtado, "Draft of the answers to the 11th and 12th questions," Pascal Thémanlys, Jerusalem.

[57]More than one deputy reminded the rabbis that it was their responsibility to prevent any instance of usury.

[58]Furtado, "Draft."

[59]*Ibid.*

[60]S. Stein, "Interest Taken by Jews from Gentiles," *Journal of Semitic Studies,* I (1956), p. 161.

[61]Jacob Katz in *Exclusiveness and Tolerance,* p. 187, illustrates not only the conflicts among the deputies but also the implications of the resolutions for

future generations of Jews.

⁶²Anchel, *Napoléon*, p. 177.

⁶³*Ibid.*, p. 179.

⁶⁴For a more detailed account of these reports, see Anchel, *Ibid.*, pp. 184–6.

⁶⁵Graetz, in describing the activities of the Assembly, unequivocally attributed the preparation of the responses to the united efforts of the Commission and the Imperial Commissioners. "This Commission handed over the chief part of their work to Rabbi David Sinzheim, the most scholarly and esteemed member of the Assembly, who in a very short time completed his task to the satisfaction of his colleagues, of the Imperial Commissioners and eventually of the Emperor. (July 30-August). His report was submitted to the Commissioners who reported it to the Emperor before it was brought up for public discussion." Heinrich Graetz, *History of the Jews* (Philadelphia: Jewish Publication Society of America, 1946), vol. V, p. 490.

Despite Graetz's assertion, and although the Commissioners may have been aware of the answers proposed by the Commission of twelve, we find it highly improbable that the Assembly voted on answers already approved by the government. In fact, on July 29th, after the Imperial Commissioners had informed the Assembly of its task, Furtado had assured his colleagues that no response would be sent to Molé, Portalis, and Pasquier without prior discussion and deliberation by the Assembly. "Avant le levée de la séance, M. le président dit qu'il n'a besoin de faire observer à l'assemblée qu'aucune réponse ne sera envoyée à MM les commissaires de sa Majesté, sans que préalablement l'assemblée l'ait discutée et en ait déliberé." *Procès-Verbal.* Of course this could have been inserted in the minutes in response to the accusations by the newspapers.

⁶⁶Archives Nationales, F¹⁹11005.

⁶⁷*Ibid.*

⁶⁸*Ibid.*

⁶⁹*Ibid.*

⁷⁰This is probably a reference to Furtado's defense of the Northeastern Jews.

⁷¹*Procès-Verbal.*

⁷²In Furtado's letter to Pery on September 11, he was already aware of the plans to convene the Sanhedrin. On September 8, 1806, however, we find the following letter sent to Furtado from Molé. Obviously Furtado was informed of Napoleon's plans after September 8. "Je reçois Monsieur, la lettre que vous avez adressée à mes collegues et à moi et je m'empresse d'y répondre. Nous pensons que le désir que manifeste une partie de l'Assemblée que vous présidez pour voir renouveler son comité, ne doit vous engager à aucune démarche; et que sur cet objet comme sur tous autres vous devez attendre les nouvelles communications que nous irons faire à l'Assemblée très prochainement." Pascal Thémanlys, Jerusalem.

⁷³*Procès-Verbal.*

⁷⁴On September 30, Champagny announced to the prefects the names of rabbis recommended by the Imperial Commissioners and members of the Assembly. The prefects were permitted, however, to choose others if they wished. The prefects encountered difficulties almost immediately. In the

department of Moselle, there was no official rabbi since the death of the last rabbi of Metz. The prefect of Meurthe could only find one rabbi among those suggested. The others were either too old or incapable. By October 27, 1806, Champagny announced that although some prefects had decided to choose Jews instructed in theology rather than the rabbis (some of whom had never participated in cultural functions) recommended by the Assembly, there were still only fourteen nominations. Finally, after assuring the payment of the expenses of the rabbis by the Jewish communities, recommending yet another list of rabbis, and witnessing recriminations on the part of different groups within the Assembly, Champagny was able to announce that the Sanhedrin would convene in February. Anchel, *Napoléon*, pp. 197–201.

[75]Archives départementales de la Gironde, Série IV, J209. Pery was obviously the son of Constantin Pery, who was condemned to death by the military Commission of Bordeaux, and executed the 16th Frimaire, an II. Constantin had been a member of the *Société de Musée*, the *Société de la Jeunesse bordelaise*, and an administrator and "procureur syndic" of Bordeaux. Feret, p. 496.

From the tone of the letter, Pery was a young man with whom Furtado had developed a warm friendship. "Votre Mère, au souvenir de laquelle je vous prie de me rappeller, ne désaprouveroit point ce voyage . . . . On y gouteroit votre esprit, votre gayeté, vos bons mots; car je vous le dis sans vouloir vous faire un compliment, il y a ici, peu d'hommes aussi intéressant que vous l'êtes en société; vous ne sauriés donc mieux faire que d'arrêter le jour même où vous recevrés ma lettre, une place dans la diligence."

[76]Archives départementales de la Gironde, Série IV, J209.

[77]Philippe Ferrère was a Bordelais lawyer (1767–1815) who was highly regarded by his peers. "Il possédait tous les talents de l'orateur et toutes les lumières du jurisconsulte, l'esprit de justice et le désintéressement du modèle des avocats." Feret, p. 245.

[78]Furtado had obviously sent the responses to all twelve questions to the Bordelais Jewish community. On September 10, 1806, about sixty prominent Bordelais Jews wrote to Paris to express their satisfaction and agreement with the answers adopted by the Assembly. "Les français soussignez professant la religion de Moïse, à Bordeaux, déclarant qu'ayant eu connaissance des douze questions proposées par Messieurs les Commissaires du Gouvernement à l'assemblée des Juifs à Paris, et des réponses qu'elle y a faites, ils n'ont rien trouvé dans ces réponses qui ne fut entièrement conforme aux opinions généralement reçues et suivies. C'est pourquoi ils approuvent en tant que besoin serait les dites réponses." Microfilm from Zosa Szajkowski.

[79]Archives départementales de la Gironde, Série IV, J209.

[80]As early as July 31, the Assembly had made known its desire to meet with Napoleon. We have located the following three letters addressed to Furtado from Champagny and dated July 31, September 3 and September 29. Pascal Thémanlys, Jerusalem.

"J'ai eu l'honneur Monsieur, de soumettre à S. M. l'Empereur le voeu exprimé par l'assemblée que vous présidez pour être admis à lui offrir toute entière ses hommages. Sa Majesté a daigné me répondre qu'elle consentiroit à la recevoir ainsi en corps lorsque ses travaux auront été assez avancés pour donner déjà quelque résultats."

"Monsieur, j'ai l'honneur de vous annoncer que Sa Majesté l'Empereur a daigné consentir à vous admettre à son audience. Monsieur le Chambellan de Service près Sa Majesté vous fera connaître le jour et l'heure de la présentation. Sa Majesté ayant daigné consentir en même temps à ce que vous soyez accompagné des membres de l'assemblée qui sont encore à Paris, je vous prie de les en prévenir et de m'envoyer leurs noms.

"S. M. l'Empereur et Roi a qui j'ai rappelée l'intention qu'Elle avait daigné m'exprimer de recevoir les membres de l'assemblée des israélites qui se trouvent encore à Paris m'a fait l'honneur de m'annoncer hier qu'Elle les admetteroit à Fontainebleau. Vous serez prévenu du jour et de l'heure par M. le Chambellan de Service."

The deputies, however, were never presented to the Emperor. "Son [Napoleon] départ précipité pour une guerre dont le but est d'éloigner pour long-temps ce fléau de l'Europe civilisée, d'y assurer et d'y garantir l'empire de la justice et de la raison, nous a privés de l'honneur d'être présentés à notre illustre bienfaiteur." *Procès-Verbal*, March 25th session.

[81]Archives départementales de la Gironde, Série IV, J209.

[82]*Ibid.* Suart (1734–1817) was a French writer of mediocre ability who supported the monarchy, collaborated with royalist journals, and ultimately became editor of the *Publiciste* from 1799–1810. He was named perpetual secretary of the *Nouvelle Académie française* on February 20, 1803, "et poursuivit plusieurs de ses collègues de rancures tenaces qu'il put enfin satisfaire lors de la Restauration." "Suart," *La Grande Encyclopédie*, vol. 30, p. 566.

Delisle (1774–1816) was an encyclopediste who produced numerous works before, during, and after the Revolution, but who never achieved lasting public recognition. "Delisle," *La Grande Encyclopédie*, vol. 30, p. 1195.

[83]Microfilm received from Szajkowski. This appears to be the cover letter which Furtado sent to the Jewish communities. We have located a printed copy of the specific instructions, September 24 (Archives départementales de la Gironde, Série I).

"Assemblée des Députés des Israélites de France et du Royaume d'Italie. Considérant que ces dépenses ne peuvent pas être à la charge du Gouvernement, puis qu'il s'agit exclusivement de l'avantage des Israélites de France et du Royaume d'Italie, et qu'il est du devoir des représentés de les acquitter: Considérant, enfin, que l'indemnité pour chaque député ne peut être fixée au-dessous de cinq cents francs par mois pour les frais de séjour, et de cinq francs par poste pour les frais de route:

"Deliberé, qu'avec l'approbation de S. E. M. le Ministre de l'intérieur, le Président de l'Assemblée écrira une circulaire à ses coreligionnaires des Départements qui ont des députés à Paris, pour les inviter à solder les frais qu'entraîne leur réunion; que Son Excellence sera suppliée de transmettre la présente délibération à MM. les Préfets desdits Départements, en les engageant à en poursuivre l'effet par tous les moyens de crédit et de persuasion qui sont en leur pouvoir."

[84]Anchel, *Napoléon*, p. 146.

[85]Pascal Thémanlys, Jerusalem. Had two more Sephardic deputies been permitted to attend the Assembly, the Bordelais Jews would have willingly paid their expenses. Supporting Northeastern deputies, however, represented far more than a financial issue.

[86]See Furtado's reply to Molé on September 18. *Procès-Verbal.*

[87]This letter, dated January 7, 1807, is in the possession of Pascal Thémanlys, Jerusalem.

[88]Many of the letters between Furtado and Champagny may be found in the possession of Pascal Thémanlys, Jerusalem.

[89]The Jewish Theological Seminary, New York, has many of the notes which Furtado signed authorizing Worms to pay the deputies. An example is the following: "Le soussigné Président de l'Assemblée des Israélites de France et du Royaume d'Italie certifie que Monsieur David Sinzheim est compris dans le tableau des dépenses ordonnancé par Son Excellence Monseigneur le Ministre de l'Intérieur pour la somme de Cinq cent vingt quatre francs cinquante centimes à payer par M. Orly Hayem Worms sur les contributions dont il est receveur." Signed, Furtado.

[90]Most of the letters merely indicate the next time the Commissioners and the Committee would meet. One such letter, however, implies that the Committee first prepared the *règlement* before conferring with the Commissioners. "Je prie M. Furtado, [Molé wrote] de me faire savoir si la Commission du neuf avance dans son travail et s'il peut m'indiquer le jour où elle pourra se réunir chez moi pour nous en donner connaissance, . . ." Pascal Thémanlys, Jerusalem.

Pasquier, in his Mémoires, states that the *règlement* was primarily the result of one long session, arranged because Molé was absent from Paris, with the Committee and other enlightened Jews. "Nous nous résolûmes, M. Portalis et moi, à une tentative qui fut couronnée d'un plein succès. Etant assurés d'un jour, où M. Molé serait absent de Paris, nous en profitâmes pour réunir chez M. Portalis le plus grand nombre possible d'hommes influents, et là, après une séance qui dura plus de six heures, nous parvînmes à force de bons raisonnements et de douces paroles, à leur faire adopter un projet de règlement aussi bon que nous pouvions le désirer." Lévi, "Napoléon 1er," p. 279 (extrait des mémoires du Chancelier Pasquier).

Substantiating Pasquier's statements is a letter from him to Furtado, dated April 8, 1807, in which the occasion of Molé's absence from Paris was used to review the minutes of the December 9 meeting. "M. Molé, étant parti hier soir pour la campagne, je vous prie en son absence de vouloir bien m'addresser le plus promptement possible l'expédition du procès verbal de l'assemblée du 9, qu'il vous avait démandé." Pascal Thémanlys, Jerusalem.

In November, the Imperial Commissioners, perhaps at the suggestion of the Committee of nine, informed Champagny that it would be best to place laymen along with rabbis in the consistorial organization. In this way the rabbis, who otherwise might escape from the surveillance of the police and the administration, would be required to share their authority with those who would be more committed to complying with the decisions of the Assembly and Sanhedrin. Archives Nationales, AFIV 1405 dr. 6.

[91]*Procès-Verbal.*

[92]*Ibid.*

[93]*Ibid.*

[94]Archives Nationales, AF[IV], Box 300, 2150.

[95]Manuscript, two pages, December 11, 1806, Thémanlys, Jerusalem.

[96]Although we have no further mention of this Commission, there is indication in the same letter sent by the Commissioners to Champagny that the Jews had successfully communicated the necessity of terminating the oppressive decree. "Quand les choses seront parvenues à ce point de maturité Sa Majesté jugera sans doute convenable de se faire rendre compte de l'Exécution de son Décret du 20 Mai (sic) 1806. Cette mesure de rigueur ne peut être prolongée sans être rendue définitive et l'équité parôit réclamer que la juste protection accordée aux débiteurs opprimés ne dégénère pas en oppression contre les créanciers de bonne foi." Archives Nationales, AF[IV], Box 300, 2150.

[97]Katz, *Exclusiveness and Tolerance*, p. 184, is the most recent of the historians to maintain this characterization. "The Sanhedrin, like the Assembly of Notables before it, was composed of representatives of various French, Italian, and German groups. In addition to enlightened Jews of the Mendelssohn school, these bodies included outright reformers holding deistic beliefs who, though they did not disavow the Bible, certainly did not accept Jewish tradition. At the other extreme, there were a number of old-type German Rabbis who were unaffected by the movement of Enlightenment. In the centre stood the tolerant traditionalists, outstanding among them being Rabbi David Sinzheim of Strasbourg and Rabbi Jacob Israele Carmi of Reggio, Italy."

[98]Anchel, *Les Juifs de France*, p. 247. It becomes clear when reading Anchel's two books, which contain the most comprehensive work yet done on the Napoleonic period, that he is more sensitive to the Ashkenazic position than true objectivity permits. Thus this conclusion must be seen in the light of Anchel's attempt to deny differences of any kind which might be interpreted as a superiority of the Sephardic Jews.

[99]Perhaps Berr Isaac Berr and some other enlightened Ashkenazic leaders were the most satisfied with the consistorial plan; yet one wonders if even they were willing to accept, in return for their quasi-communal authority, the position of their rabbis as government lackeys.

Chapter 5

[1]Pasquier, in his mémoires, states that Napoleon probably had precisely this in mind when he called for a Sanhedrin. "Il [Napoleon] s'était dit probablement qu'un tel bienfait attacherait à jamais cette race à sa fortune et que partout où elle était répandue, il trouverait des auxiliaires disposés à seconder ses projets. Il allait entreprendre une nouvelle invasion en Allemagne qui devait le conduire à travers la Pologne et dans les pays voisins, où les affaires alors se traitaient presque exclusivement par l'intermédiaire des Juifs; il était donc naturel de penser que nuls auxiliaires ne pouvaient être plus utiles que ceux-là et par conséquent plus nécessaires à acquérir." Lévi, "Napoléon 1er," pp. 272-3 (extrait des mémoïres du Chancelier Pasquier).

Pasquier was not the only one to make this assumption. Metternich too was aware of the use to which Napoleon could put the Sanhedrin, and he instructed the Austrian agents to watch every development of the Assembly and Sanhedrin. In a report to Count Stadion, dated September 24, 1806, Metternich wrote: "The impulse has been given; the Israelites of all kinds are looking toward this Messiah who seems to be freeing them from the yokes under which they find themselves; the object of all this empty talk (for that is all that it is) is not at all to loosen the reins for these citizens who profess this religion in the countries under French domination, but to prove to every nation that its true homeland is France." Rivkin, *Readings,* p. 15.

[2]Furtado, "Letter to the Imperial Commissioners," January 21, 1807, Pascal Thémanlys, Jerusalem.

[3]*Ibid.* Not even purely theological issues were to be discussed. The Sanhedrin was to delegate to the central consistory the task of revising the daily prayers of the Italians, Portuguese, and Germans, which Furtado described as being neither uniform nor in perfect harmony with the doctrinal decisions.

[4]"Letter from the Commissioners to Champagny," January 31, 1807, Archives Nationales, F[19]11005.

[5]"Letter from Champagny," February 2, 1808, Archives Nationales, F[19]11005.

[6]*Procès-Verbal,* installation et mode de délibération du Grand Sanhedrin, article XIV.

[7]Towards the end, the number of those present dwindled to sixty and "extra" deputies were called upon to participate. *Procès-Verbal.*

[8]Because of the lack of discussion in the Sanhedrin, we have no way to determine what, if any, changes were made as a result of the deputies' written remarks. All the decisions are presented in their final form at the end of the meetings, and we are given in the minutes only the speeches which introduced each decision. Although we have found three drafts of the *procès-verbal* of the Sanhedrin, they are no more illuminating. The first, located in the archives of the Jewish Theological Seminary, New York, is the most complete and includes not only all the speeches and decisions but also the signatures of the two "assesseurs" (Cologna and Segre) and the scribe (Michel Berr). This copy, written by Cologna, appears to be the draft from which the minutes were edited. Changes appear in the published minutes, however, which do not appear here. These changes, apparently made by Furtado, are found in two earlier and less complete drafts of the minutes. The first of these, located in the Archives départementales de la Gironde, Série I, is only of the March 9th session. The changes are merely stylistic. The second draft, in the possession of Pascal Thémanlys, Jerusalem, covers the February 9th to February 26th meetings. The only significant change occurs in the draft of the February 9th session, where a reference to Sephardic and Ashkenazic synagogues is deleted. The draft reads: "M.M. Blotz et Jonas tous deux Scribes, le premier dans la synagogue Allemande, le 2e dans celle des portugais ont été appelés à remplir les mêmes fonctions dans le grand Sanhedrin. M. Michel Berr, membre de la première assemblée des députés israélites, a été aussi nommé Scribe et chargé de procès-verbal." Furtado reduced this rambling sentence

to: "M. M. Blotz et Jonas ont été appelés à remplir la fonction de Scribes avec M. Michel Berr."

In every instance, the published minutes contain Furtado's changes. In none of the drafts do we find the decisions which were to be voted on and only in the JTS copy do we find the adopted doctrines and preamble.

[9]This report, also containing some of the remarks made by Furtado at the February 12th meeting, was subsequently published. *Rapport de M. Furtado au Grand Sanhedrin en lui proposant les trois premières décisions doctrinales*, Archives départementales de la Gironde, Série I.

[10]*Procès-Verbal.*

[11]*Ibid.*

[12]*Ibid.*

[13]*Ibid.*

[14]These decisions were adopted on February 26.

[15]Historians had always believed that these instructions were attached to Napoleon's letter dated November 29, 1806. Anchel has been able to prove— on the basis of Champagny's reports, Napoleon's whereabouts, and archival sources—that the instructions only arrived on February 16 or at most a few days earlier. Anchel, *Napoléon*, p. 210, note 1.

The significance of the date lies in the meaning one can give to the consistorial plan passed on December 9 and the accomplishments of the Sanhedrin up until March 2.

[16]Archives Nationales, F[19]11005. These instructions also appear in Rivkin, *Readings*.

[17]*Ibid.*

[18]Archives Nationales, F[19]11005.

[19]"Ces ordonnances apprendront aux nations que nos dogmes se concilient avec les lois civiles sous lesquelles nous vivons et ne nous séparent point de la société des hommes. En conséquence declarons,

Que la loi divine, ce précieux héritage de nos ancêtres, contient des dispositions religieuses et des dispositions politiques;

Que les dispositions religieuses sont, par leur nature, absolues et indépendantes des circonstances et des temps;

Qu'il n'en est pas de même des dispositions politiques, c'est à-dire de celles qui constituent le gouvernement et qui étaient destinées à régir le peuple d'Israël dans la Palestine lorsqu'il avoit ses rois, ses pontifes et ses magistrats;

Que ces dispositions politiques ne sauroient être applicables depuis qu'il ne forme plus un corps du nation;

Qu'en consacrant cette distinction déjà établie par la tradition, le grand Sanhedrin déclare un fait incontestable; . . ." *Procès-Verbal.*

[20]*Ibid.*

[21]Furtado's speech, quoted in full in the Minutes, was also published separately. *Discours prononcé par M. Furtado à la séance du Grand Sanhedrin du 2 Mars*, 1807, Pascal Thémanlys, Jerusalem.

[22]*Procès-Verbal.*

[23]*Ibid.*

[24]*Ibid.*

[25]Rivkin, *Readings* Document IC.

[26]This method has been used by modern nations to integrate their heterogeneous population.

[27]Rivkin, *Readings*, Document IC.

[28]Anchel, *Napoléon*, pp. 261–2.

[29]*Ibid.*, p. 263.

[30]It is highly probable that the establishment of a legal rate of interest in France was the result of the attitudes of liberal ministers who sought to prevent any particular legislation against the Jews.

[31]Archives Nationales, F¹⁹11005, February 21, 1807.

[32]*Ibid.*

[33]*Ibid.*, February 25, 1807.

[34]*Ibid.*, February 26, 1807.

[35]*Procès-Verbal.* Furtado repeated to the Assembly what the Sanhedrin had included in its preface, which, as we have shown, was the result of Napoleon's letter.

[36]*Ibid.*

[37]*Ibid.*

[38]*Ibid.*

[39]Archives départementales de la Gironde, Série I. The manuscript is unsigned. "Messieurs et Collègues, je viens au nom de la députation que vous avez nommée dans votre dernière séance pour se rendre auprès de MM. les Commissaires de S. M. . . . Chargés par l'assemblée de faire connaître à MM. les commissaires les réclamations que plusieurs d'entre nous avoient faites sur l'arrêté proposé par votre commission des neuf. . . ."

[40]*Ibid.*

[41]*Procès-Verbal.*

[42]*Ibid.*

[43]The Assembly, Molé reported to Champagny, indulged in "des discussions peu convenables et souvent orageuses." Archives Nationales, F¹⁹11005.

[44]"Observations sur le projet d'arrêté proposé à l'Assemblée hébraique par la Commission des Neuf dans les séances des 25 et 27 Mars," Archives départementales de la Gironde, Série I. Since we have found no mention of this manuscript, we assume that it was never presented to the Assembly.

[45]*Ibid.*

[46]"Cet arrêté est humiliant pour les Israélites, en ce qu'il paroit supposer qu'il leur est naturel de porter des désordres dans le commerce et dans les fortunes; que ces désordres exigent des mesures particulières et que la législation qui régit les autres français ne suffit pas pour eux; l'Assemblée est trop pénétrée des intentions paternelles du gouvernement pour craindre qu'il puisse jamais être accessible à de pareilles idées, mais elle ne peut pas se dissimuler que telle est l'interprétation que l'ignorance et le préjugé ne manqueront pas de donner à cet arrêté, surtout dans un moment où les bienfaits éclatants que S. M. vient de répandre sur tous les Israélites ont fixé sur eux l'attention et peut-être excité l'envie de quelques âmes basses et étroites qui ne peuvent voir sans chagrin toutes les mesures qui portent l'impreinte de la grandeur et de la justice." *Ibid.*

[47]The fact that the manuscript was found in Bordeaux points to the Sephardim as the authors.

[48]*Procès-Verbal.*   [49]Pascal Thémanlys, Jerusalem.   [50]*Ibid.*

[51]Furtado, "Observations sur le sursis du 30 Mai dernier et sur le mode à adopter pour le lever," Archives Nationales F[19]11005. Included in the signed manuscript are marginal notes made by M. De Gérando, Secretary General of the Interior.

Anchel, *Napoléon*, pp. 108–110, discusses this mémoire and indicates some of De Gérando's comments.

We have also found a nine page unfinished draft of this mémoire, signed by Furtado, in the Archives départementales de la Gironde, Série I. The deletions in the title are Furtado's. "Mémoire ~~sur l'usure des Juifs dans la ci-devant Alsace et~~ sur les moyens de lever le sursis." Although the draft differs little from the finished copy, Furtado does not include in the former either the list of Jewish usurers or his plans for a just solution. The introduction to the draft is crossed out and Furtado had written above his deletions a more general and less accusatory proposal:

"On se propose de rechercher dans ce mémoire-par quels moyens lever le sursis dans les Départements septentrionnaux on pourrait ~~affaiblir parmi les Juifs des Deux département du Haut~~ de l'Empire sur les créances hypothécaires dues aux Juifs par des ~~et Bas Rhin et de quelques lieux limitrophes, l'habitude de l'usure~~ cultivateurs non négocians.
~~et parvenir à remplacer cette industrie funeste à l'honneur d'une classe d'ailleurs estimables et qui habitent les autres parties de la France, par toute autre industrie.~~"

[52]"Or pour changer cette inclination il faut le concours de plusieurs moyens. L'un des premiers consisteroit à organiser les consistoires locaux et le consistoire central de Paris, et à confier à celui-ci la Surveillance sur les individus en petit nombre qui dans le nord commettraient des fraudes révoltantes à l'abri du prêt à interêt. . . . Les décisions du gd. Sanhedrin et les dispositions particulières qui seront prises par l'autorité publique, n'exerceront leur influence que sur la Jeunesse, en sorte que le changement des habitudes et des moeurs ne pourra s'opérer que par l'effet du temps." Furtado, "Observations."

[53]Furtado, *Mémoire . . . sur l'état des Juifs.*

[54]De Gérando disagreed with Furtado's explanations for the behavior of the Jews and was unimpressed by Furtado's statistics.

[55]De Gérando agreed with Furtado's plan for police action and called his list of usurers, "note précieuse."

[56]Furtado, "Observations." Although Furtado's *mémoire* appears to be less than supportive of the Northeastern communities, it differs little from a manuscript written by the Ashkenazic Jews at the time of the May 30 decree and apparently intended for Napoleon. We have been unable to locate any official reference to this "Petition" and we assume, based on its content and the fact that it was found in Bordeaux, that Furtado made some use of it in preparing his "Observations." "Petition à Sa Majesté L'Empereur et Roi,"

undated, unsigned, Archives départementales de la Gironde, Série I. There is no doubt that this Petition was written immediately after the promulgation of the May 30 decree and before the first meeting of the Assembly of Notables. "Les projets qu'elle [Napoleon] a concus, les intentions qu'elle vient de manifester, les événements qu'elle prépare, la convocation qu'elle a ordonnée des représentants de la Nation juive, tout annonce à cette nation. . . ."

Although more emotional in its defense of the Jews of Haut- and Bas-Rhin, the Petition is similar to Furtado's "Observations" in its explanation of the causes for the financial transactions of the Jews. Also similar is the desire on the part of these Northeastern Jews to punish those who had used their credit dishonestly and fraudulently. They did not, however, list the names of those known for their usurious activities.

[57]Archives Nationales, F[19]11005, April 2, 1807.

[58]Pascal Thémanlys, Jerusalem.   [59]*Procès-Verbal.*

[60]*Exhortation aux Israélites de France et du Royaume d'Italie,* in the possession of the author.

According to Furtado, in the minutes of the April 6th meeting, the *Exhortation* was written by "un membre de l'Assemblée." This is only partially true. We have located a manuscript of the *Exhortation,* microfilmed for the author by Zosa Szajkowski. While the first pages were only corrected by Furtado, the last several pages were written by him. A letter from Pasquier to Furtado, written on April 9, indicates, moreover, that the *Exhortation* also reflected some "slight" changes suggested by the Imperial Commissioners. "J'ai communiqué Monsieur à M. Portalis votre lettre du 6 et le procès-verbal de votre séance du 6 qui y étoit joint. Nous pensons qu'il y a quelques legers modifications à apporter à l'exhortation." Pasquier concluded his letter with an invitation to Furtado to meet with the Commissioners on the following Saturday. Letter is in the possession of Pascal Thémanlys, Jerusalem.

[61]*Exhortation.* [62]Pascal Thémanlys, Jerusalem. [63]Anchel, *Napoléon.* pp. 265-6.

[64]*Ibid.,* pp. 269–70. [65]*Ibid.,* pp. 110–111.

[66]*Ibid.,* p. 257. The date December 10 may have been an error, or, despite the account in the minutes, the *règlement* may have been accepted not on December 9, but on the following day.

[67]*Ibid.,* pp. 272–3.

[68]"Letter to Napoleon," signed among others by Furtado, Rodrigues, Isaac Mayer Marx, Levy, and Schmoll; Pascal Thémanlys, Jerusalem.

We have found no mention of either this letter or the following one. We are assuming by their contents that they were written rather early in the struggle. Although this letter mentions the fact that the Council had submitted its projects to Napoleon, which actually didn't occur until February, 1808, the tone of the letter does not reflect the nine months of letters, *mémoires,* and reclamations by the Jews which preceded the Council's actions. Thus while we recognize the discrepancy, we believe that the information concerning the Council's actions was more an assumption by Furtado of the logical procedures rather than an accurate statement of fact. If on the other hand, the letter was in fact written as late as February or March, then it must be viewed as one of the last attempts to prevent the March 17 decree.

[69]*Ibid.*

[70]"Letter to Napoleon," Archives départementales de la Gironde, Série I. "Les israélites français soussignés, l'exposent humblement à votre Majesté Imperiale et Royale, qu'ayant été informés, que les projets des Décrets transmis par Son Excellence le Ministre de l'Intérieur, au Conseil d'Etat, n'avoient pas été adoptés, ils ont appris avec douleur que le Conseil lui-même en proposoit d'autres non moins contraires aux espérances que nous avions conçues, . . . C'est ce qui nous détermine à déposer nos alarmes aux pieds de votre Majesté, et à supplier respectueusement de daigner nous entendre avant de nous juger."

Interestingly, Furtado had written a sentence distinguishing the Jews of the Southwest from those of the Northeast. He apparently thought better of it, however, and deleted it. Perhaps this deletion indicates that among those signing it, were some Ashkenazic Jews. "Jusqu'à présent, tous les israélites de l'Empire, ~~ceux du nord et de l'est, depuis quinze ans, ceux du midi depuis deux cent cinquante,~~ avoient été soumis aux lois communes: aujourd'hui, l'assimilation à leurs concitoyens d'une autre religion, à tous les étrangers de quelque pays que ce soit n'existeroit plus, si les projets présentés étoient adoptés."

[71]*Ibid.* Furtado was in favor of having the state pay the salaries of the rabbis and in his *mémoire* written against the 1808 decrees, he specified his reasons. The Council of State, however, had dismissed this as a possibility. Anchel, *Napoléon*, p. 257.

[72]*Ibid.*

[73]"Réclamation des Juifs Portugais, Espagnols, et Avignonnais de Paris, de Bordeaux, de Bayonne et du Midi de la France," Archives Nationales F^{19}11008, registered on June 13, signed by the following: Cremieux (Southern France), B. Rodrigues (Paris), Patto jeune (Bayonne), Furtado and Rodrigues (Bordeaux).

[74]*Ibid.*

[75]"Letter to Napoleon," July 19, 1807, Pascal Thémanlys, Jerusalem.

[76]Anchel, *Napoléon,* p. 282, gives the following account. "Accompagné du Nancéien Maurice Lévy, il partit pour la Pologne, vers le mois de Juin 1807, et obtint audience de l'Empereur à Tilsit. Le Souverain l'aurait accueilli avec bienveillance et même lui aurait promis que les droits des Juifs ne recevraient aucune atteinte." Anchel's reference is Graetz, *Histoire des Juifs,* trad. M. Bloch, t. 5, p. 337. "L'infatigable Furtado, accompagné de Maurice Lévy, de Nancy, ne craignit pas de se rendre jusqu'aux bords du Niemen pour informer Napoléon de ce qui se tramait. L'Empereur les accueillit avec bienveillance et leur promit de laisser jouir les Juifs des mêmes droits que les autres citoyens."

Graetz, upon whom Anchel relies exclusively, based his statements on an anonymous and inaccurate biography of Furtado which appeared in 1841. Graetz, *Geschichte der Juden von den ältesten Zeiten bis auf die Gegenwart* (Leipzig: O. Leiner, 1897-1911), vol. ll, p. 283, note 2.

The biography, "Furtado, Biographie," *Archives Israélites, II* (1841), p. 366, gives the following account; "Il [Furtado] se rendit avec son collègue, Maurice

Lévy, de Nancy, jusqu'au Niemen; arrivé auprès de l'Empereur, lui remit un Mémoire rédigé avec toute la force de son éloquence et de son talent. Il ne fut heureux qu'en partie."

[77]"A l'exception du voyage en Pologne, [Furtado refers to the borders of Poland before the partitions] c'est à mes frais que tout s'est fait." Léon, pp. 191–2. This letter to be cited in detail later, was written on March 15, 1808.

[78]From a purely geographic consideration, a trip which led from Königsberg to Dresden seems unlikely to have ended up so far east as Tilsit. In addition, it is significant that neither Furtado's letter to Patto jeune nor the following account of the journey, delivered at the meeting of the central consistory following Furtado's death, mentions *seeing* Napoleon. "Que tel fut l'attachement qu'il partait à ses coreligionnaires, qu'il n'hésita point à traverser, au milieu d'une saison rigoureuse, les plus rudes climats pour aller exposer leurs demandes et leurs besoins au chef du gouvernement, . . ." "Minutes of the central consistory," Jewish Theological Seminary, New York.

[79]Furtado, *Mémoire sur les projets de décrets présentés au Conseil d'Etat concernant les Israélites,* Paris 1808, Bibliothèque Nationale, Ld[18]482. A copy of this printed edition may also be found in the Archives départementales de la Gironde, Série I.

[80]Furtado, "Mémoire sur les projets de décrets présentés au Conseil d'Etat concernant les Israélites," manuscript, Archives départementales de la Gironde, Série I. There is no question that this was the draft Furtado used for his printed *mémoire.* Although the *mémoire* is dated 1808, it is directed against the projects proposed by Champagny and therefore was probably written in May or June, 1807.

[81]Furtado, *Mémoire,* p. 2.

[82]Furtado pointed out that the Jews would use Christians as middlemen to lend money on their behalf, that instead of engaging in agriculture and the arts and professions, they would become further estranged; and that finally no Jew who entered the army could feel committed to the France he was asked to defend.

[83]Furtado, *Mémoire,* p. 15.

[84]"Report by the Secretary of State," March 1808, Archives Nationales AF[IV] Box 300, 2150. It is interesting to note that the secularist opinions attributed to Furtado and his associates were detrimental to their being considered true representatives of the Jews. "Les personnes qui font valoir ces raisons sont du petit nombre des Israélites qui voudraient voir effacer jusqu'au nom de Juif, qui ne tiennent point à leurs coreligionnaires par leurs vices et qui, dans la réalité, n'y tiennent pas par leurs idées religieuses."

[85]Anchel, *Napoléon,* pp. 259–60.

[86]Léon, pp. 191–2.

[87]*Ibid.*

[88]Napoleon had been dissatisfied with the Council's projects, and apparently did not trust the liberal attitudes of its members. Rather than return the projects to the Council, he decided to send them to his Secretary of State, Maret, and thus avoid any further opposition to his suggestions. The final form of the decrees was the result of Maret's efforts. Archives Nationales, AF[IV]

Box 300, 2150.

[89]Archives Nationales, AF[IV]pl 2151, n° 136. In English in Rivkin, *Readings*, Documents I–D, I–E, I–F.

[90]*Ibid.*, Title I, article 4.

[91]*Ibid.*, Title I, article 5.

[92]*Ibid.*, Title I, article 6.

[93]*Ibid.*, Title II, articles 7, 8, 9.

[94]*Ibid.*, Title III, article 16.

[95]*Ibid.*, Title III, article 17.

[96]*Ibid.*, Title III, article 18.

[97]*Ibid.*, Title III, article 19.

[98]Furtado, "Copie de la lettre écrite à M. Maret ministre et Secrétaire d'Etat," April 17, 1808, Archives départementales de la Gironde, Série I. The same letter, but undated, may be found in the Archives Nationales, F[19]11007. Anchel, *Napoléon*, p. 296, was unaware of this copy in Bordeaux and assumed that the letter was written around August 1808. It is highly probable that Napoleon's and Maret's visit to Bordeaux in April 1808 stimulated Furtado to write this letter. We do not know if Furtado presented it in person. We do know, however, that Napoleon visited the Raba brothers in Bordeaux and that the Bordelais municipal council sent a delegation to Napoleon. Although Furtado was not a member of the delegation, as a municipal councilor he signed the address presented to the Emperor. E. Rousselot, "Napoléon à Bordeaux," *Revue Historique de Bordeaux*, I (1908), pp. 204–28; 281–304; 428–54.

Furtado's letter to Maret was known to the Jews, for on April 27, 1808, he received a letter from the community of Nice thanking him for his efforts to exempt them from the March 17 decree. Archives départementales de la Gironde, Série I.

[99]Furtado, "Copie de la lettre."

[100]Archives Nationales, F[19]11007.

[101]Furtado, "Copie de la lettre."

[102]A law of I Brumaire, an VII, had decreed that all those engaged in commerce were subject to a license. Thus, questions arose as to whether the additional license needed by the Jews was to follow the form of the general one. Despite the intervention of the Council of State for clarification and the interpretations offered by the Minister of Interior, the municipal councils provided various and contradictory decisions. The prefects, often asked to resolve issues such as whether they could deliver licenses despite the refusal of the councils, acted without any excessive rigor. Anchel, *Napoléon*, pp. 300–335.

In addition to making it difficult to obtain licenses, the municipal councils strove to prevent Jews from the Haut- and Bas-Rhin from leaving the areas. So hostile were these councils that they also interpreted the measures on residence to exclude the settlement of brides. Anchel, *Napoléon*, pp. 337–347.

[103]Furtado, "Copie de la lettre."

[104]For a complete list of those departments exempted, the number of Jews in each and the dates for their exemption, see the charts in Anchel, *Napoléon*, pp. 372–3.

[105]"Il suit nécessairement que le nom générique de Juif employé dans le Décret, est un outrage gratuit fait à un grand nombre de gens probes, irréprochables, plus propres à servir d'exemple à beaucoup de leurs concitoyens Chrétiens qu'à les prendre pour modèles." Furtado, "Copie de la lettre."

Bibliography

Archives

Archives départementales de la Gironde, Bordeaux.
Archives municipales de Bordeaux.
Archives Nationales, Paris.
Bibliothèque de la ville de Bordeaux.
Bibliothèque Nationale, Paris.
Jewish Historical General Archives, Jerusalem.
Jewish Theological Seminary, New York.
Private archives of the late M. Alain d'Anglade, archivist at the Departemental archives in Bordeaux. Bordeaux, France.
Private archives of the late Joseph Cohen, Grand Rabbi of Bordeaux. Bordeaux, France.
Private archives of Pascal Thémanlys. Jerusalem, Israel.
Private archives of M. Robert Weill. Talence, France.

Manuscripts

Bethencourt, L. Cardozo de. "Fonds de Cardozo de Bethencourt," Archives municipales de Bordeaux.
Furtado, Abraham. "Copie de la lettre écrite à M. Maret Ministre et Secrétaire d'Etat." Archives départementales de la Gironde, Série I.
————. "Draft of the Answers to the 11th and 12th Questions." Pascal Thémanlys, Jerusalem.
————. "Folie de jeunesse" Pascal Thémanlys, Jerusalem.
————. "Furtado-Rodrigues Marriage Document Before Rauzan, Notary in Bordeaux." Archives départementales de la Gironde, 3E21702.
————. "Journal à Paris." Pascal Thémanlys, Jerusalem.
————. Lettre à un ami, 12 octobre, 1784." Pascal Thémanlys, Jerusalem.
————. "Letter Concerning the Assembly of Notables." Pascal Thémanlys, Jerusalem.
————. "Letter to Pery." Archives départementales de la Gironde, Série IV, J209.
————. "Mémoire d'Abraham Furtado sur l'état des Juifs en France jusqu'à la Révolution." Pascal Thémanlys, Jerusalem.

————. "*Mémoires* d'un patriote proscrit." Bibliothèque de la ville de Bordeaux, ms. 1946.

————. "Mémoire sur les moyens de lever le sursis." Archives départementales de la Gironde, Série I.

————. "Mémoire sur les projets de décrets présentés au conseil d'état concernant les Israélites." Archives départementales de la Gironde, Série I.

————. "Observations sur le sursis du 30 Mai dernier et sur le mode à adopter pour le lever." Archives Nationales, F¹⁹11005.

————. "Pensées." Pascal Thémanlys, Jerusalem.

"Journal of the Bordeaux Jewish Commission in Paris, 1788." Jewish Historical General Archives, Jerusalem Zf 1.

"Journal of the Bordeaux Jewish Delegation to Paris, 1790." Jewish Historical General Archives, Jerusalem, Zf 6.

Lopes-Dubec, S. "Autobiographical Account." Jewish Historical General Archives, Jerusalem, Zf 5.

————. "Notes of Solomon Lopes-Dubec on the Bordeaux Delegation to Paris, 1788." Jewish Historical General Archives, Jerusalem, Zf 3.

"Mémoire présenté par MM Lopes-Dubec père et Furtado aîné, députés des Juifs de Bordeaux, à M. de Malesherbes ministre d'état, en Juin 1788." Archives départementales de la Gironde, Série I.

"Observations sur le projet d'arrêté proposé à l'Assemblée hébraïque par la commission des Neuf dans les séances des 25 et 27 Mars." Archives départementales de la Gironde, Série I.

"Pétition à Sa Majesté l'Empereur et Roi." Archives départementales de la Gironde, Série I.

"Réclamation des Juifs portugais, espagnols et avignonnais de Paris, de Bordeaux, de Bayonne et du midi de la France." Archives Nationales, F¹⁹11008.

"Registre des délibérations de la nation portugaise depuis 11 May 1710, tiré des anciens livres pour servir au besoin, lequel registre servira pour y coucher toutes celles qui seront passées de l'avenir dans le corps commencé du sindicat de sieur David Lameyera à Bordeaux le premier Juin 1753. Le présent registre a été continué jusqu'au 22 Mars 1787, époque de la nomination de Abraham Furtado l'aîné pour syndic, les fonctions duquel ont duré jusqu'au mois de Mars 1788." Archives départementales de la Gironde, Série I.

"Registre des procès-verbaux des séances de l'assemblée des députés français professant la religion juive." Archives départementales de la Gironde, 3JI1.

"Répertoire extrait des délibérations de la nation juive depuis 1710 jusqu'au février 1790." Archives départementales de la Gironde, Série I.

Printed, Primary

Berr, Berr Isaac. *Lettre du Sieur Berr Isaac Berr, manufacturier, membre du Conseil municipal de Nancy, à M. Grégoire, Sénateur à Paris.* Nancy: P. Barbier, 1806.

————. *Lettre du Sieur Berr Isaac Berr, négociant à Nancy, Juif, naturalisé en vertu des Lettres Patentes du Roi, à Monseigneur l'Evêque de Nancy, député à l'Assemblée Nationale, 1790,* reprinted in *Lettres, Mémoires et Publications Diverses, 1787–1806.* Paris: Editions d'Histoire Sociale, 1968.

Berr, Michel. *Eloge de M. Abraham Furtado.* Bibliothèque Nationale, Ln²78099A (47 pages).

————. *Eloge de M. Abraham Furtado.* Bibliothèque Nationale, Ln²78099 (34 pages).

Bonald, Louis Gabriel. "Sur les Juifs." *Mercure de France,* February 8, 1806, 249–67.

Bordeaux, *Livre des Bourgeois de Bordeaux XVII et XVIII siècles.* Bordeaux, MDCCCXCVIII.

Bordeaux. *Inventaire Sommaire des Registres de la Jurade:* 1520–1783. Bordeaux, 1896– .

Dohm, Christian Wilhelm. *Über die bürgerliche Verbesserung der Juden.* Berlin and Stettin: Friedrich Nicolai, 1781.

France. *Archives parlementaires de 1787 à 1860.* Paris, 1868.

France. *Recueil général des anciennes lois françaises depuis l'an 420 jusqu'à la révolution de 1789.* Paris: Librairie de Plon Frères.

Furtado, Abraham. *Discours prononcé par M. Furtado à la séance du Grand Sanhedrin du 2 Mars, 1807.* Pascal Thémanlys, Jerusalem.

————. "Lettre au Rédacteur." *Journal de Bordeaux et du Département de la Gironde.* June 16, 1790.

————. *Mémoire d'Abraham Furtado sur l'état des Juifs en France jusqu'à la Révolution.* Edited by Gabrielle Moyse. Paris: Librairie Durlacher.

————. *Mémoire sur les projets de décrets présentés au Conseil d'état concernant les Israélites.* Paris, 1808. Bibliothèque Nationale, Ld¹⁸⁴82.

Gergeres Fils, M. *Adresse aux défenseurs de l'humanité, sur le décret rendu par l'Assemblée Nationale, en faveur des Juifs.* Bordeaux: 1790. Bibliothèque de la ville de Bordeaux.

Gironde. *Inventaire sommaire des archives départementales antérieures à 1790.* Bordeaux, 1928.

Godard, Jacques. *Discours prononcé le Janvier 1790 par M. Godard, avocat au Parlement.* Bibliothèque de la ville de Bordeaux.

Grégoire, Henri. *Essai sur la régénération physique, morale et politique des Juifs.* Metz: Claude Lamort, 1789.

————. *Observations nouvelles sur les Juifs et spécialement sur ceux d'Allemagne.* Bibliothèque Nationale, Ld¹⁸⁴65.

Journal de Bordeaux et du Departement de la Gironde. 1790.

Lettre, adressée à M. Grégoire, Curé d'Emberménil, Député de Nancy, par les députés de la Nation juive portugaise de Bordeaux. Bibliothèque Nationale, Ld¹⁸⁴29.

L'Indicateur (Bordeaux Journal), 1804.

Mendelssohn, Moses. *Jerusalem: A Treatise on Ecclesiastical Authority and Judaism.* Translated by M. Samuels. London: Longman, Orme, Brown and Longmans, MDCCCXXXVIII.

P.ˣˣˣˣˣ, Moyse. *Réponse à un article sur les Juifs de M. de Bonald.* Bordeaux: 1806.

Procès-Verbal des séances de l'Assemblée des Députés français professant la religion juive; imprimé d'après le manuscrit communiqué par M. le Président. Paris: Desenne, 1806.

Printed, Secondary

Allison, John M. S. *Malesherbes*. New Haven: Yale University Press, 1938.
Anchel, Robert. *Les Juifs de France*. Paris: 1946.
————. "Les Lettres patentes du 10 Juillet, 1784," *Revue des études juives*, 93 (1932), 113–134.
————. *Napoléon et les Juifs*. Paris: Presses Universitaires de France, 1928.
Baer, Yitzhak. *Galut*. New York: Schocken Books, 1947.
Baron, Salo W. "Newer Approaches to Jewish Emancipation," *Diogenes*, 26 (1960), 56–81.
Beaufleury, Louis Francia de. *Histoire de l'établissement des Juifs à Bordeaux et à Bayonne depuis 1550*. Paris: 1799.
Bécamps, Pierre. "Les relations avec les neutres au temps de la Révolution: l'agence commerciale de Bordeaux," *Revue historique de Bordeaux*, IV (1955), 305–14.
————. *La Révolution à Bordeaux (1789-1794). J. P. M. LaCombe, président de la commission militaire*. Bordeaux: 1953.
Bernadau, M. *Histoire de Bordeaux depuis l'année 1675 jusqu'au 1836*. Bordeaux: Imprimérie de Balarac Jeune, 1837.
Bethencourt, L. Cardozo De. "Le trésor des Juifs sephardim," *Revue des études juives*, XX (1890), 287–300; XXV (1892), 97–110, 235–245; XXVI (1893), 240–56.
"Biographie, Abraham Furtado." *Archives Israélites*, II (1841), 361–68.
Bloch, C. "L'opinion publique et les Juifs au XVIIIᵉ siècle en France," *Revue des études juives*, 35 (1897), 112–114.
Blumenkranz, Bernard. *Bibliographie des Juifs en France*. Paris: Centre d'études juives, 1961.
Bright, Rev. James F. *Joseph II*. London: Macmillan Company, 1897.
Brinton, Craine. *A Decade of Revolution 1789–1799*. New York: Harper and Row, 1963.
Cahen, Abraham. "L'émancipation des Juifs devant la société royale des sciences et des arts de Metz en 1787 et M. Roederer," *Revue des études juives*, I (1880), 83–104.
Cavignac, J. "Les assemblées au désert dans la région de Sainte-Foy au milieu du XVIIIᵉ siècle," *Revue historique de Bordeaux*, XVI (July–December, 1967), 97–119.
Charles, Albert. *La révolution de 1848 et la seconde république à Bordeaux et dans le département de la Gironde*. Bordeaux: Belmas, 1945.
Chobaut, H. "Les Juifs d'Avignon et du Comtat et de la révolution française," *Revue des études juives*, 101 (1937), 5–52; 102 (1937), 3–39.
Cirot, Georges. *Les Juifs de Bordeaux*. Bordeaux: Feret et Fils, 1920.
————. *Recherches sur les Juifs espagnols et portugais à Bordeaux*. Bordeaux: 1920.
Cobban, Alfred. *The Social Interpretation of the French Revolution*. Cambridge: University Press, 1968.

"Delisle," *La Grande Encyclopédie*, vol. 30, 1195.

Detchevery, Ad. *Histoire des Israélites de Bordeaux*. Bordeaux: 1850.

Ettinger, S. "Jews and Judaism as Seen by the English Deists of the 18th Century, *Zion*, XXIX (1964), 182–207.

Feret, E. *Statistique générale du département de la Gironde*. Bordeaux: 1889.

Feuerwerker, David. "L'émancipation des Juifs en France," Unpublished Ph. D. dissertation, Sorbonne, 1961.

Genevray, Pierre. "Les Juifs des Landes sous le premier empire," *Revue des études juives*, 74 (1922), 127–47.

Gershoy, Leo. *The Era of the French Revolution*. New Jersey: D. Van Nostrand, 1957.

Ginsburger, E. "Les Juifs et la Révolution française," *Revue des études juives*, CIV (1938), 35–69.

Ginsburger, M. "Arrêtés du Directoire du Haut-Rhin relatifs aux Juifs," *Revue des études juives*, 75 (1922), 44–71.

_____. "Les familles Lehman et Cerf Berr," *Revue des études juives*, 59 (1910), 106–113.

Godechot, Jacques. "Les Juifs de Nancy de 1789 à 1795." *Revue des études juives*, 86 (1928), 1–35.

Graetz, Heinrich. *History of the Jews*. Philadelphia: Jewish Publication Society of America, 1946.

Graetz, Heinrich. *Geschichte der Juden von den ältesten Zeiten bis auf die Gegenwart*. Leipzig: O. Leiner, 1897–1911.

Grosclaude, Pierre. *Malesherbes témoin et interprète de son temps*. Paris: Librairie Fischbacher, n.d.

Gruenebaum-Ballin, P. "Grégoire convertisseur? ou la croyance au 'retour d'Israel'," *Revue des études juives*, CXXI (1962), 383–98.

Hertzberg, Arthur. *The French Enlightenment and the Jews*. New York and London: Columbia University Press, 1968.

Higounet, Charles, ed. *Histoire de Bordeaux*. Bordeaux: Fédération Historique du Sud Ouest, 1962.

Hildenfinger, P. "Actes du district de Strasbourg relatifs aux Juifs (1790–an III)," *Revue des études juives*, 60 (1910), 235–55; 61 (1910), 102-23, 279–284.

_____. "L'adresse de la commune de Strasbourg à l'assemblée nationale contre les Juifs," *Revue des études juives*, 58 (1909), 112–128.

Hubrecht, G. "Notes pour servir à l'histoire de la Franc-Maçonnerie à Bordeaux," *Revue historique de Bordeaux*, (Janvier-Mars, 1954), 143–150.

Jullian, Camille. *Histoire de Bordeaux depuis les origines jusqu'en 1895*. Bordeaux: Feret et fils, 1895.

Katz, Jacob. "A State Within a State," *Proceedings of the Israel Academy of Sciences and Humanities*, IV, N° 3, 29–58.

_____. *Exclusiveness and Tolerance*. New York: Schocken Books, 1962.

_____. "To Whom was Mendelssohn Responding in his *Jerusalem*," *Zion*, XXIX (1964), 112–32.

Labadie, E. *La Presse bordelaise pendant la Révolution*. Bordeaux: 1910.

Levi, Israel. "Napoléon Ier et la réunion du grand Sanhédrin," *Revue des études juives*, 28 (1894), 265–280.

Lefebvre, Georges. *The Coming of the French Revolution*. New York: Random House, 1947.

Léon, Henry. *Histoire des Juifs de Bayonne*. Paris: Armand Durlacher, Librairie, 1893.

Lheritier, Michel. *La fin de l'ancien régime*. Paris: 1942.

————. "La Révolution à Bordeaux de 1789: la transition de l'ancien au nouveau régime," *Revue historique de Bordeaux*, VIII (1915), 130–45.

————. *La Révolution à Bordeaux dans l'histoire de la Révolution française*. Paris: Presses Universitaires de France, 1942.

————. *Les débuts de la Révolution à Bordeaux*. Bordeaux: 1919.

————. *Liberté (1789–1790). Bordeaux et la Révolution française*. Paris: 1947.

Liber, Maurice. "Les Juifs et la convocation des états généraux," *Revue des études juives*, LXIII (1912), 185–210; LXIV (1912), 89–108, 244–77; LXV (1913), 89–133; LXVI (1913), 161–212.

————. "Napoléon et les Juifs," *Revue des études juives*, LXX (1920), 127–47; LXXI (1921), 1–23, 135–162.

Madelin, Louis. "Napoleon," *The European Past* vol. I. New York: Macmillan, 1970.

Mahler, Raphael. *A History of Modern Jewry*. New York: Schocken Books, 1971.

Malvézin, Théophile. *Histoire des Juifs à Bordeaux*. Bordeaux: Charles Lefebvre Librairie, 1875.

————. *Histoire du Commerce de Bordeaux depuis les origines jusqu'à nos Jours*. Bordeaux: Imp. Nouvelle A. Bellier et Cie., 1892.

Manuel, Frank. *The New World of Henri Saint-Simon*. Massachusetts: Harvard University Press, 1956.

Marion, Marcel. *Dictionnaire des institutions de la France aux XVIIe et XVIIIe siècles*. Paris: A. Picard, 1923.

————. "Du rôle des Juifs dans la vente des Biens nationaux dans la Gironde," *Actes de l'académie nationale des sciences, belles lettres et arts de Bordeaux*, 3e série (1908), 5–19.

Maupassant, Jean de. *Abraham Gradis (1699–1780): Un grand armateur de Bordeaux*. Bordeaux: Feret et Fils, 1917.

Michel, Francisque. *Histoire du commerce et de la navigation à Bordeaux*. Bordeaux: Imprimérie de J. Delmas, 1870.

Monin, H. "Les Juifs de Paris à la fin de l'ancien régime," *Revue des études juives*, XXIII (1891), 85–98.

Monographe du Culte Israélite à Bordeaux. Bordeaux: G. Gounouilhon Imprimeur, 1892.

Mornet, Daniel. *Les origines intellectuelles de la Révolution française*. Paris: 1934.

Moyse, Gabrielle. "Abraham Furtado. Notice biographique," *Foi et Réveil*, I (1913–14), 376–79.

————. "Les pensées inédites de Furtado," *La revue littéraire juive*, VI (1931), 456–69.

Parisit, Francois-Georges. *Bordeaux au XVIIIe siécle*. Bordeaux: 1968.

Pery, G. *Histoire de la Faculté de Médecine de Bordeaux, et de l'enseignement médical dans cette ville*. Paris: O. Douin, 1888.

Pietri, Francois. *Napoléon et les Israélites*. Paris: Berger-Leviault, 1965.

Posener, S. "The Immediate Economic and Social Effects of the Emancipation of the Jews in France," *Jewish Social Studies*, I (1939), 271–326.

Rabi. *Anatomie du Judaïsme français*. Paris: Editions de Minuit, 1962.

Reuss, Rod. "L'antisémitisme dans le Bas-Rhin pendant la révolution (1790-1793)," *Revue des études juives*, 68 (1914), 246–263.

_____. "Quelques documents nouveaux sur l'antisémitisme dans le Bas-Rhin de 1794–1799," *Revue des études juives*, 59 (1910), 248–276.

Revah, I. S. "Les Marranes," *Revue des études juives*, CVIII (1959-60), 29-77.

Rivkin, Ellis, ed. *Readings in Modern Jewish History*. Cincinnati: Hebrew Union College - Jewish Institute of Religion, 1957.

Roth, Cecil. *A History of the Marranos*. Philadelphia: Jewish Publication Society of America, 1947.

_____. "The Religion of the Marranos," *Jewish Quarterly Review*, XXII (1931-2), 1–33.

Rousselot, E. "Napoléon à Bordeaux," *Revue historique de Bordeaux*, I (1908), 204–28; 281–304; 428–54.

Scoville, Warren C. *The Persecution of Huguenots and French Economic Development 1680–1720*. California: University of California Press, 1960.

Stern, Selma. *The Court Jew*. Philadelphia: Jewish Publication Society of America, 1950.

Stein, S. "Interest Taken by Jews from Gentiles," *Journal of Semitic Studies*, I (1956), 141–64.

_____. "The Development of the Jewish Law on Interest from the Biblical Period to the Expulsion of the Jews from England," *Historia Judaica*, XIII (1955), 3–40.

Suart," *La Grande Encyclopédie*, vol. 30, 566.

Sydenham, M. J. *The Girondins*. London: The Athlone Press, 1961.

Szajkowski, Zosa. *Agricultural Credit and Napoleon's Anti-Jewish Decrees*. New York: 1953.

_____. "Anti-Jewish Riots During the Revolutions of 1789, 1830 and 1848," *Zion*, XX (1955), 82–102.

_____. *Autonomy and Jewish Communal Debts During the French Revolution of 1789*. New York: 1959.

_____. "French Jews in the Armed Forces During the Revolution of 1789," *Proceedings of the American Academy of Jewish Research*, XXVI (1957), 139–60.

_____. "Internal Conflicts Within the Eighteenth Century Jewish Community," *Hebrew Union College Annual*, XXXI (1960), 167–80.

_____. "Jewish Autonomy Debated and Attacked During the French Revolution," *Historia Judaica*, XX (1958), 31–46.

_____. "Jewish Emigration from Bordeaux During the Eighteenth and Nineteenth Centuries," *Jewish Social Studies*, XVIII (1956), 118–24.

_____. "Jewish Emigrés During the French Revolution," *Jewish Social Studies*, XVI (1954), 319–34.

_____. "Jewish Participation in the Sale of National Property During the French Revolution," *Jewish Social Studies*, XIV (1952), 291–316.

_____. "Judaica-Napoleonica: a Bibliography of Books, Pamphlets and Printed Documents, 1801–1815," *Studies in Bibliography and Booklore*, II

(June, 1956), 107–152.

_____. "Notes on the Demography of the Sephardim in France," *Hebrew Union College Annual,* XXX (1959), 217–32.

_____. "Notes on the Languages of the Marranos and Sephardim in France," *For Max Weinreich* (1964), 237–244.

_____. "Occupational Problems of Jewish Emancipation in France 1789–1800," *Historia Judaica,* XXI (1959), 109–32.

_____. "Population Problems of the Marranos and Sephardim in France, from the Sixteenth to the Twentieth Centuries," *Proceedings of the American Academy for Jewish Research,* XXVII (1958), 83–105.

_____. "Protestants and Jews of France in Fight for Emancipation," *Proceedings of the American Academy for Jewish Research,* XXV (1956), 119–35.

_____. "Relations Among Sephardim, Ashkenazim and Avignonese Jews in France from the 16th to the 20th Centuries," *YIVO Annual* X (1955), 165–96.

_____. "Religious Propaganda Against Jews During the French Revolution of 1789," *Proceedings of the American Academy for Jewish Research,* XXIV (1955), 137–64.

_____. "Synagogues During the French Revolution of 1789–1800," *Jewish Social Studies,* XX (1958), 215–29.

_____. "Trade Relations of Marranos in France with the Iberian Penisula in the Sixteenth and Seventeenth Centuries," *Jewish Quarterly Review,* I (1959–60), 69–78.

_____. "The Attitude of French Jacobins Toward Jewish Religion," *Historia Judaica,* XVIII (1956), 107–20.

_____. "The Comtadin Jews and the Annexation of the Papal Province by France, 1789–1791," *Jewish Quarterly Review,* XLVI (1955), 181–93.

_____. "The Delegation of the Jews of Bordeaux to the Malesherbes Commission (1788) and to the *Assemblée Nationale* (1790)," *Zion,* XVIII (19530, 31–79.

_____. "The Demographical Aspects of Jewish Emancipation in France during the French Revolution," *Historia Judaica,* XXI (1959), 7–36.

_____. "The Emancipation of Jews during the French Revolution: a Bibliography of Books, Pamphlets and Printed Documents 1789-1800," *Studies in Bibliography and Booklore,* III (1957–8), 55–68, 87–114; IV (1959), 21–48.

_____. *The Economic Status of the Jews in Alsace, Metz and Lorraine (1648–1789).* New York: 1954.

_____. "The Growth of the Jewish Population of France," *Jewish Social Studies,* VIII (1946), 179–96, 297–318.

_____. "The Jewish Community of Marseilles at the End of the Eighteenth Century," *Revue des études juives,* CXXI (1962), 367–82.

_____. "The Jewish Problem in Alsace, Metz and Lorraine on the Eve of the Revolution of 1789," *Jewish Quarterly Review,* XLIV (1954), 205–43.

_____. "The Jewish Status in Eighteenth Century France and the *Droit d'aubaine,*" *Historia Judaica,* XIX (1957), 147–61.

_____. "The Marranos and Sephardim of France," *The Abraham Weiss Jubilee Volume* (1964), 107–27.

_____. "The Sephardic Jews of France During the Revolution of 1789," *Proceedings of the American Academy for Jewish Research*, XXIV (1955), 137–64.

Thémanlys, Pascal. "Abraham Furtado personnalité centrale de l'histoire de l'émancipation juive en Occident," *Tesoro de los Judios Sefardies*, III (1960), XLI–LVIII.

_____. "L'oeuvre connue et l'oeuvre inconnue d'Abraham Furtado," *Le Judäisme Séphardi*, I (No. 5, 1932), 76–77.

_____. "Un écrivain et un sociologue: Abraham Furtado," *Les cahiers de l'Alliance Israélite*, 89 (1955), 3–9.

Vivie, A. *La terreur à Bordeaux*. Bordeaux: 1877.

Weil, J. "Contribution à l'histoire des communautés alsaciennes au XVIIIe siècle," *Revue des études juives*, 81 (1925), 169–180.

Index